Experience in Healthcare Innovation

Health and Innovation Set

coordinated by
Corinne Grenier

Volume 5

Experience in Healthcare Innovation

Fad or New Paradigm?

Edited by

Luigi Flora
Corinne Grenier
Frédéric Ponsignon

iSTE

WILEY

First published 2024 in Great Britain and the United States by ISTE Ltd and John Wiley & Sons, Inc.

ISTE Ltd
27-37 St George's Road
London SW19 4EU
UK

www.iste.co.uk

John Wiley & Sons, Inc.
111 River Street
Hoboken, NJ 07030
USA

www.wiley.com

Library of Congress Control Number: 2024931120

British Library Cataloguing-in-Publication Data
A CIP record for this book is available from the British Library
ISBN 978-1-78630-845-0

Contents

Foreword by Vincent Dumez

This book proposes an international kaleidoscope of the current deployment of the notion of patient experience and consequently that of patient partnership through the combined perspectives of patients and health professionals. Each of the experiments presented here constitutes an invaluable source of innovation through the engagement mechanisms developed as much as through the results observed on the strategic, tactical and operational levels. They also cut across the major missions of our health systems, namely care, teaching and research, showing that we are undoubtedly in the midst of large-scale systemic organizational and cultural change with multiple impacts.

At the heart of these experiments is the fundamental question of the mobilization of patient knowledge in different forms and by different means. This knowledge, still poorly known, underestimated and consequently underused, is nevertheless the main "fuel" of the innovation driven by this movement of change that we discover in this work through the achievements of actors from extremely varied horizons. From the engagement initiative of a large private health organization like Kaiser Permanente, to the pioneering initiative of a living laboratory in the clinical context of a public university hospital, to advocacy in the context of Alzheimer's disease, "patient" knowledge is highlighted again and again as a lever for innovation at the very heart of patient experience.

To support this critical effort to mobilize patient knowledge, an organizational transformation must of course be supported by inspired leadership and a vision of humanist care. Our health institutions have most of the time been structured above all to support the practices of health professionals putting the experience of patients and their families second. The reversal of this logic to aim for a better balance requires us to rethink certain hitherto unshakable fundamental operational pillars. Several avenues of innovation are proposed for this purpose in this work, particularly in terms of supporting the most vulnerable populations which are too often on the margins of our systems, as well as in terms of profound and necessary change in the philosophy of care or even the digital revolution, an irresistible and radical lever for modifying the practices of all health stakeholders including patients and their families. Through these structuring innovations, the patient experience is therefore lastingly transformed, inviting an in-depth questioning of institutional modes of operation and the way in which we orchestrate communication and collaboration and therefore, consequently, the sharing of knowledge and power.

Finally, in this proliferation of innovations characteristic of major emerging transformation movements, it remains essential to implement mechanisms to fully understand their nature, their systemic ramifications, their impacts in fine on health and possibly also, their limits. We must therefore evaluate initiatives as systematically as possible and produce research to develop the science of patient experience and partnership with a view to the "intelligent" scaling of innovations. This work also offers some significant avenues for reflection on this very critical question, on how this science can help us to transfer and scale innovations in a precise and adapted way, as well as on what it teaches us in terms of the evolution of roles, the development of capacities or of an organizational model.

Happy reading!

Vincent DUMEZ
Member of the National Order of Quebec
Partner patient
Co-director of the Center of Excellence on
Patient and Public Partnership (CEPPP)
University of Montréal

Foreword by David Darmon

The care partnership with the patient is considered an important social innovation because it strengthens patients' engagement and responsibility in their own care. This can improve health outcomes, patient satisfaction and quality of life. Care partnerships are based on transparent communication and active collaboration between patients and healthcare professionals, allowing care plans to be personalized and taking into account patients' unique preferences and needs. It can also reduce healthcare costs by minimizing medical errors and unnecessary hospitalizations. Technological innovations are also important, but the care partnership emphasizes the human connection and collaboration to achieve optimal health outcomes.

In a world where new techniques and technologies have taken a prominent place in our lives, it is increasingly important to understand how they can be used to improve the quality of medical care. This book examines the importance of patient participation in care using, among other things, innovations to facilitate communication, collaboration and decision-making. It demonstrates how patients can become active partners in their own care by using the digital tools available to them to collect and share information, monitor their health and better understand treatment options. Perspectives from healthcare professionals, patients and technology experts are explored to provide a comprehensive picture of the use of new technologies in medical care. This book is a valuable guide for those seeking to understand how new technologies can help improve care for partner patients. The example of mobile health applications is an illustration of this in that they can enable the autonomy of patients, when and if they wish, by giving them access to information on their state of health and advice on how to manage their illness, as well as allowing them to monitor their progress and communicate with their doctor and other health and medico-social professionals. It also values their experiential knowledge by giving them an active role in managing their health and recognizing their expertise with regard to their own body and its symptoms.

Corinne Grenier, through her systemic vision, and Luigi Flora, as a patient researcher and pioneer of the vision of partnership (with whom I have the pleasure of directing the Center for Innovation in Partnership with Patients and the Public at the University of Côte d' Azur), offer through this collective work a reflection on the evolution of care and on what there is to come as well as a desirable future.

Once you have taken the path of partnership, it is difficult to turn back, as you will notice when reading this book.

Introduction

This book, entitled *Experience in Healthcare Innovation: Fad or New Paradigm?*, follows the international conference held in June 2021 on health innovation through shared perspectives, and even experiences combining the knowledge of each person. Through this book, the opportunity is given to contributors (who may or may not have participated in the conference) to, shed light on the subjects covered. In-depth studies can, for some, take up questions asked during the discussions following the communications presented during the 2021 conference.

The 2021 conference was the result of an initiative born in 2008. The KEDGE Business School health conferences are organized by Corinne Grenier[1] in partnership with the social work research institutes (IRTS) of Provence-Alpes-Côte d'Azur-Corsica and Nouvelle Aquitaine, with the support of the ARAMOS association. They question actors, organizations and public authorities in the health and social action sectors using a multidisciplinary approach to better understand their dynamics. In 2021, after the brand new Center for Innovation in Partnership with Patients and the Public (CI3P) of the Faculty of Medicine of Côte d'Azur University (Flora et al. 2020) proposed two communications at the previous conference[2], the 2021 conference pursues the ambition of questioning innovation by partnering with the CI3P, an innovation center co-directed by a doctor–patient tandem, through the perspective of *the experience of stakeholders: new perspectives on health innovation.*

Introduction written by Luigi FLORA, Corinne GRENIER and Frédéric PONSIGNON.

1 Coordinator of the "*Innovation, Healthcare and Inclusive Society*" Lab.

2 Two communications which resulted in publication (Flora 2021).

According to the book *Terminologie de la pratique collaborative et du partenariat patient en santé et services sociaux* (Direction collaboration et partenariat patient (DCPP-CIO, UdeM 2016)), the patient experience is defined as:

> The overall knowledge drawn from situations experienced living with the disease which have an impact on the patient, as much on their ways of taking care of themselves, of interacting with those involved, as on their way of using health services and social services (Ibid., p. 17).

The place and role of the people concerned (patients, people with disabilities and caregivers) in their relationship to the experience of living with illness or a disability situation have attracted the interest of the human and social sciences since the 1950s, in particular with regard to the first works focusing on relationships between health professionals and patients in order to explain care trajectories and the organizational and managerial structuring allowing for the delivery of care (Strauss 1992). Anthropology (Laplantine 1986) has also been concerned with the way in which patients experience their illness by emphasizing the social and cultural elements, which permeate their experience of their illness and their recovery. It was firstly with the emergence of pathologies such as AIDS (Epstein 1996) in the third sector health environment and the perspective of community health, for example, that the experience was questioned in its collective dynamics. This was, however, a societal movement, which was made broader with the birth of popular epidemiology in the 1970s, through population reactions to attacks on health due to local pollution in the USA, and which has since spread across the planet as populations gradually sense or perceive risks to their health, which are factors of public health problems (Brown 1987, 1997).

To better understand what has become a social fact in the 20th century, the following have appeared or been recovered (Flora 2012; Flora et al. 2014; Jouet 2014) in the sense given to them by the father of sociology Emile Durkheim (1894), concepts such as *empowerment or recovery* and capability (Le Gales and Bungener 2015), coming *from* the field of North American psychiatry and taken up by French researchers (Greacen and Cadeau 2012) which now irrigate the work on experience (Troisoeufs 2020). Other *concepts* come from the political sciences and evoke the question of *citizen participation.* Multiple user participation and professionalization initiatives exist, such as the *Montreal model* (Vanier et al. 2014; Pomey et al. 2015), the expert patient program in England (Rogers et al. 2008) or the model of *narrative medicine* (Charon 2015).

Many terms have come to enrich the roles that patients can endorse in the health system: the expert user (Jouet et al. 2010); the trainer-patient (Flora 2010); the resource-patient developed by the French Association of Hemophiliacs since the beginning of the century[3]; the researcher-patient (Godrie 2017); the health mediator-peer (Roelandt et al. 2016); the expert-patient (Tourette-Turgis 2015); the teacher-patient (Gross and Gagnayre 2017); the partner-patient (Pomey et al. 2015); and the tracer-patient (HAS 2014).

At the international level, multiple initiatives for the participation and professionalization of patients, relatives and health users have existed for several years. For example, in France, experiences of peer health mediators supported by the WHO can be identified (see the report from the World Health Organization Collaborating Center (WHOCC) (Roelandt et al. 2015)). More broadly, we finally talk about the professionalization of patients/users to configure participatory health systems.

This trend, the social fact of recognizing patients' knowledge, is thus carried by patients and relayed by international (Consortium APPS 2020) and national (HAS 2020) agencies as well as by major Evidence Based Medicine journals (EBM) (Richards et al. 2013). These different models are based on a renewed partnership between patients and professionals. The latter are challenged on two counts: a) because their practices are questioned by what patients, beneficiaries and citizens tell them; b) as well as because the experience of professionals counts just as much and their lived experience of their work needs to be integrated into innovation approaches.

Thus, the chapters issued from the 2021 conference consider the experience of patients, relatives and/or segments of the population just as much as the experience of professionals to address the question of innovation in health. This perspective thus adopts the point of view of the organization or its representatives and would be the primary cause of the power to act.

As a result, it is possible through the insights offered throughout the chapters to apprehend and understand how *experience* is now reinvested when each of the parties is interested in innovation approaches and in the capacity of health organizations and the health system to innovate in partnership with patients, relatives and citizens. The relationship appears a priori to be virtuous: taking into account the lived experience of the people concerned (patients, beneficiaries, caregivers, professionals, volunteers, citizens, etc.) so as to imagine, design and deploy interventions, organizations or services that are more appropriate and

3 See: https://afh.asso.fr/je-me-forme/leducation-therapeutique-des-patients/patientsparents-ressources/programme-patients-parents-ressources/.

appropriable by these actors. The recognition of experience, and of citizen participation in the creation and deployment of public policies, raises complex questions, some of which the chapters proposed in this work shed light on.

References

Brown, P. (1987). Popular epidemiology: Community response to toxic waste-induced disease in Woburn, Massachusetts and other sites. *Science, Technology, and Human Values*, 12(3/4), 76–85.

Brown, P. (1997). Popular epidemiology revisited. *Current Sociology*, 45(3), 137–156.

Charon, R. (2015). *Médecine narrative. Rendre hommage aux histoires de maladies* (translated from the English version published by Oxford University Press in 2006). Sipayat, Paris.

Consortium INTERREG APPS (2020). Orienter les soins vers le patient partenaire : un livre blanc pour la grande région Consortium APPS/Octobre 2020. White paper, Fonds européen de développement régional.

DCPP, CIO (2016). Terminologie de la pratique collaborative et du partenariat patient en santé et services sociaux. DCPP/CIO/Université de Montréal.

Durkheim, E. (1988). *Les règles de la méthode sociologique*. Flammarion, Paris [Original published 1894].

Epstein, S. (1996). *Impure Science, Aids, Activism and the Politics of Knowledge*. University of California Press, Berkeley.

Flora, L. (2010). Le patient formateur auprès des étudiants en médecine : un concept effectif. *Revue générale de droit médical*, 34, 115–135.

Flora, L. (2012). Le patient formateur : élaboration théorique et pratique d'un nouveau métier de la santé. PhD Thesis, Université Vincennes Saint Denis, Paris.

Flora, L. (2021). Recognition of patients' experiential knowledge and co-production of care knowledge with patients and citizens in the 21st century. In *Altering Frontiers: Organizational Innovations in Healthcare*, Grenier, C. and Oiry, E. (eds). ISTE Ltd, London, and John Wiley and Sons, New York.

Flora, L., Jouet, E., Las Vergnas, O. (2014). Contribution à la cartographie des publications établissant le fait social de la reconnaissance des savoirs des malades. In *Nouvelles interventions réflexives dans la recherche en santé : du savoir expérientiel des malades aux interventions des professionnels de santé*, Jouet, E., Las Vergnas, O., Noel-Hureaux, E. (eds). Archives contemporaines, Paris, 235–236.

Flora, L., Darmon, D., Benattar, J.-M. (2020). Le Centre d'Innovation du partenariat avec les patients et le public : un moteur du développement de la culture du partenariat de soin avec le patient, avec les patients et le public en Europe. *Le partenariat de soin avec le patient : analyses*, CI3P, Université Côte d'Azur, 1, 138–163.

Godrie, B. (2017). Rapports égalitaires dans la production des savoirs scientifiques. L'exemple des recherches participatives en santé mentale. *Vie sociale*, 20, 99–116.

Greacen, T. and Jouet, E. (2012). *Pour des usagers de la psychiatrie acteurs de leur propre vie*. Erès, Toulouse.

Gross, O. and Gagnayre, R. (2017). Caractéristiques des savoirs des patients et liens avec leurs pouvoirs d'action : implication pour la formation médicale. *Revue française de pédagogie*, 201, 71–82.

HAS (2014). Le patient traceur en établissement de santé. Méthode d'amélioration de la qualité et de la sécurité des soins guide méthodologique. Haute Autorité de Santé [Online]. Available at: https://www.has-sante.fr/jcms/c_1661702/fr/le-patient-traceur-en-etablissement-de-sante.

HAS (2020). Soutenir et encourager l'engagement des usagers dans les secteurs social, médico-social et sanitaire. Haute Autorité de Santé.

Jouet, E. (2014). La reconnaissance des savoirs des malades : de l'émergence au fait social. In *Nouvelles interventions réflexives dans la recherche en santé : du savoir expérientiel des malades aux interventions des professionnels de santé*, Jouet, E., Las Vergnas, O., Noel-Hureaux, E. (eds). Archives contemporaines, Paris, 9–21.

Jouet, E., Flora, L., Las Vergnas, O. (2010). Construction et reconnaissance des savoirs expérientiels des patients. *Pratique de formation/Analyses*, 58/59, 13–94.

Karazivan P., Dumez V., Flora L., Pomey M.-P., Del Grande C., Guadiri S., Fernandez N., Jouet E., Las Vergnas O., Lebel P. (2015). The patient as partner in care: Conceptual grounds for a necessary transition. *Academic Medicine*, 90(4), 437–441 [Online]. Available at: http://journals.lww.com/academicmedicine/Fulltext/2015/04000/The_Patient_as_Partner_Approach_in_Health_Care_A.15.aspx.

Laplantine, F. (1986). *Anthropologie de la maladie*. Payot, Paris.

Le Gales, C. and Bungener, M. (2015). *Alzheimer : préserver ce qui importe. Les "capabilités" dans l'accompagnement à domicile*. Presses Universitaires de Rennes, Rennes.

Pomey, M.-P., Flora, L., Karazivan, P., Dumez, V., Lebel, P., Vanier, M.-C., Débarge, B., Clavel, N., Jouet, E. (2015). Le "Montréal model" : enjeux du partenariat relationnel entre patients et professionnels de santé. *Santé publique*, 41–50.

Richards, T., Montori, V.M., Godlee, F., Lapsley, P., Paul, D. (2013). Let the patient revolution begin. *BMJ*, 346, f2614–f2614.

Roelandt, J. and Staedel, B. (2016). *L'expérimentation des médiateurs de santé/pairs : une révolution intranquille*. Doin, Paris.

Rogers, A., Kennedy, A., Bower, P., Gardner, C., Gately, C., Lee, V., Reeves, D., Richardson, G. (2008). The United Kingdom Expert Patients Programme: Results and implications from a national evaluation. *MJA*, 189(10) [Online]. Available at: https://www.mja.com.au/system/files/issues/189_10_171108/rog10822_fm.pdf.

Strauss, A. (1992). *La trame de la négociation. Sociologie qualitative et interactionnisme.* L'Harmattan, Paris [Original published 1978].

Tourette-Turgis, C. (2015). Les patients experts et les soignants, vers des relations de réciprocité. *Soins*, 796, 35–37.

Troisoeufs, A. (2020). Patients intervenants, médiateurs de santé-pairs : quelles figures de la pair-aidance en santé ? *Rhizome*, 75/76(1/2), 27–36.

Vanier, M.-C., Dumez, V. Brault I., Boucher, A. (2014). Partners in interprofessional education: Integrating patients-as-trainers. In *Partnering with Patients, Families, and Communities to Link Interprofessional Practice and Education.* Josiah Macy Jr. Foundation, New York, 73–84.

PART 1

Crossed Perspectives on Experiential Knowledge

Introduction to Part 1

The first part of the book *Experience in Healthcare Innovation: Fad or New Paradigm?* is made up of six chapters combining different views, perspectives and areas in order to deepen the notion of experience.

Geneviève Cyr and **Marie-Pascale Pomey** offer us the first chapter entitled "User Knowledge, a Key Ingredient for Health Innovation and the Sustainability of our Health Systems".

Here, it is the patients and caregivers who are at the heart of the authors' chapter, developing experiential knowledge related to their health condition and the use of both health and medico-social services. This knowledge is considered to be an important resource in health innovation approaches; their active engagement is recognized as an essential element of a learning health system and as one of the necessary conditions for redesigning the health system (Carman et al. 2013). With the description of a few concrete cases, the authors deepen the distinction between patient participation (and that of their caregivers) and citizen participation in the evolution of the health system, all of this according to different levels of participation, allowing new ways to create value for the system.

Open innovation is defined with regard to three complementary perspectives: centered on users and the response to their needs, centered on the organization and the creation of value through the search for new market opportunities, and centered on the ecosystem, looking at spaces and places for generating new ideas. This form of innovation is necessarily collaborative, participatory and very often emergent. In the field of health, the search for value takes on particular meanings such as: improving the efficiency, effectiveness, quality, safety and/or affordability of health care (WHO 2023). It is about improving or transforming treatment, diagnosis,

---

Introduction written by Corinne GRENIER, Luigi FLORA and Frédéric PONSIGNON.

education, awareness, prevention, research quality and delivery, and access to health care (Kimble and Massoud 2017).

The authors look with interest at a particular case of innovation, so-called responsible innovation (RIH, responsible innovation in health), defined as a collaborative approach by which stakeholders commit themselves to clarify and implement a set of principles and values as well as ethical, economic, social and environmental requirements in order to respond to the challenges and needs of health systems in a sustainable manner (Silva et al. 2018). RIH targets five areas of value: for the population, for the health system, the economy, the organization and the environment. The objectives are all the more achieved when the participation of individuals is strong. Cyr and Pomey then rely on the typology of Arnstein (1969), which defines the degree of citizen participation in eight levels (manipulation, education, information, consultation, involvement, partnership, delegation of powers and control of citizens) to propose a similar scale for the participation of patients and health users. The authors also rely on Kaulio's model (1998) to understand the modalities of user involvement in innovation processes.

These methodological approaches for working with patients and caregivers' voices and making them heard are illustrated by different examples of spaces such as hackathons and "living laboratories" (Niitamo and Leminen 2011), those of the LIO (research laboratory in imaging and orthopedics, CHU Montreal, Canada) and of the Living Lab LUSAGE (Broca Hospital, Paris, France), for example.

Anaïs Cheneau and **Valérie Fargeon** focus on caregivers of the elderly in the second chapter entitled "The Experience of Caregivers in Supporting People with Neurodegenerative Diseases", wondering if their particular position (neither patients nor professionals) does not make their experiences and their forms of involvement and participation specific. The authors study the cases of caregivers of people with Parkinson's disease or amyotrophic lateral sclerosis (ALS).

This work is a continuation of initial work on the production of care by caregivers (Bungener 1987), particularly through the capabilities approach (Le Galès et al. 2015), which allows us to understand what they do, for what reasons and the conditions for carrying out their activities. It aims to understand the particular case of the participation of relatives and caregivers, with regard to the modalities of patient involvement and participation in care, and, for example: on an information–consultation–collaboration–partnership continuum (Pomey et al. 2015) for the micro level of care and the clinical relationship, or with regard to the work of Scholl et al. (2014) for a more global approach, focusing on access to care, its coordination and continuity, as well as teamwork.

Cheneau and Fargeon conclude their study by showing that the participation of loved ones, ranging from dialogue with professionals to co-production in care actions, varies depending on the loved ones and the components of support during the care process. This variability reflects situations where involvement or noninvolvement is sometimes desired, sometimes constrained, in particular to overcome the difficulties of access to professionals or of hospital organization. It also reveals the weakness of the psychosocial approach in the health system. The involvement and participation of loved ones are the expression of two non-convergent logics: an institutional logic of cost reduction and a logic where loved ones seek to strengthen their capacity to act.

Ruth-Laure Alamarguy and **Pauline Lenesley** deepen the experience of people with Alzheimer's disease by focusing on the spiritual dimension of this experience. Their chapter is entitled: "The Experiential Approach and Alzheimer's Disease: Including the Spiritual Dimension for a More Global Approach". It is here a multidimensional approach to the sick person is considered, since "spirituality fundamentally responds to the need to find meaning and reason for the events of life (Jobin 2012)" (quoted by Gaillard Desmedt and Shaha (2013, p. 1)). This is frequently defined as "an aspect of humanity that refers to the way individuals seek and express meaning and purpose, and the way they experience their connection to the moment, to themselves, to others, to nature, and to the signifier or the sacred" (Appleby et al. 2018).

However, several studies show that the spiritual dimension of support and care is little taken into account due to the lack of time or to the discomfort of distinguishing between spirituality and religion. From then on, Alamarguy and Lenesley wonder how to reconcile this issue of quality of care with the embarrassment caused by the evocation of the spiritual; and how to understand the spiritual dimension in a healthcare situation, beyond the strong influence of a biomedical vision of disorders. The first meta-analysis (Edward et al. 2010) has already revealed that it is above all the relationship that is decisive in taking spiritual needs into account.

Based on ethnographic research in EHPADs[1], the authors first highlight the important role of the establishment's commitment to taking the spiritual experience of residents into account when supporting professionals. However, they engage in it in three proactive ways, at the explicit request of the resident, some more in the background; positions depending on the way in which the professional views their own spirituality. They conclude their work by proposing some recommendations.

---

1 EHPAD: accommodation establishment for dependent elderly people (or medicalized nursing home) specific to France.

In the fourth chapter "Rethinking the Organization of SDCCs in Light of the Experience of Volunteers in a State of Great Social Precariousness", **Corinne Grenier** analyzes the regulatory work within an *accueil de jour* (ADJ), or day center, started by a team of around 10 social workers to ease tensions, support the quality of the work and allow those welcomed to truly find a haven of peace and comfort. This day center, called Boutique Solidarité, is managed by the Abbé Pierre Foundation and is located in one of the districts of Marseille (France) known as one of the poorest in Europe. Those welcomed are people in great social and economic precariousness. This organization is mainly defined by its welcoming mission "in unconditionality" and as a space of relationship and expression which is open to all and where people create meaning and commonality together; it is intentionally a place of very weak control regulation (Martinez-Perez 2013). However, the multiplicity of incidents, sometimes serious, was putting more and more strain on the team and those welcomed, including the volunteers, who, support the salaried team in their activity for around two mornings per week. The bet is that this work can contribute to their recovery process.

The author conducted action research at the request of the foundation in order to rethink the framework of the action, thus asking the research question by mobilizing the theory of regulation (Reynaud 1997) and the notion of experiential knowledge: "to what extent does the experiential knowledge of volunteers contribute to the regulatory work within a day center?". This articulation was observed around the establishment of a new system, the Mutual Agreement Contract (MAC), which defines the framework for action of volunteers with those welcomed and with the team. We have also defined the method of management of the MAC (signature, discussion time to take focus in on volunteers and their activities) as well as a better organization of the activity of the Boutique in general. For the Boutique, the MAC had to be a tool that participates in the volunteer's recovery process, by supporting their behavior, as well as their experiential knowledge. This knowledge is built in the experience of being welcomed at the Boutique, in being with others, identifying or analyzing situations or more generally in knowing what to do and what to say in certain circumstances.

The process of implementing the MAC has made it possible to bring about a "peaceful" joint regulation, wherein volunteers and teams interact more to know how to act in the face of any situation. The capacity of volunteers to put forward their knowledge and the attention paid by employees were possible thanks to the establishment of several regulatory spaces, allowing a "long and repeated practice of an activity which allows the emergence of the experienced individual" (Demailly and Garnoussi, 2015, p. 58). This being said, this joint regulation still proves to be unstable, in particular because the team has not managed to support a space specific to volunteers, and still remains uncertain about the reason to support and use the experiential knowledge of volunteers, for the proper functioning of the Boutique or for their good recovery.

In their chapter "Professional, Team and Digital Identity: The Impact on Patient Experience", **Stephanie Best**, **Ann Dadich** and **Sharon Williams** examine how new forms of collaboration, particularly through digital tools, impact the identity of caregivers and medico-social workers, and consequently the way in which the patient experience is taken into account by the latter.

The way of apprehending this is generally founded on PROMs and PREMs measures[2]. The first allow patients to express their opinion on their care and support; the latter to capture their experience (in relation in particular to their circulation in the health system, their involvement in decisions, the quality of communication with professionals, etc.).

The authors endeavor to define digital identity, which emerges in a fluid manner, through the use of digital tools such as consultation, coordination, communication and collaboration platforms. It develops through socialization between actors, their use reinforcing it in return.

The authors identified nine major articles that allow the investigation of the relationship between digital team identity and patient experience (in particular), through lexical analysis (Gephart 2004). This reveals that the patient health–identity–experience relationship is very little studied in the literature. The authors suggest avenues for research.

In the last chapter of this first part, **Éléonore Ségard** and **Philippe Chervin** examine "Mobilizing the Experience of People with Disabilities: A Necessity in the Transfer of Innovations". Disability is seen as the situational result of an interaction between a person who is physically or functionally different and a specific physical and social environment (Fougeyrollas 2002). The Convention on the Rights of Persons with Disabilities (CRPD) adopted in 2006 by the United Nations recognizes disability as a human rights issue and questions their inclusion in society and the recognition of disabled peoples' experience. In particular, the authors question the role of experiential knowledge in social innovations carried out to transform the medico-social field, and their transfer (swarming), to accelerate (or scale up) this –transformation; a dynamic which remains little explored in this field, described by Ségard (2022) in four processes: evaluation, capitalization, transferability and implementation. The authors describe each of the four processes with regard to the experience of people with disabilities. They show that the experience of disabled

2 PROMs: Patient Reported Outcome Measures; PREMs: Patient Reported Experience Measures.

people can be thought of at two levels in the transfer of innovations: a) the experience of people who participate, upstream, in the design of the innovation and b) the experience of people who benefit from and experience the innovation in the original context and then in a new context following its transfer.

References

Appleby, A., Wilson, P., Swinton, J. (2018). Spiritual care in general practice: Rushing in or fearing to tread? An integrative review of qualitative literature. *Journal of Religion and Health*, 57(3), 1108–1124.

Arnstein, S.R. (1969). A ladder of citizen participation. *Journal of the American Institute of Planners*, 35(4), 216–224.

Bungener, M. (1987). Logique et statut de la production familiale de santé. *Sciences sociales et santé*, 5(2), 45–59.

Carman, K.L., Dardess, P., Maurer, M., Sofaer, S., Adams, K., Bechtel, C., Sweeney, J. (2013). Patient and family engagement: A framework for understanding the elements and developing interventions and policies. *Health Affairs*, 32(2), 223–231.

Demailly, L. and Garnoussi, N. (2015). Le savoir-faire des médiateurs de santé pairs en santé mentale, entre expérience, technique et style. *Sciences & Action Sociales*, 1, 51–72.

Edwards, A., Pang, N., Shiu, V., Chan, C. (2010). The understanding of spirituality and the potential role of spiritual care in end-of-life and palliative care: A meta-study of qualitative research. *Palliative Medicine*, 24(8), 753–770.

Fougeyrollas, P. (2002). L'évolution conceptuelle internationale dans le champ du handicap : enjeux socio-politiques et contributions québécoises. *Perspectives interdisciplinaires sur le travail et la santé*. doi: 10.4000/pistes.3663.

Gaillard Desmedt, S. and Shaha, M. (2013). La place de la spiritualité dans les soins infirmiers : une revue de littérature. *Recherche en soins infirmiers*, 115, 19–35.

Gephart, R.P. Jr. (2004). From the editors: Qualitative research and the Academy of Management Journal. *Academy of Management Journal*, 47(4), 454–462.

Jobin, G. (2012). *Des religions à la spiritualité. Une appropriation biomédicale du religieux dans l'hôpital*. Lumen Vitae, Brussels.

Kaulio, M.A. (1998). Customer, consumer and user involvement in product development: A framework and a review of selected methods. *Total Quality Management*, 9(1), 141–149.

Kimble, L. and Massoud, M.R. (2017). What do we mean by Innovation in Healthcare. *European Medical Journal*, 1, 89–91.

Le Galès, C., Bungener, M., Groupe Capabilités (2015). *Alzheimer : préserver ce qui importe. Les "capabilités" dans l'accompagnement à domicile de la maladie*. Presses Universitaires de Rennes, Rennes.

Martinez-Perez, C. (2013). L'usage des plans de dessin industriel et la régulation du travail ouvrier. *La nouvelle revue du travail*, 3 [Online]. Available at: https://hal.univ-reims.fr/hal-02108619v1.

Niitamo, V.P. and Leminen, S. (2011). Living Labin historia. In *Innovoi(tko) yhdessä asiakkaittesi kanssa-näkemyksiä Living Lab-toimintaan*, Nyström, A.-G. and Leminen, S. (eds). Painosalama OY, Turku.

Pomey, M., Flora, L., Karazivan, P., Dumez, V., Lebel, P., Vanier, M., Jouet, E. (2015). Le "Montréal model" : enjeux du partenariat relationnel entre patients et professionnels de la santé. *Santé Publique*, HS(S1), 41–50.

Reynaud, J.-D. (1997). *Les règles du jeu. L'action collective et la régulation sociale*. Armand Colin, Paris.

Scholl, I., Zill, J.M., Harter, M., Dirmaier, J. (2014). An integrative model of patient-centeredness. A systematic review and concept analysis. *Plos One*, 9(9), e107828 [Online]. Available at: https://journals.plos.org/plosone/article?id=10.1371/journal.pone.0107828.

Ségard, E. (2022). *Le transfert des innovations dans le domaine du handicap – Quelles approches opérationnelles pour soutenir le transfert sur le terrain*. FIRAH, Paris.

Silva, H., Lehoux, P., Miller, F.A., Denis, J.L. (2018). Introducing responsible innovation in health: A policy-oriented framework. *Health Research Policy and Systems*, 16(1), 1–13.

WHO (2023). WHO Innovation Hub [Online]. Available at: https://www.who.int/teams/digital-health-and-innovation/who-innovation-hub.

1

User Knowledge, a Key Ingredient for Health Innovation and the Sustainability of our Health Systems

1.1. Introduction

Our societies and health systems face several 21st century challenges including an aging population, the preponderance of chronic diseases, climate change and the appearance or resurgence of infectious diseases. These significant transformative pressures require health systems to be agile to face these new challenges. However, organizations working alone no longer have the knowledge, capabilities or resources needed to meet these contemporary challenges and find solutions. Health innovation is no longer reserved for a restricted group of specialists. Today, it relies on the principles of open innovation and the creative spark of collectives, rather than on the solitary genius of an individual (Brunet and Malas 2019). Participation in innovation ecosystems then becomes a means of responding to this reality.

This participation allows organizations to find new ways to create value by creating relationships with new collaborators. In recent years, the importance of taking into consideration the experiential knowledge of users (patients and caregivers) has become apparent. Indeed, patients suffering from chronic illnesses are developing knowledge and skills related to their health condition and the use of health services, as well as caregivers who support them through this process. In order to integrate the knowledge and creative potential of users[1], the open innovation model is proposed.

Chapter written by Geneviève CYR and Marie-Pascale POMEY.

1 This includes patients and caregivers.

This chapter first presents the evolution of open innovation with a focus on the health sector. Then, we address the concept of responsible innovation in health (RIH) and discuss more specifically the importance of the inclusion of different stakeholders in the innovation process. Finally, a distinction will be made between patient/caregiver and citizen participation as well as between the different levels of participation. Before concluding, we will describe, through concrete cases, open innovation practices allowing patients, caregivers and citizens to contribute to innovation processes.

1.2. Innovation

The term "innovation" is a widely used buzzword in many different fields. To date, there is no consensus on how to define it. Different sciences, such as economics, public health, geography and sociology, offer slightly different concepts. Schumpeter was one of the first economists to recognize the relevance of innovations for economic systems. He describes innovation as any change in the mode of production, in the manufacturing of new products, of business structures or of entry into a new market and as the "creative destruction" which underlies any progress in a capitalist market regime (Schumpeter 1934).

Innovation is not synonymous with invention. While invention describes the emergence of a new idea or product, an innovation is considered to be the commercial implementation of a new idea as well as the economic optimization of knowledge use. A distinction can be made between invention as the generation of ideas and the first technical achievement (e.g. a prototype) and innovation as a more complete process starting with the generation of ideas and ending with the successful acceptance of use by potential users (adoption). Without dissemination of the product or process on the market and without the effective use of the new organizational method on the ground, we cannot speak of innovation.

Innovations are therefore new ideas that are put into practice, creating value for users or customers. These innovations can be disruptive (radical), by completely changing the way things are done, or continuous (progressive), by making improvements in comparison to what existed before (Brunet and Malas 2019).

1.2.1. *Linear innovation model*

The linear model of innovation is a model designed to understand the relationship between science and technology that begins with basic research and focuses on applied research, development and diffusion (Godin 2006). It poses scientific research as the basis of innovation which ultimately leads to economic growth. According to Greer (1977), there are three major stages in the innovation process: invention, adoption and diffusion. These stages were identified by Greer based on the conceptual frameworks of Rogers (1962), Hage and Aiken (1967) and Zaltman et al. (1973)[2].

The linear model has been criticized by researchers over the decades. These critiques highlight its limitations in capturing the sources of the process and the effects of innovation. These models ignore the many feedback loops that occur between different stages of the innovation process. Gaps and failures that arise at different stages can also lead us to reconsider the previous stages, which can result in innovation.

1.2.2. *Contemporary vision*

More recent works tend to break with these classic visions. In this new contemporary vision, the future "user" is most often involved in the innovation process. This means that the user does not just "adopt" an invention already stabilized before the moment of its diffusion, but instead participates in the entire process of creating an innovation. These phenomena of user participation in the very process of innovation are particularly present in the case of information and communication technologies (ICT) where users have greater room for maneuver (Doray et al. 2015).

1.3. Towards open innovation

Two main innovation management models exist, that of closed innovation and that of open innovation. Closed innovation is characterized by innovation development carried out exclusively within a single organization (van de Vrande et al. 2009). The organization mainly relies on its own internal resources to develop or market products and services (Gassmann 2006). In this closed innovation model, the "know-how", the technology, the processes and the intellectual property remain under the control of the organization and of research and development professionals.

Organizations have traditionally relied on closed innovation models, relying on internal knowledge and skills to drive innovation (Chesbrough 2003; Gassmann 2006). The literature has focused on the knowledge and work of research and development professionals, its boundaries and how they produce scientific and

2 Hage, J. and Aiken, M. (1967). Relationship of centralization to other structural properties. *Administrative Science Quarterly*, 72–92; Rogers, E.M. (1962). *Diffusion of Innovations*. Free Press of Glencoe, New York; Zaltman, G., Duncan, R., Holbek, J. (1973). *Innovations and Organizations*. Wiley, New York/Toronto.

technological innovation (Lifshitz-Assaf 2018). Professionals establish knowledge boundaries to gain legitimacy and help distinguish experts from laypeople as well as distinguish experts from different disciplines (Lamont and Molnar 2002). As a result, this can lead to the rejection of innovations proposed by individuals outside these knowledge boundaries (Lifshitz-Assaf 2018). To be able to face these challenges, the open innovation model is proposed. This model, born over the last two decades, proposes that the organization makes a strategic choice to acquire and integrate the knowledge and creative potential of external and internal partners in order to foster an environment conducive to development and growth and to the adoption of innovation.

According to the literature, three main perspectives characterize open innovation (see Figure 1.1). Firstly, the user-centered perspective which takes into account the needs of users in the development of new products (e.g. Open Source software where users transform existing products to give them new functions or adapt them to their needs). The second perspective, centered on the organization, is interested in the needs to generate value in organizations and focuses mainly on the mechanisms that allow opportunities to be developed in the market. This perspective seeks external partners, with the objective of taking advantage of the contribution of knowledge (e.g. multi-firm collaboration agreement, an open business model). The third perspective, centered on the ecosystem, comes from studies in economics and sociology which are interested in how organizations function in their context, by looking at such as spaces and places to generate ideas from (e.g. the emergence of the Silicon Valley). Despite their differences, these three perspectives emphasize that talent and value are distributed, that organizations cannot have the best "brains" and that innovative processes are collaborative (KE Dionne, personal communication, lecture from March 30, 2020).

Figure 1.1. *Opening up innovation – three perspectives. For a color version of this figure, see www.iste.co.uk/flora/experience.zip*

The main reasons for organizations to adopt open innovation practices are: i) the development of complex innovations which requires a diversity of skills; ii) contemporary markets that are rapidly demanding new solutions, which the organizational structures of large companies are not well suited to provide for; iii) users who exert pressure to participate in the development process. Furthermore, in an open innovation model, the simultaneous presence of different ecosystem players makes it possible to:

– create new relationships (Lakhani et al. 2012);

– share and benefit from knowledge, resources and capacities (Lakhani et al. 2012);

– accelerate internal innovation, to position ourselves in new markets and disseminate innovations more widely (Chesbrough 2003);

– create solutions in line with the real needs of the user (von Hippel 2005; Baldwin and von Hippel 2011);

– reduce innovation costs (von Hippel 2007).

1.4. Health innovation

The World Health Organization's (WHO) health innovation group (2023) explains that health innovation is the development or improvement of health policies, systems, products, technologies and services that improve people's health, with a focus on the needs of vulnerable populations. The group emphasizes that health innovation aims to add value in order to improve the efficiency, effectiveness, quality, safety and/or affordability of health care. Therefore, innovations in health care should produce scalable solutions and improvements in health policies, systems, products, technologies, services and delivery methods, to improve treatment, diagnosis, education, awareness, prevention, research quality and delivery, and access to health care (Kimble and Massoud 2017). These innovations often involve several innovations simultaneously. For example, the successful launch of a technological innovation requires the development of complementary technologies, new business models, new processes, new roles for patients and clinicians, or policy changes.

1.5. Responsible health innovation

Over the last decade, a new concept has emerged: responsible innovation in health (RIH). RIH consists of a collaborative approach within which stakeholders commit to clarifying and applying a set of ethical, economic, social and environmental principles, values and requirements when they design, finance, produce, distribute and use sociotechnical solutions in order to respond to the challenges and needs of health systems in a sustainable manner (Silva et al. 2018).

RIH looks at the technology as well as the organization that develops it and makes it available to users. The principles, values and requirements of RIH apply themselves throughout the technology life cycle, promoting the best environmental and social practices. RIH also considers accountability and responsiveness in the operations and decision-making of organizations, including the suppliers and distributors those organizations rely on to produce and disseminate technology.

Silva et al. (2018) propose a conceptual framework (see Figure 1.2) to define the five values to be integrated throughout the life cycle of an innovation: 1) population health; 2) health systems; 3) economic; 4) organizational; and 5) environmental processes. Table 1.1 presents these value areas, the definitions and dimensions.

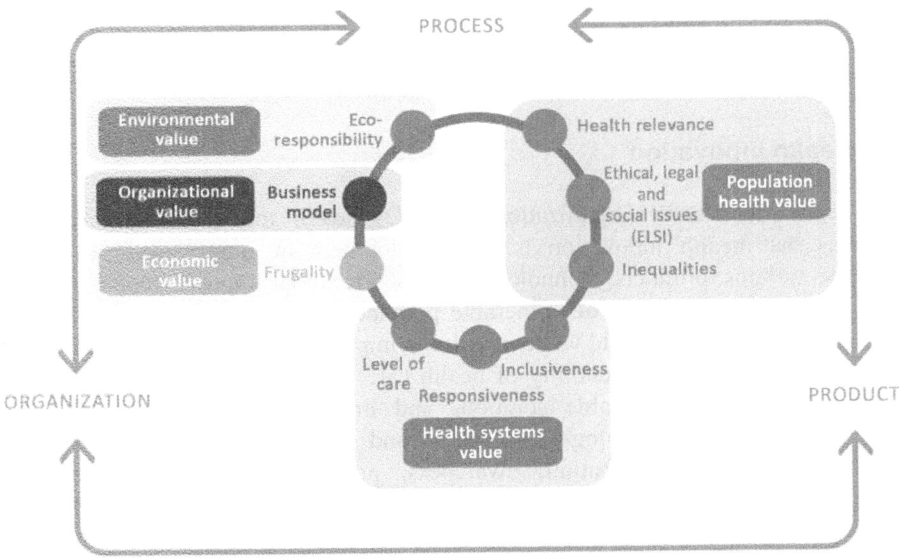

Figure 1.2. *Conceptual framework for responsible innovation in health (RIH) (In Fieri (2022) inspired from Silva et al. (2018)). ELSI = ethical, legal and social issues. For a color version of this figure, see www.iste.co.uk/flora/experience.zip*

Value	Definitions	Dimensions
Population health value	Increasing our capacity to meet collective needs while combating health inequalities	**Health relevance**: Does the innovation address a relevant health problem? **Ethical, legal and social issues**: Was the innovation developed by seeking to mitigate ethical, legal and social issues? **Health equity**: How does the innovation promote health equity?

Health system value	Having an innovation that provides an appropriate response to the contemporary challenges of health systems	**Inclusiveness**: Was the innovation development process inclusive? **Responsiveness**: Does the innovation provide a dynamic solution to a health system challenge recognized as being of the highest importance in the target region? **Level of care**: Is the level of care required by the innovation compatible with the sustainability of the health system?
Economic value	Providing products that are both efficient and affordable in order to promote equity and sustainability	**Frugality**: To what extent does innovation deliver more value to more people using fewer resources?
Organizational value	Fostering business strategies through which a company brings value to innovation users, buyers and society	**Business model**: Does the organization producing the innovation seek to offer more value to users, buyers and society?
Environmental value	Reducing the negative impacts of health innovations on the environment as much as possible throughout their life cycles	**Eco-responsibility**: Does the innovation seek to limit its environmental impact throughout its life cycle?

Table 1.1. *Value domain of the responsible innovation in health (RIH) model (Silva et al. 2018; In Fieri 2022)*

The "health system" value includes three dimensions, one of which is related to user knowledge, that of inclusiveness. This dimension examines the extent to which innovation processes and results are "inclusive" of multiple societal actors (Silva et al. 2018). This dimension is important for democratic reasons and also to broaden and diversify sources of expertise and perspectives. Inclusion makes it possible to specify all the individuals and institutions who should contribute to the design, development and pilot stages of an innovation (e.g. clinicians, managers, patients and caregivers, citizens, etc.) (Silva et al. 2018).

It also appears to be essential to define the engagement methods to be deployed in order to capture their expectations, needs and interests, and to assess their value and importance. This dimension of inclusiveness is both process and product-focused and is based on a principle which states that, although stakeholder engagement may differ from one type of innovation to another, processes and outcomes must be held accountable (Silva et al. 2018).

1.6. Participation of patient-caregivers and citizens in innovation

It should be noted that the scientific literature distinguishes between citizen participation versus the participation of patient-caregivers. The patient-caregiver addresses how experiencing an illness, a condition, a treatment or a health intervention leads individuals to use (or likely to use) health services and social services. Their participation is desired in order to mobilize their experiential knowledge with the aim of having decisions that are relevant, acceptable and applicable to their needs. For their part, citizens are recognized as belonging to a community that adheres to common norms, including rights and duties (Pomey and Langlet 2019). Their participation is required to guarantee respect for a society's values and transparency in decision-making. They help to raise or anticipate decision-making and societal issues, and they participate in decisions to ensure that they are fair and reasonable. Table 1.2 summarizes and presents the distinction between these two types of users.

	Patient-caregiver	Citizen
Definition	**Patient**: a person who has experience with a disease, condition, treatment or intervention. Using or likely to use health and social services. **Caregiver**: someone who takes care of a person experiencing loss of autonomy which is caused, among other things, by the aging process, an illness or a physical disability, and who maintains close relationships with the people concerned by the health of this person.	Person belonging to and participating in the community and who adheres to a set of common norms including rights and duties.
Outlook	From an experience (personal or of a loved one) relating to an illness, a condition, a technology, or an intervention in health or social services. Individual (and collective) interests in improving the health system and social services.	Emerging from a personal understanding of the diverse interests, priorities and values of the community. Collective (and individual) interests in improving the health system and social services.
Contributions sought in the field of innovation	Curative and illness/disability. Self-monitoring, systematization and performance. Self-management.	Prevention and well-being. Self-monitoring, systematization and performance.
Expected contributions	Use of experiential knowledge generated by the experience of the illness, condition, treatment or use of health or social services (by the patient or a caregiver). Development of a critical sense towards the object of evaluation: advantages and limits, impacts on the patient, on others and on the system, appropriation, economic issues, ethical dilemmas, etc.	Highlighting social and ethical issues (and associated dilemmas) regarding technologies and methods of intervention in health and social services. Societal (systemic) and external viewpoint providing a certain perspective on the object of evaluation: social acceptability,

	Patient-caregiver	Citizen
		public aspects, clear communication of stakes at hand, etc. Support for the legitimacy, transparency and accountability of a public body (public dimension of evaluation).
Stakes	Recovery of patient/caregiver voices for commercial purposes. Utilization of their contribution, because it is much less expensive than other sources. Selection of patients/caregivers who participate in the innovation project.	Representativeness of citizens.

Table 1.2. *Distinction between the patient, the caregiver and the citizen (inspired by Pomey and Langley (2019) and Demers-Payette et al. (2020))*

1.6.1. *Level of participation*

In the field of healthcare, active user engagement is recognized as an essential element of a learning health system, as well as being one of the necessary conditions for redesigning the health system (Carman et al. 2013). For citizen participation, one of the best-known scales is that of Arnstein (1969), which propose eight levels: manipulation, education, information, consultation, involvement, partnership, delegation of powers and citizen control.

For patient and caregiver engagement, Carman et al. (2013) and Pomey et al. (2015) propose a continuum similar to that of citizens. User involvement in a partnership process can take several forms and be located at different levels: clinical, organizational and strategic (Pomey and Lebel 2016). In a clinical context, patients and their loved ones can receive documents including information about their illness (information), be asked to make a judgment about care (consultation) or even discuss the decisions concerning them with health professionals (collaboration), and, finally, are led to find solutions to the problems encountered by being considered as full members of the team (co-construction). This having been said, these models do not highlight the different levels of engagement in innovation processes.

From a design perspective, Kaulio (1998) defines three degrees of user involvement that reflect the levels of participation in innovation processes: design *for* users, *with* users and *by* users. Design *for* users (user-centered design) is an approach to product development in which products are designed on behalf of customers, but where users are involved in the testing phase. Designing *with* users (participatory design) enables the development of customer-centric products, using data about their preferences, needs and requirements, and includes proposals for different solutions/concepts to which customers can respond. Finally, design *by* users offers product development where customers are actively involved and participate in the design of their own products (co-creation). Users can thus participate in several forms at the different stages of the product development process.

1.7. Open innovation practices to bring patient-caregivers and citizens to contribute to innovations

This section highlights some of the methods used to implement open innovation and enable collaboration between external (e.g. patient-caregivers, citizens) and internal partners in the ecosystem.

1.7.1. *Hackathon*

The word hackathon is a combination of the words hack and marathon, where hack signifies experimental and creative problem solving with a fun approach and marathon signifies the duration of the event. The hackathon has its origins in software and hardware engineering, but the concept is also applied in other fields to develop innovative solutions.

A hackathon lasts between 24 and 48 hours and is dedicated to a specific topic or challenge. Participants work in small groups in an environment that encourages creative thinking and leads to new innovative concepts, ideas and prototypes. The result of the hackathon is a finished prototype for a product, service or innovative business model.

The hackathon formula is well known in the digital and technology world, but is also starting to be used in the field of health. As an example, Hacking Health (founded in Montreal, Canada) is now active in over 50 cities. This international movement's mission is to catalyze collaboration and enable actors from diverse backgrounds to create innovative, concrete solutions together that respond to health challenges (Vézina et al. 2019). Hacking Health is thus a social architect who designs environments within which people from different disciplines, hierarchical positions and industries can share and combine their knowledge and passions in order to find useful solutions for their community (Vézina et al. 2019). In order to be effective and have a concrete effect in the context of healthcare, its methodology must be refined. It must ensure the inclusion of patients, citizens and clinicians at the heart of projects, integrate a period of research into the problems encountered in the field as well as their clear and precise articulation in short and inspiring pitches (Vézina et al. 2019).

1.7.2. *Living Labs*

The Living Lab (LL) concept originated at the Massachusetts Institute of Technology (MIT) Media Lab in the late 1990s and was further developed by the European Network of Living Labs (ENoLL) in 2006 (Niitamo and Leminen 2011). LLs were initially designed to address innovation challenges encountered primarily for information and communication technology (ICT) (Hossain et al. 2019). The LL makes it possible to take into account the needs of the people who will benefit from the innovation and to mobilize their knowledge and ideas in real time, in order to improve the innovation throughout its development process (Pallot et al. 2010). In fact, the beneficiaries of an innovation become full partners of the team. They participate fully in the design of the innovation, its adoption, its diffusion and its valorization. Thanks to its agility, the LL makes it possible to create solutions that are in line with real needs, by integrating for this purpose from the start all the different actors representing the complexity of the health environment (Berthou and Picard 2017). Below, we present healthcare LL where patients-caregivers are involved in the innovation process.

1.7.2.1. *Imaging and Orthopedics Research Laboratory (LIO) – Montreal University Hospital Center (CHUM), Montreal, Canada*

The LIO is a participatory health technology innovation ecosystem that brings together researchers, clinicians, patients and businesses, and is located in a hospital environment. The LIO offers technological responses to the problems brought forward by clinicians or patients. Its work focuses on the development of 3D imaging technologies to improve the diagnosis and treatment of cancer, cardiometabolic, immunopathological and neurological diseases. The LIO team adopts a model of innovation illustrated by the double helix of DNA structure. Ideas, new products, services and processes therefore circulate in a nonlinear manner (Picard and de Guise 2015).

Among the LIO's projects, we find a project that focuses on patients suffering from head and neck cancer, who need a synthetic facial prosthesis following a dilapidating facial surgery at the CHUM. These patients face great physical and psychological distress linked to the loss of a part of their face along with challenges regarding the reconstruction of their identity. Currently, these patients receive very little emotional/psychological support and do not have access to new technologies.

To respond to this problem, an LL project was created to bring together patients and caregivers, health professionals (stomatologist, plastic surgeon, psychiatrist, public health professional, prosthodontist), as well as specialists in social sciences (management, identity, patient partnership, ethics, economics), decision-makers, engineers (3D imaging and 3D printing), technological arts specialists, an industrialist and an artist. This team was able, through co-creation, to develop a new care trajectory in order to introduce technological, psychological, artistic and social support for patients who need facial reconstruction using a replacement facial prosthesis.

1.7.2.2. *Laboratory of usages in gerontechnology, Broca Living Lab (LUSAGE) – Broca Hospital, Paris, France*

LUSAGE is a research laboratory specializing in the evaluation, design and development of technological solutions for health, autonomy, the quality of life of the elderly and support from their informal and professional caregivers (Pino et al. 2012). This laboratory brings together diverse knowledge and skills, concerning the technological aspects and the cognitive aspects of neurodegenerative pathologies. LUSAGE received ENoLL certification in 2012 as part of the sixth wave of certification. LUSAGE is also one of the testing laboratories of the Centre d'expertise national (CEN) in cognitive stimulation, the CEN STIMCO, set up thanks to the support of the National Solidarity and Autonomy Fund (CNSA). The objective of these CENs is to accelerate the development and use of technical aids or innovative and quality devices, integrating ICT in particular, and helping to compensate for disabilities. Design and development processes benefit from the contribution of different stakeholders within a multidisciplinary and collaborative environment. In this dynamic, each stakeholder (research teams, private or public companies, organizations, groups of potential users) brings their own ideas and therefore participates in the construction of solutions.

1.7.2.3. *Suan-Lien Living Laboratory – Sanzhi, New Taipei, Taiwan*

The Suan-Lien LL was established by the Center of Innovation and Synergy for Intelligent Home and Living Technology of the National University of Taiwan (INSIGHT) and the Suan-Lien Center for elderly care in Northern Taiwan in 2009 (Kang 2012). As a multidisciplinary platform in the development of innovation of products and services, the Suan-Lien LL involves users, including patients, to participate in the first stages of product development, facilitates cooperation between the industry and academia and enhances industries in healthcare, nursing, entertainment and information technology. The lab aims to promote the well-being of elderly people's lives while capturing social trends, identifying needs and securing market entry points.

1.7.2.4. *"Lo-fi" living laboratory – Bendigo Hospital, Bendigo, Victoria, Australia*

This is a research project where designers, occupational therapists and inpatients from a mental health unit collaborated to develop the prototype of an "arts and health practice" program for recovery. When developing this project, they created a "lo-fi"[3] living laboratory, a collaborative platform resulting from the combination of collaborative design, which allows healthcare personnel to do their work creatively and create platforms for user participation in the design of health services (Sanin et al. 2021). The establishment of this laboratory within Bendigo Hospital allowed the research team to initiate a process of democratic participation and active collaboration with occupational therapists and service users.

1.8. Conclusion

This chapter unravels the intricacies of innovation in the healthcare landscape, offering a nuanced understanding. Navigating the complexities of health innovation is no small feat. Open innovation is a dynamic approach that weaves together the diverse interests of stakeholders, transforming challenges into collaborative opportunities. Through this chapter, we have observed the transformation of innovation models, evolving from linear and non-iterative approaches to more open frameworks. This evolution embraces inclusivity, welcoming new actors into the ecosystem, fostering a collaborative and comprehensive vision. Responsible Innovation in Health (RIH) strengthens this model by prompting us to contemplate the diverse impacts of innovations across various dimensions, integrating these considerations into our decision-making processes. In this dynamic ecosystem, amplifying the voices of patients, caregivers, and citizens becomes paramount for optimal outcomes and value creation. Leveraging methodologies such as hackathons and living laboratories facilitates the organic integration of diverse knowledge, including the invaluable experiential insights of users. The sustainability of our health systems hinges on creating value through the active engagement of patients, caregivers, and citizens.

1.9. References

Arnstein, S.R. (1969). A ladder of citizen participation. *Journal of the American Institute of Planners*, 35(4), 216–224.

3 Definition of the "lo-fi" LL: according to Sanin et al. (2021), it is a collaboration platform, a space similar to any living laboratory, but where simplistic and improvised co-creation takes place. Having a lo-fi approach to the LL means that power shifts from the research team to the participants.

Baldwin, C. and von Hippel, E. (2011). Modeling a paradigm shift: From producer innovation to user and open collaborative innovation. *Organization Science*, 22(6), 1399–1417.

Berthou, V. and Picard, R. (2017). Les Living Labs, ces leviers d'innovation en santé publique. *Annales des Mines-Réalités industrielles*, 2, 68–72.

Brunet, F. and Malas, K. (eds) (2019). *L'innovation en santé : réfléchir, agir et valoriser*, 2nd edition. Éditions Sainte-Justine, Montreal.

Carman, K.L., Dardess, P., Maurer, M., Sofaer, S., Adams, K., Bechtel, C., Sweeney, J. (2013). Patient and family engagement: A framework for understanding the elements and developing interventions and policies. *Health Affairs*, 32(2), 223–231.

Chesbrough, H.W. (2003). *Open Innovation: The New Imperative for Creating and Profiting from Technology*. Harvard Business Press, Boston, MA.

Demers-Payette, O., Ganache, I., Goetghebeur, M., Pomey, M.P., Roy, D. (2020). Valoriser une voix citoyenne en santé et en services sociaux. In *L'État du Québec 2020*, Busso, D. (ed.). Institut du Nouveau Monde, Quebec.

Dionne, K.E. (2020). Innovation ouverte. Note, Cours ENTE 61012 Management de l'innovation, HEC, Montreal.

Doray, P., Niosi, J., Proulx, S. (2015). Diffusion de la technologie et des innovations. In *Sciences, technologies et sociétés de A à Z*, Bouchard, F., Doray, P., Prud'homme, J. (eds). Presses de l'Université de Montréal, Montreal. doi: 10.4000/books.pum.4284.

Gassmann, O. (2006). Opening up the innovation process: Towards an agenda. *R&D Management*, 36(3), 223–228.

Godin, B. (2006). The linear model of innovation: The historical construction of an analytical framework. *Science, Technology & Human Values*, 31(6), 639–667.

Greer, A.L. (1977). Advances in the study of diffusion of innovation in health care organizations. *The Milbank Memorial Fund Quarterly Health and Society*, 55(4), 505–532.

von Hippel, E. (2005). *Democratizing Innovation: Users Take Center Stage*. MIT Press, Cambridge, MA.

von Hippel, E. (2007). Horizontal innovation networks – by and for users. *Industrial and Corporate Change*, 16(2), 293–315.

Hossain, M., Leminen, S., Westerlund, M. (2019). A systematic review of living lab literature. *Journal of Cleaner Production*, 213, 976–988.

In Fieri (2022). Ce qu'est L'IRS [Online]. Available at: http://infieri.umontreal.ca/#section-ce-quest-lirs.

Kang, S.C. (2012). Initiation of the Suan-Lien living lab – A living lab with an elderly welfare focus. *International Journal of Automation and Smart Technology*, 2(3), 189–199.

Kaulio, M.A. (1998). Customer, consumer and user involvement in product development: A framework and a review of selected methods. *Total Quality Management*, 9(1), 141–149.

Kimble, L. and Massoud, M.R. (2017). What do we mean by innovation in healthcare. *European Medical Journal*, 1, 89–91.

Lakhani, K.R., Tushman, M.L., Baldwin, C., Grandori, A., von Hippel, E. (2012). Open innovation and organizational boundaries: The impact of task decomposition and knowledge distribution on the locus of innovation. Harvard Business School Working Paper, Boston, 12–57.

Lamont, M. and Molnár, V. (2002). The study of boundaries in the social sciences. *Annual Review of Sociology*, 28(1), 167–195.

Lifshitz-Assaf, H. (2018). Dismantling knowledge boundaries at NASA: The critical role of professional identity in open innovation. *Administrative Science Quarterly*, 63(4), 746–782.

Niitamo, V.P. and Leminen, S. (2011). Living Labin historia. In *Innovoi(tko) yhdessä asiakkaittesi kanssa-näkemyksiä Living Lab-toimintaan*, Nyström, A.-G. and Leminen, S. (eds). Painosalama OY, Turku.

Organisation mondiale de la santé (OMS) (2023). Pôle d'innovation de l'OMS [Online]. Available at: https://www.who.int/teams/digital-health-and-innovation/who-innovation-hub.

Pallot, M., Trousse, B., Senach, B., Scapin, D. (2010). Living lab research landscape: From user centred design and user experience towards user cocreation. *First European Summer School "Living Labs"*.

Picard, R. and de Guise, J. (2015). Un exemple d'écosystème d'innovation en technologies de la santé. Laboratoire de recherche en imagerie et orthopédie de Montréal, 3.

Pino, M., Cristancho-Lacroix, V., Kerhervé, H., Boulay, M., Legouverneur, G., Wu, Y.H., Rigaud, A.S. (2012). Le laboratoire LUSAGE : un exemple de Living Lab dans le domaine des gérontechnologies. *Les cahiers de l'année gérontologique*, 4(4), 386–393.

Pomey, M.P. and Langlet, M.F. (2019). L'innovation du point de vue du patient-famille et du citoyen. In *L'innovation en santé : réfléchir, agir et valoriser*, 2nd edition, Brunet, F. and Malas, K. (eds). Éditions Sainte-Justine, Montreal.

Pomey, M.P. and Lebel, P. (2016). Patient engagement: The Quebec path. *Healthcare Papers*, 16(2), 78–83.

Pomey, M.P., Ghadiri, D.P., Karazivan, P., Fernandez, N., Clavel, N. (2015). Patients as partners: A qualitative study of patients' engagement in their health care. *PloS One*, 10(4), e0122499.

Sanin, J., Spong, L., McRae, C. (2021). Creative wellbeing. Prototyping an arts-health practice program for mental health recovery. *Design for Health*, 5(1), 61–81.

Schumpeter, J.A. (1934). *The Theory of Economic Development: An Inquiry Into Profits, Capital, Credit, Interest, and the Business Cycle*. Harvard University Press, Cambridge, MA.

Silva, H., Lehoux, P., Miller, F.A., Denis, J.L. (2018). Introducing responsible innovation in health: A policy-oriented framework. *Health Research Policy and Systems*, 16(1), 1–13.

Van de Vrande, V., De Jong, J.P., Vanhaverbeke, W., De Rochemont, M. (2009). Open innovation in SMEs: Trends, motives and management challenges. *Technovation*, 29(6/7), 423–437.

Vézina, I., Dionne, K.E, Sirois, L. (2019). Pratiques pour susciter la créativité collective et l'innovation en santé : l'approche structurée de Hacking Health. In *L'innovation en santé : réfléchir, agir et valoriser*, 2nd edition, Brunet, F. and Malas, K. (eds). Éditions Sainte-Justine, Montreal.

2

The Experience of Caregivers in Supporting People with Neurodegenerative Diseases

2.1. Introduction

Since the 1990s, we have observed a renewal in the consideration of patients within the health system, which is linked to several movements: medical and technological innovations; the search for quality and productivity gains in healthcare; a transformation of care needs (due to demographic and epidemiological changes) (Mougeot 2018). The new consideration of patients is manifested in the recognition of their experience, kowledge and expertise, as well as the pursuit of tailored care. Moving from a passive role wherein the patient receives care and health professionals, holders of medical expertise, make decisions, it is about recognizing and supporting an active role for patients in managing their health. Patient involvement in managing their illness helps to improve their experience of the illness, their adherence to treatment, to reduce the costs of their care and can be clinically effective (Coulter et al. 2008; Oshima and Emanuel 2013). In France, the laws of January 2, 2002, renovating social and medico-social action and of March 4, 2002 relating to the rights of patients and the quality of the health system are the institutional markers of this new place for patients. The "hospital, patient, health, territories" law strengthened this movement in 2009 by developing therapeutic education for patients with chronic illnesses. We expect a more "patient-centered" health system from these directions, where the "patient experience" would be considered more. While the recognition in health institutions of knowledge developed by the patient through the daily experience of illness marks an evolution

Chapter written by Anaïs CHENEAU and Valérie FARGEON.

in the representation of health, the role and experience of caregivers and those around them are less documented (Jouet et al. 2010).

Since the 2000s, numerous studies have observed the involvement of patients in their health and care. However, the engagement of relatives is less known even though they play an essential role in the mediation and management of the patient's care journey, particularly in the case of chronic diseases (Fantino et al. 2007; Zigante 2018). Surveys (such as SHARE, HSM-HSA and CARE) have revealed the help provided by caregivers in daily activities, but their role in care pathways is less known (Coudin 2005; Campéon et al. 2012; Bragstad et al. 2014; Buthion and Godé 2014). It can be noted, however, that programs based on the patient care partnership approach are being implemented in Quebec in different care contexts and are based on the experiential knowledge developed by patients and their caregivers (Boivin et al. 2017).

The challenge of understanding this domestic production of care (Bungener 1987; Le Galès et al. 2015) and the "caregiver experience" associated with it is important. There is an increasing demand for relatives to provide care due to chronic illnesses, the shift to ambulatory care, policies oriented towards social inclusion for individuals with disabilities, as well as due to the shortage of nursing staff. A better understanding of the action abilities of informal caregivers, as well as their knowledge and skills also allows us to consider relatives in their contribution to improving support and the quality of care. This knowledge is necessary to define and deploy support policies for informal caregivers. It appears essential to determine the degree of involvement that relatives wish to have in supporting their sick loved ones and what possibilities they have to do so. In order to support the continued participation of family members, it is important to examine how the health system and professionals value their experience of caring.

In this chapter, we study the experience of a specific audience, caregivers, based on their involvement in supporting their sick loved ones and the co-production of care with health professionals. (Batalden et al. 2016). Does their particular position – as neither patients nor professionals – make their forms of involvement and participation specific? Is the caregiving experience specific? To do this, we process data from interviews with informal caregivers of people with Parkinson's disease or amyotrophic lateral sclerosis (ALS)[1].

1 This study is part of the IRS-Expé-Patient (Initiatives de Recherches Stratégiques) research funded as part by the IDEX-Université Grenoble-Alpes program. The study also received financial support from the UNAF (Union Nationale des Associations Familiales). We thank everyone who participated in the study and the interviews.

2.2. Theoretical framework

Wolf et al. (2014) identify three dimensions of "patient-approaches" to reflect on the organization of services and of the health system: 1) Patients and families are care partners who have layman knowledge and capacity for action; 2) focusing on the needs, preferences and values of the patient implies a personalization of care; 3) during the patient's care journey, the care experience extends beyond the singular care relationship and involves interactions between the individual and various organizations. Thus, "taking care" is a co-production that mobilizes multiple actors beyond just medical care providers, and the patient and those around them are co-producers of it.

Works on the production of care for loved ones (Bungener 1987; Le Galès et al. 2015) have produced knowledge on the practices, characteristics and logics of this type of care work. In particular, the *capabilities* approach (Le Galès et al. 2015) provides an analytical and methodological framework for studying what caregivers do, why they do it, and the conditions for carrying out their activities. It allows us to analyze their freedom to get involved in the support, and constraints, and resources for their engagement.

The involvement and participation of patients in care are modeled along a *continuum* that goes from information (knowledge) to power (capacities): information, consultation, collaboration and partnership (Coulter 1997; Charles et al. 1999; Carman et al. 2013; Pomey et al. 2015). While the models mainly analyze how professionals take patients into account in decision-making and care pathways, Thompson's model (2007) has the advantage of giving a place to the patient as an actor in their own participation: this is co-determined both by their behavior and preferences as well as by those of professionals. This approach distinguishes between the involvement desired by patients, the positioning and relationships with health professionals and participation co-determined and co-constructed by patient–health professional relationships.

The model distinguishes four degrees of patient involvement in consultations which depend on patients' preferences and what they are prepared to do to receive/give/use information (Table 2.1). The model distinguishes five degrees of determined professional involvement depending on how professionals position patients in consultations. These positions range from the paternalistic position of doctors – excluding patients or simply transmitting the information they deem necessary – to a position of informed decision-making which requires a transfer of knowledge, skills and responsibilities to the patient and their loved ones. The intermediate levels cover consultation and the professional as an agent, where the health professional takes into account the expertise, point of view and preferences of patients in the final decisions. Each level reflects a relative position of patient power.

Participation[2] corresponds to forms of involvement co-determined by patients' and professionals' preferences and behaviors towards patients. This participation presupposes the relationships between patients and healthcare professionals: if the patient makes a decision without discussing it with the healthcare professional, we cannot speak of participation. We can identify two forms: dialogue between patients, relatives, and professionals (which involves both a transmission of information from the patient and/or caregivers and consultation from professionals), and shared decisions, particularly about therapeutic preferences (which involve the transmission of information and the taking into account of the patient's preferences by the professional).

While this model offers a dynamic approach to patient involvement and participation, it remains focused on micro-level care and the clinical relationship. Other works make it possible to complete it (Carman et al. 2013; Scholl et al. 2014; Pomey et al. 2015; Ortiz Halabi et al. 2020) and to take into account the role of organizational and institutional characteristics in the involvement and participation of patients and relatives. The integrative model of patient-centered approaches from Scholl et al. (2014) identifies five meso-level dimensions that operate as facilitators for the implementation of patient-centered care: clinician–patient communication, the integration of medical and non-medical care, teamwork, access to care, coordination and continuity of care.

From these models, we study the involvement and participation of caregivers in supporting the care journey of their sick loved ones, by analyzing the patient–professional–caregiver relationship. The dynamics of the involvement and participation of relatives is based on: 1) the articulation between the preferences and behaviors of the triad: caregivers/patient and health professionals where communication and the patient/caregiver/professional relationship are central to the possibility of co-production of care; 2) influencing factors, both at the personal level and at the organizational and socio-political levels. The objective is to study the specificities of the participation of relatives.

2 The engagement and participation terms of the patient are often used interchangeably in the literature to describe active patients. We distinguish between patient involvement which has been independently determined by the patient and the healthcare professional, and patient participation co-determined by the patient and the healthcare professional (Thompson 2007; Fumagalli et al. 2015).

Degree of patient involvement	Patient's side		Co-determined PARTICIPATION	Professional's side	
4	Development of skills and motivations (empowerment) ↑	Autonomous decision-making		Informed decision	Transfer of competencies and responsibilities ↑
3			**Shared decisions**	Professional as an agent	
2		Transmission of information	**Dialogue**	Consultation	
1		Search for information		Transmission of information	
0		Non-participation		Exclusion	

Patient-professional relationships

Table 2.1. *Degrees of patient involvement. Codetermined forms of participation (according to Thompson (2007) and Fumagalli et al. (2015))*

2.3. Data and method

While the majority of studies focus on caregivers of elderly patients (Clayman et al. 2005; Ishikawa et al. 2005), our study focuses on the situation of caregivers for adults suffering from two neurodegenerative diseases: Parkinson's and amyotrophic lateral sclerosis (ALS, Charcot disease). These very debilitating illnesses often occur in fairly young patients. While Parkinson's disease progresses quite slowly, ALS progresses quickly. These diseases require multidisciplinary and complex monitoring which requires a significant capacity for adaptation and self-management (Mosley et al. 2017; Holkham and Soundy 2018). Relatives play a vital role in care pathways.

To study the trajectories of the involvement of relatives and the dynamics of their participation, we conducted 19 semi-structured interviews with caregivers of people with Parkinson's or ALS between September 2018 and January 2019 in Isère (see Box 2.1). The interviews enable the recognition of patients and their relatives as active change agents within their relationships with healthcare professionals and the wider health system. The adopted approach is comprehensive and narrative-based, aimed at exploring the experiences of caregivers and their care recipients. The objective is to understand the actions of relatives in the patient care pathway (what they do), the context of their actions, and the reasons that motivate them (why they do it). It is also a question of identifying the dynamics of their participation, the moments of rupture, of choice between several possibilities as well as the constraints and resources linked to their involvement.

The sample of caregivers interviewed was constituted thanks to the mediation of France Parkinson Isère, of the Centre de référence des maladies neuromusculaires (CRMN) and the ALS center of the Grenoble University Hospital (CHU). The average duration of the interviews is 1 hour 23 minutes, and some were conducted in the presence of the person cared for. They were fully transcribed and analyzed using the NVivo textual data processing software.

Among the 19 relatives interviewed, 8 help a person with Parkinson's and 11 a person with ALS. 60% of the sick people are men. The stages of the disease vary. The majority of people with Parkinson's are still independent. For people with ALS, they are in an advanced stage of the disease and some people had died at the time of the interview. 68% of caregivers, aged 56 years old on average at the time of the survey, are women. Six caregivers are employed, eight are retired, three are on sick leave, and two are unemployed. The situations are diverse about the bond between the person being cared for and the caregiver in the presence of friends, spouses, parents and children. However, spouses are the majority, representing 74% of dyads. Some caregivers have a medical background, others do not.

Box 2.1. *Interviews with caregivers and sample*

2.4. Results

2.4.1. *The components of care and the meaning of involvement*

From the interviews, we can characterize the support of caregivers, their layman production of care and its logic and the context as well as the context in which these activities are carried out. The interviews also reflect the lived experience of those close to them. The analysis of the specificity of their involvement based on the patient–caregiver–professional triad sheds light on the unique position of caregivers. They act with but also in the place of the sick person just as they act with but also in the place of professional caregivers, indicating a complementary and/or substitutive relationship (Table 2.1).

The interviews made it possible to identify four components of support, which are common to caregivers with regard to both illnesses. They vary depending on the caregivers and the disease progression stage.

2.4.1.1. *Supportive care and support for self-managing the disease*

Supportive or compensatory care, not involving medication, refers to all actions outside of therapeutic treatment aimed at relieving pain, slowing the progression of the disease, reducing its effects and improving the quality of life and comfort of patients.

For caregivers of people with Parkinson's, it is about encouraging social and sports activities and supporting the motivation of sick people, because doing sports helps to create dopamine:

> […] he tended to close in on himself and so I had to tell him, we're going to see friends, hey, we're going to do that when I come back from work. […] you always had to stimulate him a little… (Park-5F).

For caregivers of people with ALS, nutrition is an important part of supportive care:

> So I focused all my energy on anything that was gentle therapy, food, anything that could help him feel better […]. Above all, he really should not have been losing too much weight […]. So I spent weeks studying nutrition. […] In this disease diet […] is approximately 50% of the treatment. […] From the moment the patient loses weight his general condition deteriorates rapidly and this can also affect muscles which are vital (ALS-7F).

It is also about maintaining communication:

> I learned language [...] with my eyes. [...] Until the end [...] we were still talking (ALS-2F).

The comprehensive approach of the interviews makes it possible to highlight this component of support (which statistical surveys do not allow) by grasping the meaning that caregivers give to their actions: they consider these activities as an integral part of the treatment of the disease to slow its progression and improve the quality of life of patients.

Involvement in supportive care by caregivers implies complementarity: complementary to the sick person's involvement and treatment and medical care. It is a component valued by relatives/informal caregivers, who demand recognition of support activities and care by the health system and its professionals.

2.4.1.2. *Medical care*

When the illness progresses, the involvement of loved ones in medical care is common. In the sample, the majority of information caregivers to people with ALS participates in medical care and perform technical procedures such as noninvasive ventilation, connection/disconnection of the gastric tube, nasal suction, chest physiotherapy or the preparation of certain medications. In the case of Parkinson's disease, relatives sometimes help with drug treatment, by organizing or supervising the taking of medications at a fixed time and several times in a day. Some relatives also participate in physiotherapy exercises with the sick person.

Participation in the production of medical care by relatives most often has a substitutional implication with regard to professionals. If some relatives do not wish to get involved in this type of activity (and are able to), others carry them out, due to a lack of professionals or to be able to deal with emergency situations. For certain actions, the sick person also prefers that their relative, in whom they have more confidence, intervene.

2.4.1.3. *Support for the medical journey*

Accompanying patients on their medical journey involves organizing and accompanying them to medical appointments, as well as helping them with the management of day hospitalizations as well as returning home, and administrative and financial procedures (monitoring reimbursements, research and monitoring of financial aid if applicable). The evolution of the disease with more significant damage to the sick person leads relatives to become more involved in this component (in the case of ALS in our sample).

If relatives get involved in supporting the medical journey, it is both to obtain information on the illness and the treatments, and to transmit information on the effects of the treatments on a daily basis, on the side effects and on compliance. They, at times, play an alert role in emergency situations, as well as mediate with the sick person. With regard to the organization of hospitalizations, their involvement aims to overcome the difficulties linked to hospital organization in particular (by, for example, coming along with the sick person's home care assistants during hospitalization, in the case of ALS). Relatives often report a difficult experience with this component of support, linked to a lack of confidence in what will happen in the hospital and to questions of coordination and continuity of hospital care. This implies both complementary support for the sick and substitution in emergencies.

2.4.1.4. *Decisions on therapeutic strategies*

The involvement of loved ones in decisions on therapeutic strategies takes different forms: decisions relating to the implementation and adaptation of treatments (in the case of Parkinson's disease); end-of-life decisions; and decisions concerning advance directives (particularly in the case of ALS). The involvement of relatives in therapeutic decisions aims to seek information and transmit it, at times in emergency situations, while also aiming to assert the preferences and values of their sick loved one.

In certain cases, relatives mediate and manage conflicts between the sick person and health professionals, particularly when there is opposition and conflict between the medical profession and the patient. In interviews, relatives speak of a "battle" with health professionals to ensure patients' end-of-life choices are respected. It is then an implication of substitution or intermediation for the sick person.

The interviews show that the family and relatives are involved in the care journey of their sick loved one, to maintain their functional and social capacities and to "preserve what is important to [them]" (Le Galès et al. 2015).

2.4.2. *The dynamics of the involvement of informal caregivers and their challenges*

The dynamics of the participation of informal caregivers in the care pathway highlights the relational issues between relatives and professionals, professionals and patients as well as patients and caregivers, in terms of information, consultation, skills and decisions.

Components of informal care	The reasons and motivations	Position about professionals
Support in the self-management of illness and participation in the production of supportive care	Maintaining the functional and social abilities of their sick loved one	Implication of complementarity
Participation in the production of medical care	Dealing with emergencies Addressing the lack of professionals Trust of the sick person	Implication of substitution
Support for the medical journey	Emergency alerts, if applicable Research in order to find information Transmission of information on the effects of everyday treatments, on side effects, on therapeutic compliance issues Mediation with the sick person Overcoming the difficulties linked to the organization of care, particularly in hospitals No confidence in hospital care	Implication of complementarity and/or substitution
Decisions on therapeutic strategies	Emergency situations, if applicable Research in order to find information Transmission of information on the sick person's preferences and values Promoting consideration for psychosocial aspects and effects on daily life Mediation Promoting the preferences and values of the sick person during decisions and their implementation	Implication of complementarity and/or substitution

Table 2.2. *Positioning of informal caregivers: an implication of complementarity and/or substitution*

2.4.2.1. *Information about the disease and medical and nonmedical treatments*

The participation of relatives presupposes that they have information – about the illness, the treatments, the patient's care journey, etc. – and that professionals transmit this information.

Some relatives highlight the difficulty in obtaining information and explanations from specialist doctors, neurologists in particular. The qualities of the clinician partly explain this:

> A very good neurologist but very uncommunicative. [...] to get the information it was very, very, very difficult, you know in the old-fashioned way (Park-8H).

> Yes, sometimes they talk too medically (ALS-6F).

This is also explained by the approach of certain doctors, focused on medication-based treatments, without a more global vision of the quality of life of patients and what could relieve them on an everyday basis (supportive and compensatory care). This is particularly problematic at specific points of care (diagnosis and end of life):

> [...] Diagnosis in this disease is essential [...]. It first determines the understanding of what is happening, then the way we must go about it, and how we will act. Because the first thing we are told is that it is an illness that cannot be cured, without any more explanation than that (ALS-7F).

> Neurologists provide very little information on everything available that is available to help the patient, that is to say without talking about treatments, simply diet, followed by relaxation sessions [...]. That is to say, when you are very ill, everything that is compensation is essential, everything that provides pleasure, comfort. [...] And unfortunately, doctors don't work on that. They only relieve the symptoms but do not work on other parameters (ALS-7F).

This leads some caregivers not to accompany their loved one to medical consultations:

> [...] It has happened that I accompany him but... there is nothing to expect. The visit to the neurologist only means renewing prescriptions [...] (Park-3H).

Loved ones and patients then seek information online, from patient associations (France Parkinson, ARSLA, etc.) or in their family and friendship networks.

In addition to the issue of information, the lack of coordination – particularly in hospitals where several specialized professionals are involved in care – harms the reception and understanding of information by relatives.

2.4.2.2. *Dialogue: the consultation of relatives and transmission of information by relatives*

The first level of participation in the care pathway is the dialogue between health professionals, patients and their caregivers. Dialogue implies that professionals consult relatives and patients and that the latter transmit information to professionals. The construction of this three-way dialogue is not straightforward. It raises specific issues of legitimacy and responsibility for caregivers and sometimes of conflicts between the preferences of the patient and those of the caregiver.

2.4.2.2.1. Recognizing the place of relatives in the care relationship

Health professionals consulting with loved ones involves recognizing their specific place alongside sick people. The interviews show that at the beginning of the illness, relatives are not always consulted and can be excluded from the care relationship, centered on the patients:

> [...] there is no three-way meeting in the end, in fact the caregiver is completely excluded from the process (Park-1F).

> Because until now I left it to him... I was there all the time but the conversation was between him and the neurologist, I was next door; she asked me a few questions but it was mainly between the two of them, [...] it's normal, it's his health, it's up to him to manage (Park-5F).

As the disease progresses (worsening of the disease for ALS or even side effects of treatments for Parkinson's), relatives become intermediaries between patients and doctors.

2.4.2.2.2. What legitimacy do relatives have in transmitting information?

The transmission of information is particularly important in monitoring treatments involving medication. Relatives are able to provide information on developments or changes in patients' behavior which may be a sign of adverse effects of medications or of over/under dosage. Caregivers have a particularly therapeutic alerting and monitoring role.

However, the transmission of information to health professionals by relatives is neither straightforward nor natural, due to their specific position, as neither patients nor doctors:

> And in fact I realized that he [her husband] said only what he wanted to, but not everything. [...] As he does not want to fall into this molecule he is going to lie a little to say it is finally going well; but I

> don't live it like that at all. [...]. On the other hand, if I go there and speak on his behalf, I don't know if the neurologist will accept what I'm going to tell him. [...] Having said that, what measures he will take between the patient and the spouse, I do not know. And somehow by doing this I substitute myself for my husband and I almost betray him. So there is also this problem of saying what legitimacy I have in saying things in his place (Park-1F).

2.4.2.3. *Towards a co-production of care: professionals in an agent role and loved ones in an active role*

In certain cases, professional–informal caregivers relationships go beyond simple dialogue and consist of producing care together, which includes supportive care, medical care, the organization of the care pathway and therapeutic decisions. The co-production of care, conjunct and recognized by health professionals, can contribute to the evolution of care, ways of caring and treatments. Interviews show that some patients and their informal caregivers become "experts" in living with the disease, and seek alternative treatments or new treatments, often abroad (such as stem cell treatments, food supplements or even access to Édaravone treatment for ALS in France):

> [Relationship with a neurologist, on food supplements] She follows us, we work together on it, all the ideas I have, I bring to her, she tells me whether it's OK or not, whether it's effective or not, whether specific treatments are duplicated, whether it's of no use, whether the body can synthesize certain food supplements or not. What interests me is finding a synergy where we can all work together [...] (ALS-7F).

> So we made an appointment with this neurologist [in the United States], [...] she named different treatments, including Édaravone, which is a very powerful anxiolytic and which initially treated strokes. We had already contacted our neurologist at the CHU who told us "there is no problem [...] if you go see her I am interested and I will help you, I will follow you, I will have interviews with her in English". [...] So it's our neurologist, who in his corner, all alone wrote the requests for an ATU [temporary authorization for use] and ensured that we could obtain priority, but that all the recently diagnosed patients could also have access to this treatment if they wished (ALS - 7F).

This co-production of care assumes an agent role for professionals and an active role for the patient and their loved ones.

2.4.2.3.1. Listening to informal caregivers and recognizing their knowledge

On the side of health professionals, this requires that they consult informal caregivers, that they listen to their information, their observations, and that they recognize their expertise:

> [...] This year, I saw it was starting again. However, as I noticed it immediately, I went to see the doctor following him at the medio-psychological center. He gave him antidepressants again, and since then, it has improved, and there has not been a big clash like before (Park-2F).

> We usually see [the neurologist] every six months but since the overdose problem the communication has gone through me; it's "I'll leave it to you, call me if necessary" whereas before it was C. [her husband] and that was normal, but now she's started listening […] and now every time she asks questions because there are things of which C. is not aware of (Park_5F).

The consideration of information from informal caregivers is not systematic, and they emphasize health professionals' failure to listen. We can cite the wife of a Parkinson's patient who had warned doctors of side effects linked to her partner's treatment and who was not heard:

> […]they are not attentive enough to the people in contact with the patient all the time. […] Because you know nothing about it you are not a doctor and that doesn't go down well, because you know it already (Park-2F).

2.4.2.3.2. Skills and know-how

Family members must have the necessary skills and resources to be co-producers or medical care providers.

The interviews highlight the conditions for learning these technical gestures and the transfer of skills and responsibilities. While some relatives acquire these skills in the hospital, from nurses or from patient associations, they also often learn through experience. It is common for relatives to impart lay expertise to caregivers or acquaintances by sharing their acquired experiences of caring for a sick loved one. This knowledge is then positioned with respect to the sick individual:

> No, I'm not trained for a tracheotomy either. I will learn as I have learned everything, with him, the transfers, [...] I am the one who introduces the medication (ALS-8F).

2.5. Conclusion

This knowledge constructed during the experience of illness and everyday life with the illness of their loved one, particularly regarding the observation of symptoms, their interpretation, and treatment, redefines the clinic (Jouet et al. 2010). Although this experiential knowledge demonstrates that care is a co-production between the patient, their entourage, and health professionals.

Some patients and their informal caregivers become "experts" in living with the disease and taking this expertise into account by professionals and the health system can contribute to improving support and access to new treatments by changing the ways of "taking care", as the study shows for ALS. In order to formalize and have this expertise recognized, the role of patient associations is essential. The work on HIV has shown how third-sector mobilization has contributed to promoting the figure of an active patient (Barbot 2002).

The study also shows that if the caregiver experience is specific, it is within the interactions with health professionals and medical and social organizations, due to their unique positioning. This raises questions of legitimacy and accountability for relatives. A legal framework exists with the possibility of designating a trusted person, who plays the role of a privileged witness in end-of-life procedures and decisions. However, in the daily support of the sick person, the skills, knowledge and expertise of relatives which are complementary to the medical skills of professionals and those of patients are more difficult to have recognized. Several recommendations from the Haute Autorité de santé (French High Authority for Health) and the plan to combat neurodegenerative diseases (2014–2019) recommend formalizing the place of loved ones, particularly in hospitals and in medico-social establishments. Studying the point of view of professionals in relation to their interactions with caregivers and their expertise is one of the extensions of this research.

Finally, the study shows that the participation of relatives, which ranges from dialogue with professionals to co-production in care actions, varies depending on the relatives and the components of support in the care process. This variability reflects situations where involvement or noninvolvement is sometimes desired and sometimes forced to overcome difficulties in accessing professionals or hospital organizations. It also reveals the weakness of the psychosocial approach in the healthcare system. The involvement and participation of loved ones are the expression of two non-convergent logics: an institutional logic of cost reduction and a logic where relatives seek to strengthen their capacity to act. Furthermore, while the participation and experience of loved ones are influenced by individual factors, organizational and sociopolitical factors also play an important role. Without simultaneous action on these different levels, encouraging the participation of relatives can reinforce inequalities in health and support between patients, as it depends on the economic, cultural, and social resources of families.

The participation of the patient and those around them in the process of co-production of care constitutes a potential for transforming the healthcare system and finding new designs (Batalden 2016) for it, which presupposes a transformation of relationships with health professionals and organizations (information and training, development of therapeutic education[3] for loved ones), a transformation of health organizations (integration of medical and nonmedical care, coordination and continuity of care, etc.) and new measures of health outcomes (psychosocial perspective of health which integrates quality of life).

2.6. References

Barbot, J. (2002). *Les Malades en mouvement. La médecine et la science à l'épreuve du sida*. Balland, Paris.

Batalden, M., Batalden, P., Margolis, P., Seid, M., Armstrong, G., Opipari-Arrigan, L., Hartung, H. (2016). Coproduction of healthcare service. *BMJ Qual. Saf.*, 25, 509–517.

Boivin, A.P., Flora, L., Dumez, V., L'Espérance, A., Berkesse, A., Gauvin, F.P. (2017). Co-construire la santé en partenariat avec les patients et le public : historique, approche et impacts du "modèle de Montréal". In *La participation des patients*, Hervé, C. and Stanton-Jean, M. (eds). Dalloz, Paris.

Bragstad, L.K., Kirkevold, M., Foss, C. (2014). The indispensable intermediaries: A qualitative study of informal caregivers' struggle to achieve influence at and after hospital discharge. *BMC Health Serv. Res.*, 14(331). doi: 10.1186/1472-6963-14-331.

Bungener, M. (1987). Logique et statut de la production familiale de santé. *Sci. Soc. Santé*, 5(2), 45–59.

Buthion, V. and Godé, C. (2014). Les proches-aidants, quels rôles dans la coordination du parcours de soins des personnes malades ? *Journal de gestion et d'économie médicales*, 32(7), 501–519.

Campéon, A., Le Bihan-Youinou, B., Martin, C. (2012). La prise en charge des personnes âgées dépendantes en Europe : le vécu des aidants familiaux. *Vie Soc.*, 4, 111–127.

3 Therapeutic education is mainly aimed at the patient and "aims to make the patient more autonomous through the appropriation of knowledge and skills so that they become the actor of their behavioral change during major care events (initiation of treatment, modification of treatment, intercurrent events, etc.), but also more generally throughout the care project with the objective of having a quality of life which is acceptable to them" (Saout et al. 2008, p. 171).

Carman, K.L., Dardess, P., Maurer, M., Sofaer, S., Adams, K., Bechtel, C., Sweeney, J. (2013). Patient and family engagement: A framework for understanding the element and developing interventions and policies. *Health Aff.*, 32(2), 223–231.

Charles, C.A., Gafni, A., Whelan, T. (1999). Decision-making in the physician-patient encounter: Revisiting the shared treatment decision-making model. *Soc. Sci. Med.*, 49, 651–661.

Clayman, M.L., Roter, D., Wissow, L.S., Bandeen-Roche, K. (2005). Autonomy-related behaviors of patient companions and their effect on decision-making activity in geriatric primary care visits. *Soc. Sci. Med.*, 60(7), 1583–1591.

Coudin, G. (2005). Les familles de malades atteints de maladie d'Alzheimer et leur réticence par rapport à l'aide professionnelle. *Sci. Soc. Santé*, 23(3), 95–104.

Coulter, A. (1997). Partnerships with patients: The pros and cons of shared clinical decision-making. *J. Health Serv. Res. Policy*, 2, 112–121.

Coulter, A., Parsons, S., Askham, J. (2008). Où sont les patients dans la prise de décision concernant leurs propres soins de santé ? *Conférence ministérielle européenne de l'OMS sur les systèmes de santé : "Système de santé et prospérité"*, Tallin, 25–27 June.

Fantino, B., Wainsten, J.P., Bungener, M., Joublin, H., Brun-Strang, C. (2007). Représentations par les médecins généralistes du rôle de l'entourage accompagnant le patient. *Santé Publique*, 3(19), 241–252.

Fumagalli, L.P., Radelli, G., Lettieri, E., Bertele, P., Masella, C. (2015) Patients empowerment and its neighbours: Clarifying the boundaries and their mutual relationshop. *Health Policy*, 119(3), 384–394.

Guadagnoli, E. and Ward, P. (1998). Patient participation in decision-making. *Soc. Sci. Med.*, 47, 329–339.

Holkham, L. and Soundy, A. (2018). The experience of informal caregivers of patients with motor neurone disease: A thematic synthesis. *Palliat. Support. Care*, 16(4), 487–496.

Ishikawa, H., Roter, D.L., Yamazaki, Y., Takayama, T. (2005). Physician-elderly patient-companion communication and roles of companions in Japanese geriatric encounters. *Soc. Sci. Med.*, 60(10), 2307–2320.

Jouet, E., Flora, L.G., Las Vergnas, O. (2010). Construction et reconnaissance des savoirs expérientiels des patients : note de synthèse. *Pratiques de formation/Analyses*, 58/59, 13–94.

Le Galès, C., Bungener, M., Groupe Capabilités. (2015). *Alzheimer : préserver ce qui importe. Les "capabilités" dans l'accompagnement à domicile de la maladie*. Presses Universitaires de Rennes, Rennes.

Mosley, P.E., Moodie, R., Dissanayaka, N. (2017). Caregiver burden in Parkinson disease: A critical review of recent literature. *J. Geriatr. Psychiatry Neurol.*, 30(5), 235–252.

Mougeot, F., Robelet, M., Rambaud, C., Occelli, P., Buchet-Poyau, K., Touzet, S., Michel, P. (2018). L'émergence du patient-acteur dans la sécurité des soins en France : une revue narrative de la littérature entre sciences sociales et santé publique. *Santé Publique*, 30(1), 73–81.

Ortiz Halabi, I., Scholtes, B., Voz, B., Gillain, N., Durieux, N., Odero, A., Baumann, N., Ziegler, O., Gagnayre, R., Guillaume, M. (2020). Patient participation and related concepts: A scoping review on their dimensional composition. *Patient Educ. Couns.*, 103, 5–14.

Oshima, L.E. and Emanuel, E.J. (2013). Shared decision making to improve care and reduce costs. *N. Engl. J. Med.*, 368(1), 6–8.

Pomey, M., Flora, L., Karazivan, P., Dumez, V., Lebel, P., Vanier, M., Jouet, E. (2015). Le "Montréal model" : enjeux du partenariat relationnel entre patients et professionnels de la santé. *Santé Publique*, 27, 41–50.

Saout, C., Charbonnel, B., Bertrand, D. (2008). Pour une politique nationale d'éducation thérapeutique du patient. Report, Ministère de la Santé, Paris.

Scholl, I., Zill, J.M., Harter, M., Dirmaier, J. (2014). An integrative model of patient-centeredness. A systematic review and concept analysis. *Plos One*, 9(9), e107828.

Thompson, A.G.H. (2007). The meaning of patient involvement and participation in health care consultations: A taxonomy. *Soc. Sci. Med.*, 64, 1297–1310.

Wolf, J.A., Niederhauser, V., Marshburn, D., LaVela, S.L. (2014). Defining patient experience. *Patient Exp. J.*, 1(1), 7–19.

Zigante, V. (2018). Informal care in Europe: Exploring formalisation, availability and quality. Report, Publications Office of the European Union, Luxembourg.

3

The Experiential Approach and Alzheimer's Disease: Including the Spiritual Dimension for a More Global Approach

3.1. Introduction

Nowadays, a new care paradigm, as well as an innovative look at the caregiver–patient relationship, promotes a more active role for the sick person themselves by recognizing their knowledge about their illness and the care that is to be provided for them. Indeed, "patient engagement has for several years been seen as one of the promising avenues" for the well-being of both patient and the health system (Pomey et al. 2015, p. 49). The prerequisite for this commitment is the recognition of the "experiential knowledge" of patients which enriches and guides the professional knowledge of caregivers (Jouet et al. 2010). Faced with the "Alzheimer patient", whose memory, logic and discursive capacities are impaired, the legitimation of the experience is largely compromised. Firstly, because our experiences can be expressed through indirect or unusual means (Hirsch 2011), which remain ignored. Secondly, because the disqualification of the person themselves (Hirsch 2011) discredits their experience. Although it appears to be more difficult, access to the sick person's lived experience, as well as access to their experience of the healthcare system, nonetheless remains essential for designing appropriate support.

Chapter written by Ruth Laure ALAMARGUY and Pauline LENESLEY.

Furthermore, the awareness of the need to take the whole person into account, particularly during chronic illnesses, has grown (Smyre et al. 2018). Whole person care, holistic care, biopsychosocial approach, these neighboring terms which overlap without superimposing (Thomas et al. 2018) have a common foundation: a multidimensional approach to the sick person. Part of this dynamic, the question of spirituality in care has experienced renewed interest in recent decades (Schmit 2017) but is often thought of in the context of palliative care, as evidenced by the biopsychosocial–spiritual model, designed for end-of-life care. However, "spirituality fundamentally responds to the need to find meaning and reason with regards to life events (Potter and Perry 2010; Jobin 2012)" (in Gaillard Desmedt and Shaha (2013, p. 1)), it cannot be confined to the gates of death.

Alzheimer's disease disrupts the sick person's life experience. Sagne (2007, p. 6) describes this upheaval as "a traumatic event [which] reexamines our conception of identity, of the awareness of oneself and of the other, of the notions of recognition, and of memory, which structure our conception of the singularity of each human being". Considering the entirety of being without neglecting its essence is all the more necessary since the visible would tend to determine what the person is in the eyes of their counterpart.

But while theoretically the question of spirituality in care is unavoidable, it seems difficult to grasp concretely. Several studies show that many caregivers convinced of the merits of considering spiritual needs in caregiving put them aside (Snapp et al. 2021) due to a lack of time, as well as due to discomfort (Vermandere et al. 2011; Abdulla et al. 2019; López-Tarrida et al. 2021). How then can we reconcile this issue of quality of care with the embarrassment that the evocation of the spiritual arouses? How do we perceive the spiritual dimension in a healthcare situation? In this chapter, we propose addressing the importance of the spiritual aspect of supporting people affected by Alzheimer's disease in order to discuss both the obstacles and the perspectives for implementing a truly global approach to the sick person.

3.2. Alzheimer's disease: loss or search for meaning?

Alzheimer's disease, unknown to the general public 40 years ago, is today widely considered to be a social scourge which crystallizes fears of "aging badly". In Western societies' eyes, it represents ultimate decline (Ngatcha-Ribert 2004).

3.2.1. *At the macrosociological level: Alzheimer's disease, a predicted loss of meaning*

The pejorative representation of this disease is the result of a culture. At odds with socially praised values, the patient is discredited, and considers themselves to have fallen.

3.2.1.1. *Alzheimer's disease, a Western definition*

The clinical picture of Alzheimer's disease as described by Westerners can be observed all around the globe in all types of populations. However, it is not the subject of any medical evaluation in many cultures, because it is not necessarily experienced as abnormal. For example, like many populations with traditional cultures, Canadian Aborigines "perceive cognitive and behavioral changes as a normal consequence of the aging process. Their conception of the life cycle places aging as 'a return to the baby stage'" (Ngatcha-Ribert 2014, p. 24). Variations in behavior are therefore experienced as normal and constitutive of an existential continuum. Elsewhere, in Africa, those who are sometimes described as "déments" (demented), that is, "whose mind is undone" by Westerners can be considered as having "on the contrary more spirit, because they are decanted and the spirits speak through them" (Ngatcha-Ribert 2014, p. 20).

In the studies carried out by Western researchers and compiled by Ngatcha-Ribert, we note the pervasiveness of the filter of the biomedical vision of disorders. By biomedical, we mean the ontological approach to illness in that it has a consistency: there is an organic lesion caused by an exogenous factor; it is an attack that must be resolved (Laplantine 1993). This biological, organic approach, targeted at the disease, eclipses the patient and their experience.

There is a certain Western uniformity in the way Alzheimer's disease is approached. The primary objective for our societies frightened by this disease is de facto to find a cure for it. The "biomedicalization of dementia" has therefore imposed itself in our societies (der Linden and Juillerat 2014) and leaves little room for alternatives to explain the loss of bearings of elderly people. However, "an anthropological awareness of dementia as a social and cultural phenomenon could add an important dimension to the efforts of scientists trying to understand it" (Nubukpo et al. in Ngatcha-Ribert (2014, p. 25)). It emerges from the analyses of the speech of people affected by Alzheimer's disease that their behavior sometimes stems from self-preservation strategies, directly linked to their psychosocial context and to the reactions of those around them (Enjolras 2005). The type of view cast onto the disoriented person is imbued with cultural representations which may or may not consider behaviors deemed "suspicious" as pathological. And, while the distinction between normal and pathological is closely linked to social norms as

Canguilhem (2013) reminds us, the label of "Alzheimer's disease" imposed by Western culture is far from being neutral.

3.2.1.2. *Alzheimer's disease, a socially engaged prognosis*

The vision conveyed by Western culture of Alzheimer's disease is profoundly repulsive. Stephen Post, a physician and professor of medical ethics:

> contextualizes the concept of Alzheimer's disease within [what he calls] a 'hypercognitive' culture and society, in which nothing is more frightening than the disease of Alzheimer's because it violates the spirit of self-control, independence, economic productivity and cognitive performance which defines our dominant image of human accomplishment (Post 2000 in Ngatcha-Ribert (2012, p 68)).

The social injunction to "aging well" favors a physically and mentally healthy old age and discredits the individual who deviates from the socially established norm (Ngatcha-Ribert 2012). Its intolerance is all the greater as society cultivates the utopia of perfect health (Sfez 1995).

Furthermore, in a context of "acceleration of the pace of life", and more generally of global acceleration of time, which disqualifies the past (Deléage and Sabin 2014), how does the person destabilized in their spatio-temporal orientation, and resolutely attached to the past by the scraps of their memory, find their place? People disoriented by Alzheimer's disease are therefore considered as socially deviant individuals and, as a result, stigmatized and ostracized. The diagnosis of Alzheimer's disease therefore carries within itself something irremediable and a condemnation to irreversible exclusion from a Western society whose values are incompatible with the patient's condition. The patient's behavioral disorders in fact disturb their counterpart, whether individual or collective, seeing as

> the reflection that comes to [the counterpart] is: 'I hope that such a thing does not happen to me.' This double movement of recognition of the other as similar paired with its rejection as an impossible double underlies the root of difficulties in Alzheimer's disease in its interhuman dimension (Pitaud 2007, p 12).

The label "Alzheimer's disease" contains in itself the announcement of a loss of social status – for a person already stigmatized by their age – while also predicting an alienation of identity.

3.2.1.3. *Alzheimer's disease, a presumed inevitable loss of identity*

The perception and imagination built around Alzheimer's disease, described as neurodegenerative, are not without consequences for the person who is dehumanized and then desocialized (Ngatcha-Ribert 2004; Cavayas et al. 2012). Because beyond the alteration of the social identity of the disoriented person, it is their individual identity as a human person which is damaged in the eyes of others. The memory problems typical of Alzheimer's disease constitute "in the eyes of others, an existential handicap" (Post 2000 in Ngatcha-Ribert (2012, p.60)). "Losing one's memory is, in a way, losing one's mind, as if the person had lost all of their intellectual and mental functions, having had their head emptied of its content." Stephen Post emphasizes that asserting "I think therefore I am" is therefore equivalent to claiming that "if I do not think, I am not" (Post 2000 in Ngatcha-Ribert (2012, p. 60)). It questions here our conception of identity. A conception based both on memory as a preserver of identity over time (Nizzi 2012) and on the capacity to tell one's story, that Ricœur put forward through the concept of "narrative identity" (Ricœur 1988). This dual conception of identity explains the reasons for its presumed loss by people living with Alzheimer's disease. On the one hand, the modification of their behavior undermines the permanence of their identity. On the other hand, the loss of narrative thread due to cognitive disorders is seen as destructive of the subject's identity construction. The two constituent pillars of identity, as it is traditionally thought of, are therefore fundamentally shaken. Affected people are thus seen as deprived of their identity.

Assimilated by the patient themselves, these representations necessarily affect them and deteriorate relationships with others (Werner 2005). "This is a typical example of a self-fulfilling prophecy: those who are given a diagnosis of Alzheimer's disease now risk being observed as such, and of their every behavior being interpreted based on this fact" (Van Gorp et al. 2012, p. 61). The supposed deprivation of identity seems contained in the diagnosis itself, and is intrinsically linked to the representation that society has of it. The label which is immediately applied induces a different view of the sick individual. As soon as the diagnosis is announced, the person disappears, masked by the illness. This having been said, the supposed loss of identity, just like the loss of social status, is not the result of the illness, but really of a social construction: "the lived experience of Alzheimer's disease is social, because it is determined by the collective frameworks, by words, by ways of thinking and doing which have been built around this disease in our societies" (Béliard 2019, p. 15). While failing to be able to deconstruct these models, it is necessary to become aware of them and to objectify the reality of Alzheimer's disease.

3.2.2. *At the microsociological level: sick people in search of meaning*

Beyond social eviction and the presumed disappearance of the patient's identity, an existential loss of meaning is also predicted for them as well as for their loved ones (Institut universitaire en santé mentale 2014).

3.2.2.1. *Living with illness by rejecting nonsense*

The announcement of a serious illness constitutes an existential upheaval,

> a phase of rupture: rupture of time, between before the illness and after illness which seems uncertain; rupture of the link, link of self to self, link of self to other and link of self to a transcendence. This rupture is the crucible of a loss of meaning (Echard 2006, p. 1).

While Alzheimer's disease is in our society considered to be a serious illness, which also carries social and identity nonsense, those who are confronted with it may be led to reconstruct meaning based on their own experiences.

Thus, while the dominant representations in the collective imagination resonate with the people affected, they coexist with a diversity of individual representations which feed on scientific and media discourse while simultaneously keeping it at a distance. Béliard (2019), who conducted a sociological survey among 55 entourages (i.e. 130 interviews) of people directly affected by Alzheimer's disease, in this regard underlines the diversity of reactions to a confirmed or unconfirmed suspicion of Alzheimer's disease. While some take up the main features of medical analysis, speak of "memory disorders", of degeneration, and consider that it is the brain which malfunctions, others conceive of things in terms of "old age", of an aging which leads to inevitable deterioration, and which is not necessarily pathological. Others also mainly highlight the role of certain life accidents or emotional shocks in triggering the disorder. For some, the diagnosis of Alzheimer's disease is simply unthinkable, inconceivable.

Collective representation, linked to the "deprivatization movement of aging and health" (Meidani 2015), wishes to impose itself on the individual and claims to dictate their experience. But the individual does not remain passive in the face of the intrusion of public power into the private sphere and resists the normative formatting of collective representations by constructing their own conception of illness. This distancing is a personal attempt to give meaning to lived reality, something that dominant representations deny.

3.2.2.2. *Beyond illness, the challenge of recognizing being*

The view cast on the person affected by Alzheimer's disease is crucial as it directly impacts the progression of the disease (Ploton 2009). It is in fact reductive to conceive consistency of a person commensurate with the thickness of being we ourselves think to have, and to think of the subject only according to the experience that so-called healthy people have of them. Grosclaude thus notes that "the conviction of [the] disappearance [of the subject] arises from the misunderstanding of the psyche and the theoretical incapacity to think of the human being in other states, in other forms than one's own, both current and conscious" (Grosclaude 2017, p. 167).

In order to take the opposite view of identity traditionally conceived of as immutable, Nizzi (2012) suggests conceiving of identity as "a psychological process, a dynamic and plastic construction" (ibid, p. 54). It offers a change of perspective by arguing "that we do not "remain" ourselves so much as we "become" ourselves permanently" (ibid, p. 54). Memory is no longer conceived of as a guarantor of identity, as a collection of an "objective sum of memories", but rather as a reservoir of memories with fluctuating capacity from which identity construction takes place. Even though the person's memory is affected, they continually develop from their memories, even fragmentary ones, what makes them who they are. This explains the perceived discrepancy between the identity projected by others onto a person and the identity which they themselves construct, sometimes out of step with their age or their current environment. "Behaviors perceived as failures are those that go against what their entourage expect of the person, what they know about them, the way they define their lifestyle, their skills, their character – including in comparison with themselves" (Béliard 2019, p. 180). This having been said, while the observer perceives nonsense, the person with impaired memory capacities continues to make sense.

Several authors highlight that, despite the illness, the depth of being is preserved. Ploton (2009, p. 36) states that "clinically, the emotional foundation of the subject (the true definition of them in their deepest form of identity) seems to be respected and even preserved in a privileged sense, until the end of the disease". Grosclaude (2017), who wondered in his first writings about the eventual possibility of (re)discovering the lost subject, gives a categorical answer to this question by affirming the permanence of the subject and their psychic life. According to him,

> "'proofs of life' [are] given by the lost subject, [who is] discovered somewhere, in their corporalized places of residence where their remains, dispersed, unbound, in solution, indicating to us that they exist and where they do, *provided we look for them there*" (Grosclaude 2017, p. 167).

It is us who highlight this prerequisite, because it demonstrates the extent to which the attitude of others carries meaning or nonsense. By abandoning their "personalized judgment of abnormality" (Béliard 2019, p. 179) with regard to the disoriented person, the gaze of their counterpart contributes to bringing out the reality of their being, metamorphosed but always present. "Staring, speaking and recognizing through gazes and words, the intact sovereignty of those who have lost everything" (Bobin 2019, p. 127) is a prerequisite for any caregiving.

3.2.3. *And the spiritual in all this?*

3.2.3.1. *Quest for meaning, construction of identity, questioning of relationships with others: all spiritual needs*

In the United States, where the question of spirituality is more debated than in France, "spirituality is an aspect of humanity that refers to the way in which individuals seek and express meaning and purpose and the way in which they live their connection to the moment, to themselves, to others, to nature and to the signifier or the sacred" (Appleby et al. 2018). This definition, presented across the Atlantic as consensual, was developed during conferences of health professionals. In Europe, on the other hand, there is no consensus around a definition, but "the religion-spirituality distinction is [however] unanimous among researchers". This distinction is in fact a "novelty" in the West, spirituality once being "the prerogative of religion" (Meuli and Zulian 2014, p. 35). This partly explains the discomfort of health professionals that we mentioned in the introduction, because individual and collective representations are still marked by the spiritual/religious amalgam. The relationship with spirituality is inseparable from the cultural context in which it takes place.

The needs of people living with Alzheimer's disease mentioned in the previous sections, and concerning both the questioning of meaning, as well as of their identity and of their relationship with others, inscribe themselves into the spiritual register. Many authors (Greenstreet 2006; Puchalski et al. 2014; López-Tarrida et al. 2021) emphasize that taking spiritual needs into account in chronic illnesses leads to better quality of care. Hutchinson et al. (2009) discuss two diametrically opposed approaches to care: the curing mode and the healing mode. In curing, the patient seeks to preserve everything that made them who they were before their illness; they seek to avoid any change. The healing mode is achieved when the patient accepts the change produced by the illness and implements their own resources to access a new experience of integrity (Hutchinson 2009). Alzheimer's disease induces an irreversible upheaval which excludes the success of curing care. It involves a healing care that supports the person in living with the illness, in order to experience "a new dimension of life" (Canguilhem 2009, p. 122). Indeed, "the patient is not a passive being, they are only a patient under the medical gaze which makes them an object of care" (Delory-Momberger and Tourette-Turgis 2014, p. 2). Taking the opposite view of the apparent decline associated with the so-called Alzheimer's pathology, the caregiver can choose to see an alter ego and not a denatured double, in the person affected by the disease. They will thus legitimize "their incessant and still largely invisible activity" as a "producer of care" for themselves (Delory-Momberger and Tourette-Turgis 2014, p. 2). To do this, they must recognize not only the needs of the sick person, but also their resources, including spiritual ones.

3.2.3.2. *The spiritual dimension, the watermark of all support*

Seeking to give a schematic, operational and educational definition to spirituality, Jacquemin (2014, p. 127) suggests designating it as "the movement of existence of the human subject". This movement therefore involves a constant search for balance and echoes the dynamic process of identity construction that we mentioned above. Jacquemin (2016) notes that, disrupted in their movement of existence, the patient in search of a new balance will also surrender to the professional, in a certain sense without a precise recipient, without in-depth examination of the adequacy of the competence of the person to whom they reveal themselves, if not the availability of the person they meet. The patient's expectation and needs lie in the domain of validation of the inner process they are experiencing. The gestures and words that the patient produces attest to their effort to rediscover who they are.

So, what is the role of the caregiver? What do they have to do? "Nothing except being present for others", replies Jacquemin. Summoning Paul Ricœur, he calls for the recognition of the power of the linguistic exchange which brings the speaker to the subject that they are. The patient thus calls upon the professional to witness the process of resilience or rebalancing of their movement of existence. We could also add that the sick person shows the supporting person their work of giving life, requiring the presence of others to become themselves. While the caregiver must humbly accept not having an answer, they must allow through their "inhabited" presence to open up a space for interior progress. Patients have their own spiritual strengths and resources (Meuli and Zulian 2014). The image of the watermark seems telling to us: printed in the thickness of the paper, it is always present although invisible at first glance. While it sometimes "jumps out" to the observer, it requires special attention to be discovered. This imprint is seen through a print from which it is inseparable and which could at first glance only be considered in two dimensions. It is the fact of knowing that there is a watermark that leads us to search for it through transparency, but without guaranteeing that we will perceive it. "The goal of spiritual care is to identify and support detected resources" (Meuli and Zulian 2014, p. 30).

The caregiver may believe that they need particular knowledge, of a spiritual nature, in order to meet spiritual needs, in the same way that they acquired specific medical skills in response to certain physical needs of their patients, but it is not that simple. A meta-study (Edwards et al. 2010) underlines that it is above all the relationship which is decisive in taking spiritual needs into account.

> "It is the way in which the caregiver relates to the patient that constitutes the greatest part of spiritual care: being present, listening actively, taking time, expressing empathy, giving physical care while respecting the dignity of the person" (Meuli and Zulian 2014, p. 30).

We present a survey carried out in order to understand the obstacles that prevent the recognition of the spiritual part in the healthcare environment in order to address the conditions for developing a global approach that includes it.

We carried out an ethnographic study with four elderly people aiming to collect their experience of aging through individual interviews, then followed by a participant observation period of 15 half-days spread over four weeks in an ADJ dedicated to people affected by Alzheimer's disease. The management put forward support with an essentially functional aim, the main objective of which was to maintain the existing capacities of the patients and to slow their decline.

At the same time, given the difficulty of openly discussing the spiritual dimension in different establishments contacted, we turned to an establishment explicitly advocating holistic support. This accommodation establishment for dependent elderly people (EHPAD), with a large Alzheimer's unit, has included the search for the "spiritual well-being" of residents in its main missions. We conducted an online questionnaire survey among health professionals in this structure, and we obtained 17 responses. Our questionnaire, alternating between open and closed questions, questioned the spiritual needs of people affected by Alzheimer's disease, the responses given to them as well as the professional's relationship to spirituality and the place attributed to the spiritual in professional practice.

Box 3.1. *Method and study areas*

3.3. Obstacles to taking the spiritual dimension into account in support

Sick person, caregiver, institution: each protagonist involved in the care relationship can, at their own level, knowingly or not, close the door to comprehensive support. We will not mention the aspect of the patient, who, in a position of vulnerability and feeling themselves slipping from the status of a person to that of an object of care, risks allowing themselves to be reduced to their role as patient. We will focus on the role of the institution and that of the caregiver.

3.3.1. *Institutional side: the biomedical approach, a reductive filter*

One of the people we met testified:

> When I arrived at the hospital, I was assigned to geriatrics. Of course, when you arrive: 90 years old, 92 years old, let's go, geriatrics department! Then, they realized that [...] I was not dependent. I didn't need diapers, so that was wonderful! [...] So suddenly, I was put in another department.

This experience was very rewarding for this "upgraded" patient moved to a department other than geriatrics and the measurement of "patient experience" would certainly have given very good scores in this case. But this testimony is particularly revealing in terms of the impact of the biomedical classification of elderly people. What image will this person have of themselves if one day they become incontinent? The patient experience is consubstantial with the view that is placed on the sick person:

> In the ACD, during workshop focused on the body, those welcomed sat in a circle around the caregiver. In front of them, as if we were alone, the caregiver said to us: "we can't do much with them. We always do the same thing because they are disconnected". Out of it (pointing to her head).

This example is symptomatic of the "form of dishumanity" (Ngatcha-Ribert 2012) that others can impose on the person with impaired cognitive abilities. However, Grosclaude (2017, p. 168) recalls that "the demented person only remains a subject on the condition of being treated as such by others, as a peer, as a partner in their care, in the state of their speech, with the condition of speaking *to* them even in silence, and not *about* them". Faced with the "Alzheimer patient", the posture of the caregiver is in fact crucial, because it directly impacts the progression of the disease:

> We met Mr. B., diagnosed with Alzheimer's disease, during his first day in an ADJ. At noon, when it is mealtime, Mr. B., a little lost (it's his first day in this unusual place with all these unknown people), refuses to sit down, insistently asks to go home, and persists in going around the building to find an exit. Accustomed to supporting people at a less advanced stage of the illness, caregivers are destabilized and will perceive this behavior as disturbing. By talking with this gentleman, we come to understand that he has turned his pockets inside out, and, having noticed that he has no money to pay for the meal, simply has decided that he wants to leave.

Unaware that "any behavioral or mood disorder has a meaning " (Derouesné and Selmès 2005, p. 39), the caregivers perceived the behavior of Mr. B. as simple proof of his state of deterioration, a state which will be deemed incompatible with the care that is practiced in this establishment. However, no neuropsychological test could measure this gentleman's combination of probity and logic when he does not want to eat a meal that he cannot pay for.

The biomedical filter is in fact an obstacle to understanding the experience of the person being treated. Jacquemin (2012, p. 520) calls on William James, specifying that "meaning, "truth", does not exist by itself, outside of the experience that the subject has of it at the heart of their own existence, an experience and truth which both present themselves as the place for progressive elaboration and verification of meaning.

IMPORTANT.– When the observer is focused on behavioral disorders, they perceive nonsense, whereas the sick person, within the limits of their altered capacities, continues to make sense. The gaze of the counterpart can, however, bring out the reality of being, sometimes metamorphosed, but always present.

In fact, reestablishing the "Alzheimer patient" as a partner in care could not have as its aim to "allow them to gradually become autonomous and active in the care dynamic" (Pomey et al. 2015, p. 4). This having been said, it can be to simply accept, as Blanchard mentions, to "support the person 'room by room' by considering that the latter finally revisits the house of their life, makes a return to their past before 'being ready to leave the world's stage'" (Clause-Verdreau 2020, p. 12). The caregiver must then recognize that the patient themselves is the only competent person in guiding this visit.

3.3.2. *The caring aspect: the relationship to spirituality guides the approach of the "patient"*

If the institution does not reduce the patient's care to their body alone by denying the whole of their being, the positioning of the caregiver is itself determining in the overall support of the sick person. We were indeed able to note, during our survey, that caregivers were sensitive to taking the spiritual dimension of residents into account: they unanimously recognize the interest in seeking the spiritual well-being of the person and thus inscribe themselves in the orientation provided by the establishment's management. However, their personal investment in contributing to it is expressed as according to a very varied palette. Some respondents take a proactive approach to residents whose religious beliefs they know (e.g. offering to participate in religious services, making sacred books available, etc.), while others say they meet their needs only when an explicit request is made. Others, which are a minority, are further behind. These positions match the various degrees of commitment described by López-Tarrida et al. (2021). The results of this survey seem to confirm that the essential issue for real global care of the person lies around the free and assumed relationship with spirituality and to our own beliefs, whatever these may be.

IMPORTANT.– Relegating personal convictions to the private domain and having a distanced relationship with spirituality hinders the consideration of the potential spiritual needs of the person being supported.

To quote a caregiver: "This subject is anything but neutral", because it involves everyone personally. However, what seems interesting to us in the results of our survey is noting that taking the spiritual dimension into account is not influenced by the nature of the professionals' beliefs. More than 70% of respondents (n = 12) believe that sensitivity to the spiritual needs of residents is not correlated with personal beliefs.

Faced with needs, the responses are in fact differentiated based on those who give support, but what is particularly highlighted by caregivers is the importance of recognizing these needs:

> It seems to me that the important thing is for each caregiver to listen to spiritual needs, without feeling obliged to participate, but at least to listen.

Faced with a need of a spiritual nature, the most cited reaction in both closed and open questions is indeed to listen. More specifically, active and empathetic listening, which is the central tool of the validation™ method, developed by Feil in approaching people with Alzheimer's disease, and which the majority of caregivers are trained for in this structure.

> Naomi Feil [...] proposes tuning into the rhythm of the disoriented old man, to put one's 'steps in his footsteps', to try to enter into 'resonance' with him. It is a matter of being neither in front nor behind, but 'with' him, at his side, of joining him in his reality of the moment and exploring it together, without questioning it, so that he can feel supported (Munsch-Roux and Munsch 2008, p. 31).

"Validating" is recognizing being, the need to exist as an individual, recognizing that words – sometimes at first sight ill-fitted – silences, gestures, facial expressions, have a meaning that belongs to them, if not to discover, to at least be recognized in order to join the other. It is not an approach dedicated to the spiritual sphere, but truly a global approach to the person and their life experience.

3.4. Perspectives: ways to approach the overall lived experience

3.4.1. *Raising awareness among professionals about their relationship to the spiritual and intimate*

Recognizing the other as a person challenged by their health means knowing what deeply affects them and identifying the poles which are an anchor for them. This requires not putting aside the spiritual part of their support. But sensitivity to the inner movement of others can only be achieved through a necessary questioning by the supporting person of their own spirituality. Châtel (2007) emphasizes that "the suffering of the sick also calls us to surpass ourselves, to invent ourselves. Caring for others first of all means risking oneself in the exploration of one's own spiritual dimension" (ibid., p. 6). The spirituality of others summons our own, which forces us to position ourselves. The question of the unique relationship that is established between a caregiver and a sick person is at the heart of the issue of the global care approach. "It is the way in which the caregiver relates to the patient that constitutes the greatest part of spiritual care" (Meuli and Zulian 2014, p. 120). López-Tarrida et al. (2021) evoke a reciprocal and symmetrical relationship from person to person when doctors open the discussion onto the spiritual field.

> There is only a human and spiritual reality when the invisible of man (the hidden face of our being, our history, our feelings, etc.) takes the initiative to show itself, when the intimate of our being has enough confidence in another to truly offer itself to their presence. When we enter this dimension of 'being in truth', stripped of all certainties, we leave the order of good will, of good intentions, and so a true relationship can be established (Baud 2004, p. 69).

Support is this intentionally undertaken approach to meet another self, with awareness of our common vulnerability. But only the caregiver who is aware of their quality of moving in search of balance, of "spiritual being", can recognize this same quality in their counterpart and purposely enter into a holistic perspective of support.

3.4.2. *Initiating collective reflection*

In our survey, we noted, on the one hand, the difficulty of caregivers in citing spiritual needs, and on the other hand, the great disparity in the evaluations of these (a professional with 10 years of seniority said he "never" identified spiritual suffering among residents while a caregiver with less than two years of seniority says he spots it "often"). This highlights the subjectivity of the assessment of needs and the strong divergences that it entails, in the absence of formalized common reflection on the evaluation of spiritual well-being.

Rochat et al. (2015, p. 2055) emphasize that "the relevance of caring for the spiritual dimension of patients without proselytizing depends [not only] on the capacity of each stakeholder to address it [but also] on effective interdisciplinarity in overall care. This is where the hinge between institution and professionals can be decisive". Pujol (2017, p. 40) suggests:

> Instead of thinking about the spiritual question in the caregiver/patient register, it seems more appropriate to think about it in the institutions/people and people/people registers. Institutions/people because it is necessary for health professionals to also be recognized as people in their own right who are also on an internal journey.

3.5. Conclusion

Making room for the experience of the sick person requires becoming aware of the subjectivities at play on both sides of the encounter, between an individual established in their status as caregiver and an individual who would tend to be reduced, and sometimes to reduce themselves to an object of care. The caregiver, shaped by their professional identity, meets a sick person, anchored in their culture, their history and their own experience of illness. From the position of this caregiver, the implicit governing body of the terrain on which the relationship will be established, will result in the nature of the experience lived jointly by the person and their caregiver, but more broadly will also produce an impact on the overall experience of the sick person. The objectivation of the support offered by the caregiver is therefore essential. The rehabilitation of the spiritual part is an essential prerequisite for approaching the reality of the experience of the sick person and for being able to provide an appropriate response. It requires joint reflection among health professionals who will then be able to adopt a critical stance in the face of the risk of being locked into a biomedical logic while shedding their mistrust of the spiritual.

The challenge is to try to grasp the way in which the deterioration of a person's health affects who they are, their existential balance. This having been said, opening up to the reality of the experience lived by others necessarily means accepting the fact that every human encounter is hazardous, and that no quality approach, however, developed, can ever guarantee that the overall experience of the person confronted with the illness is a success every time. Working on the grounds of the vulnerability inherent to human nature also means consenting to being pushed around by others, a primordial condition for the encounter to be gainful for both sides.

3.6. References

Abdulla, A., Hossain, M., Barla, C. (2019). Toward comprehensive medicine: Listening to spiritual and religious needs of patients. *Gerontology & Geriatric Medicine*, 5 [Online]. Available at: https://www.ncbi.nlm.nih.gov/pmc/articles/PMC6487746/.

Appleby, A., Wilson, P., Swinton, J. (2018). Spiritual care in general practice: Rushing in or fearing to tread? An integrative review of qualitative literature. *Journal of Religion and Health*, 57(3), 1108–1124.

Baud, R.C. (2004). L'accompagnement des mourants, un chemin initiatique menant du "pour" au "parce que". *Revue Terre du Ciel*, 72, 69.

Béliard, A. (2019). *Des familles bouleversées par la maladie d'Alzheimer*. Érès, Toulouse.

Bobin, C. (2019). *La Présence pure et autres textes*. Gallimard, Paris.

Canguilhem, G. (2013). *Le normal et le pathologique*, 12th edition. PUF, Paris.

Cavayas, M., Raffard, S., Gély-Nargeot, M.C. (2012). Stigmatisation dans la maladie d'Alzheimer, une revue de la question. *Gériatrie et psychologie neuropsychiatrie du vieillissement*, 10(3), 297–305.

Châtel, T. (2007). Prise en compte du spirituel et nouvelles représentations du soin. *Médecine palliative*, 6(3), 155–216.

Clause-Verdreau, A. (2020). Reconnaître les expériences et les expertises. Retour sur les journées "Éthique, Alzheimer et maladies neuro-évolutives" (12 et 13 novembre 2019, Reims). *Revue française d'éthique appliquée*, 1(1), 144–151.

Deléage, E. and Sabin, G. (2014). Peut-on résister à l'ère du temps accéléré ? *Écologie & politique*, 48(1), 13–21.

Delory-Momberger, C. and Tourette-Turgis, C. (2014). Vivre avec la maladie : expériences épreuves résistances. *Le sujet dans la cité*, 5, 33–38.

Derouesné, C. and Selmès, J. (2005). *La maladie d'Alzheimer : comportement et humeur*. John Libbey Eurotext, Paris.

Echard, B. (2006). Fin de vie et quête de sens. *VST – Vie sociale et traitements*, 90(2), 87–90.

Edwards, A., Pang, N., Shiu, V., Chan, C. (2010). The understanding of spirituality and the potential role of spiritual care in end-of-life and palliative care: A meta-study of qualitative research. *Palliative Medicine*, 24(8), 753–770.

Enjolras, F. (2005). Incidence du pronostic sur la construction des modèles explicatifs de la maladie d'Alzheimer à l'île de la Réunion. *Sci. Soc. Santé*, 23(3), 69–94.

Gaillard Desmedt, S. and Shaha, M. (2013). La place de la spiritualité dans les soins infirmiers : une revue de littérature. *Recherche en soins infirmiers*, 115, 19–35.

Greenstreet, W. (2006). From spirituality to coping strategy: Making sense of chronic illness. *British Journal of Nursing*, 15(17), 938–942.

Grosclaude, M. (2017). Le dément : sujet extrême, sujet quand même. *NPG Neurologie-Psychiatrie-Gériatrie*, 17(99), 166–172.

Hirsch, E. (2011). Expérience d'une disqualification. *Le Journal des psychologues*, 291, 34–36.

Hutchinson, T.A., Hutchinson, N., Arnaert, A. (2009). Whole person care: Encompassing the two faces of medicine. *CMAJ: Canadian Medical Association Journal*, 180(8), 845–846.

Institut universitaire en santé mentale Douglas (2014). Maladie d'Alzheimer : conseils pour la famille [Online]. Available at: www.douglas.qc.ca/info/alzheimer-conseils-famille [Accessed 28 February 2022].

Jacquemin, D. (2012). Ethique et spiritualité dans la relation de soins. Actualité de William James. *Revue théologique de Louvain*, 43, 517–539.

Jacquemin, D. (2014). Soins palliatifs entre rationalité, spiritualité et existence. In *Manuel de soins palliatifs*, 4th edition, Jacquemin, D. and de Broucker, D. (eds). Dunod, Paris, 125–131.

Jacquemin, D. (2016). Spiritualité, besoins spirituels : de quoi parle-t-on ? *18ème journée régionale organisée par la Coordination Bretonne de Soins Palliatifs* [Online]. Available at: https://www.youtube.com/watch?v=91Cfc7Dt MCg [Accessed 15 April 2021].

Jobin, G. (2012). *Des religions à la spiritualité. Une appropriation biomédicale du religieux dans l'hôpital*. Lumen Vitae, Brussels.

Jouet, E., Flora, L., Las Vargnas, O. (2010). Construction et reconnaissance des savoirs expérientiels des patients : note de synthèse. *Pratiques de formation/Analyses*, 58/59, 13–94.

Laplantine, F. (1993). *Anthropologie de la maladie*. Payot, Paris.

der Linden, M.V. and Juillerat, A.-C. (2014). L'avènement du modèle biomédical du vieillissement cérébral et cognitif : le mythe de la maladie d'Alzheimer. *PSY-Théories, débats, synthèses*, 17–40.

López-Tarrida, Á., de Diego-Cordero, R., Lima-Rodríguez, J.S. (2021). Spirituality in a doctor's practice: What are the issues? *Journal of Clinical Medicine*, 10(23), 5612.

Meidani, A. (2015). À l'intersection du public et du privé : la médicalisation du grand âge à travers la prise en charge de la maladie d'Alzheimer en France et en Grèce. In *La santé : du public à l'intime*, Meidani, A., Legrand, E., Jacques, B. (eds). Presses de l'École des hautes études en santé publique, Rennes, 37–54.

Meuli, V. and Zulian, G. (2014). La spiritualité en soins palliatifs adultes en Europe : une recherche de littérature. *Revue internationale de soins palliatifs*, 29, 113–123.

Munsch-Roux, K. and Munsch, F. (2008). La méthode de validation™ de Naomi Feil. *Gérontologie et société*, 126(3), 189–204.

Ngatcha-Ribert, L. (2004). Maladie d'Alzheimer et société : une analyse des représentations sociales. *Gériatrie et psychologie neuropsychiatrie du vieillissement*, 2, 49–66.

Ngatcha-Ribert, L. (2012). *Alzheimer : la construction sociale d'une maladie*. Dunod, Paris.

Ngatcha-Ribert, L. (2014). Maladie d'Alzheimer : cultures, diversités, identités. *Dossier thématique de la Fondation Méderic Alzheimer*, 2.

Nizzi, M.-C. (2012). La maladie d'Alzheimer et son impact sur l'identité de la personne. In *Alzheimer, éthique et société*, Gzil, F. and Hirsch, E. (eds). Érès, Toulouse, 49–59.

Nubukpo, P. (2009). Ethnopsychiatrie et sujets âgés. *Psychologie et neuropsychiatrie du vieillissement*, 7(3), 175–183.

Pitaud, P. (2007). *Exclusion, maladie d'Alzheimer et troubles apparentés : le vécu des aidants*. Érès, Toulouse.

Ploton, L. (2009). À propos de la maladie d'Alzheimer. *Gérontologie et société*, 128/129(1), 89–115.

Pomey, M.-P., Flora, L., Karazivan, P., Dumez, V., Lebel, P., Vanier, M.-C., Débarges, B., Clavel, N., Jouet, E. (2015). Le "Montréal model" : enjeux du partenariat relationnel entre patients et professionnels de la santé. *Santé publique*, 1, 41–50.

Post, S.G. (2000). The concept of Alzheimer disease in a hypercognitive society. In *Concepts of Alzheimer Disease: Biological, Clinical, and Cultural Perspectives*, Whitehouse, P.J., Maurer, K., Ballenger, J.F. (eds). Johns Hopkins University Press, Baltimore, MD, 245–256.

Potter, P.A. and Perry, A.G. (2010). *Soins infirmiers. Tome 1. Fondements généraux*, 3rd edition. Chenelière, Montreal.

Potter, P.A., Perry, A.G., Hall, A., Stockert, P.A. (2009). *Fundamentals of Nursing*, 7th edition. Elsevier, Mosby.

Puchalski, C.M., Vitillo, R., Hull, S.K., Reller, N. (2014). Improving the spiritual dimension of whole person care: Reaching national and international consensus. *Journal of Palliative Medicine*, 17(6), 642–656.

Pujol, N. (2017). La spécificité de l'accompagnement spirituel dans le monde des soins. In *L'accompagnement de l'expérience spirituelle en temps de maladie*, Jobin, G., Pujol, N., Legault, A. (eds). PUL, Louvain-La-Neuve, 35–42.

Ricœur, P. (1988). L'identité narrative. *Esprit*, 140/141(7/8), 295–304.

Rochat, E., Vollenweider, E., Truchard, C. (2015). Prendre en compte la dimension spirituelle du patient : plus pertinent à plusieurs. *Revue médicale suisse*, 11, 2055–2057.

Sagne, A. (2007). La question de l'intime dans la vie actuelle du malade Alzheimer. *Gérontologie et société*, 30(122), 181–191.

Schmit, A.-C. (2017). Évaluation de l'attitude des soignants face à la spiritualité des patients en fin de vie : enquête réalisée au sein de 4 services hospitaliers de l'aire toulonnaise. PhD Thesis, Université d'Aix-Marseille.

Sfez, L. (1995). *La santé parfaite, critique d'une nouvelle utopie*. Le Seuil, Paris.

Smyre, C.L., Tak, H.J., Dang, A.P., Curlin, F.A., Yoon, J.D. (2018). Physicians' opinions on engaging patients' religious and spiritual concerns: A national survey. *J. Pain Symptom Manage.*, 55(3), 897–905.

Snapp, M. and Hare, L. (2021). The role of spiritual care and healing in health management. *Advances in Mind Body Medicine*, 35(1), 4–8.

Thomas, H., Mitchell, G., Rich, J., Best, M. (2018). Definition of whole person care in general practice in the English language literature: A systematic review. *BMJ Open*, 8(12), e023758.

Van Gorp, B., Rondia, K., Gombault, B. (2012). "Je suis toujours la même personne". Réflexions sur la communication à propos de la maladie d'Alzheimer. In *Alzheimer, éthique et société,* Gzil, F. and Hirsch, E. (eds). Érès, Toulouse, 60–71.

Vermandere, M., De Lepeleire, J., Smeets, L., Hannes, K., Van Mechelen, W., Warmenhoven, F., Van Rijswijk, E., Aertgeerts, B. (2011). Spirituality in general practice: A qualitative evidence synthesis. *Bristish Journal of General Practice*, 61(592), e749–e760.

Werner P. (2005). Social distance towards a person with Alzheimer's disease. *Int. J. Geriatr. Psychiatry*, 20(2), 182–188.

4

Rethinking the Organization of SDCCs[1] in Light of the Experience of Volunteers in a State of Great Social Precariousness

4.1. Introduction

Created in 1988, the Abbé Pierre Foundation (APF) has been recognized as a public utility since February 1992. Its mission is to provide housing to the most deprived people and to fight against their exclusion, promoting the construction of very social housing, and fighting against substandard housing. The foundation financially supports charities which pursue these objectives. It also manages so-called "in house" actions, including SDCCs called Boutiques Solidarité (BS).

BS appeared in the 1990s in order to deal with the scale of the phenomenon of "homelessness" by offering

> a welcome for all, an anonymous but warm welcome around a coffee for a discussion, a shower, a little bit of rest. It is a place for conversation, an address, a house, perhaps one that we did not have, a springboard to leave with better chances [...] By creating the Boutiques Solidarité, we have had the audacity that politicians did not have. There are both forces of selfishness and compassion in society. There must be private, insolent initiatives that denounce the emergency so that public opinion can take an interest in it and put pressure around it (extract from the social project of the BS 2017).

Chapter written by Corinne GRENIER, with the contribution of employees and certain volunteers from the Boutique Solidarité de Marseille of the Abbé Pierre Foundation.

1 Social day care centers.

This study here focuses on the Boutique Solidarité de Marseille (BSM).

The BSM is located in the Saint-Mauront – Belle de Mai neighborhood, which is an area with a reputation of being one of the poorest in France and Europe. It opened in November 1991 as one of the first achievements of the Abbé Pierre Foundation. Every morning, it welcomes more than 100 people in a state of great social, economic and psychological precariousness. Approximately 8 to 10 employees run the BS, and they rely on volunteers for greeting the service users in the morning. No definition of volunteering[2] is specified in French law. However, in 1993, the Conseil Economique, Social et Environnemental (Economic, Social and Environmental Council in France) characterized it as follows: "A volunteer is any person who freely commits to carrying out non-salaried action benefiting others and outside of their own professional and family time."[3]

At the Boutique, volunteers are individuals who have been welcomed and who wish to assist the salaried team in their activities for approximately two mornings per week. The idea is that this work will participate in the recovery process of those welcomed: "the BS helped me to calm down. I was a little violent; and now I see things in another way"; "I hope to have legal documents, to build a family. Because I have too many problems" (VII[4]).

The rise in social and economic issues, particularly in Marseille, explains the rise in tensions and incidents during welcoming hours at the BSM, causing employees to feel exhausted, as well as questioning the benefit of this type of volunteering for those welcomed and for the organization itself. A particularly dramatic event in 2017 meant that the BSM had to close its doors for several weeks and give itself a long period of reflection to revisit its mode of organization as well as its activities. It is within this context that the organization engaged in intervention research, co-carried out with the author of this chapter. The line of questioning was empirical: *how do we continue to bring to life fundamental values (such as that of unconditionality) for the sake of those welcomed into BSM from very precarious conditions, while paying attention to the organization's professionals, who are constantly subjected to incidents, as well as much bigger crises?*

---

2 According to the ministère du Travail, des Relations sociales, de la Famille, de la Solidarité et de la Ville (Ministry of Labor, Social Relations, Family, Solidarity and the City), a volunteer is defined as "one who freely commits to carrying out non-salaried action benefiting others and outside of their own professional and family time".

3 Published in the JO Sénat from 01/04/2010, page 835.

4 VII: volunteer individual interview; (later) IEI: individual employee interview; IIES: individual interview with external stakeholders (extract from notes written in the logbook).

Our intervention-research (IR) consisted of questioning the organization of work, which was weakly prescribed, as well as the role of volunteers (knowledge bearers) who could contribute to the proper functioning and mission of the BSM. During this IR, one main tool was developed, the Mutual Agreement Contract (MAC) aiming to define the framework for the morning intervention of volunteers (during welcome hours), as well as during certain afternoons with BSM employees (meeting times). The management method of the MAC was also defined (signature, discussion time to explain their role to the volunteers) as well as a better organization of the activity of the Boutique in the afternoon (dedicated to the activities of the salaried team). For the Boutique, the MAC had to be a tool that participates in the volunteer's recovery process, by supporting their behavior, as well as their experiential knowledge. This knowledge is built through the experience of welcoming customers to the Boutique, being with others, identifying or analyzing situations, or more generally knowing what to do and what to say in certain circumstances.

Studying the work of small groups of boilermaking workers, Martinez-Perez (2013) analyzes a situation similar to this: an organization of work with very weak control regulation. She noted that the multiplicity of micro-coordinations within these groups, nourished by the practices and knowledge of the workers, formed an autonomous regulation (rules that the actors give themselves) which made it possible to counterbalance the control regulation (rules prescribed and imposed on the actors), to ensure that the general work objectives were respected. The BSM is also marked by deliberately weak control regulation; but the employees, on the contrary, had the intuition that they needed to reinforce a certain stability within the BSM, to namely, "rethink the framework", as they said.

We will thus discuss the work of regulation (Reynaud 1979, 1997; de Terssac 2012) within organizations and ask the following research question: *To what extent does the experiential knowledge of volunteers contribute to the work of regulation within an SDCC?*

Our work allows us to enrich the numerous other works that have relied on social regulation, by bringing forward two little-explored perspectives: a) by focusing on the experiential knowledge (Gardien 2017) of a particular category of actors, volunteers – mobilized in interactions between actors – while most work focuses on the interests to be defended as an explanatory factor of regulations (Bréchet 2008; de Terssac 2012); b) by exploring a situation of very weak prescription, like Martinez-Perez (2013), while works examine much more how joint regulation lifts the weight of control regulation.

We first present our theoretical framework, then our field, the Boutique Solidarité de Marseille. After having presented the IR methodology carried out by the author, the following two parts will present and then analyze the transformation carried out with the implementation of the MAC.

4.2. Theoretical framework: social regulation and experiential knowledge

4.2.1. *Regulation work*

Reynaud's theory of social regulation (1979, 1997) focuses on the creation of rules to facilitate and legitimize collective action. The epistemical position adopted is to consider that these rules are created and renewed in the exchange and interactions between actors. Thus: "social exchange, through the learning it covers, creates the rules of exchange and contributes to the establishment of the trust necessary for exchange which takes place over time" (Brechet 2008, p. 17). In regulation, actors develop their intentions, construct the meaning of their actions and regulate their interdependencies. From then on, the unit of analysis and interest focuses on the regulation activity, "by which individuals construct their constraints [i.e. rules], accept them or call them into question" (from Terssac (2012, p. 12)). Three forms of regulation are then proposed by Reynaud (in Bréchet (2008, pp. 19–20)):

– Control regulation: "corresponds to the prescription of tasks [...] by management and specialized services in a situation of rigorous subordination and marked cognitive asymmetry".

– Autonomous regulation: "manifests that the actors onto whom control is applied can oppose it, have an autonomy which allows this opposition. In doing so, it recognizes the gap between the theoretical schema and the reality of practices"; meaning that "the social actor never allows itself to be completely imprisoned within dependence frameworks" (de Terssac 2012, point 23).

– Joint regulation: is based on rules developed jointly "without necessarily eliminating opposition between sources of regulation, but taking into account the concerns and interests of each person". In this way, it is an "agreement" (Reynaud 1979, 1997) between the different parties. Joint regulation seeks to propose solutions to "contradictions" (Molinier 2008) in the organization of work.

These forms of regulation lead to a plurality of rules, developed in different actor spheres (internal and external) which make up or act with any organization, often relating to different levels of power, influence or hierarchy.

However, "a rule is not in itself a control rule or an autonomous rule" (de Terssac 2003, p. 104). The rule acquires its qualification by the way in which it has been developed and by the use made of it; thus "control and autonomy designate a use of the rule not its nature" (ibid.). The actors react to pressure "from above" (control) by seeking to find a certain balance between control and autonomy, in autonomous rules, by which the values of one and the other should be reaffirmed as legitimate action frameworks. Thus, Droz-Mendelzweig et al. (2011) show that, within healthcare establishments, joint regulation aims to preserve the values of intervention among the treated or supported populations, as well as to preserve social cohesion between different professional groups, as a "practical necessity linked to the concern of preserving community order" (ibid., p. 53).

The literature has often analyzed situations where joint regulation could act as a counterpoint to strong, top-down control regulation. On the contrary, Martinez-Perez (2013) studied an industrial design workshop, where, due to the very nature of this work, control regulation was weak, if not nonexistent. While the industrial plan can be considered as a form of control for the work of designers (because it is defined by management, or even with clients), the author, in the context studied, considers it to be a pool of knowledge mobilized by these professionals; the initial industrial plan is then reinterpreted, or even modified with certain specifications, with a view to carrying out the tasks. A joint regulation thus emerges at the interface between reading and following plans (prescription) and professional practice (autonomy based on this experience).

4.2.2. *Experiential knowledge*

The recognition of users' knowledge has a certain tradition anchored in different theoretical streams, and stemming from different terminologies, including, in particular, the notion of "layman knowledge" (Rabeharisoa and Callon 1998). It emerged with the arrival of new pathological situations (AIDS (Epstein 2001), neuromuscular diseases, rare diseases, chronic diseases, etc.) when, faced with insufficient (or almost nonexistent) medical knowledge, patients or their families "knew" and had more to say about what they were experiencing and how they understood the evolution of their situation. This recognition also implied the need for another look at the illness, not as a strictly medical fact, but as "a constant challenge in health management" (Flora 2015, p. 96) by the patient on a daily basis.

This (slow) recognition reflects an evolution in the "status" of the patient, which changes from passive to expert regarding their own illness and their daily life with their illness: "recognized as a care provider in the same way as health professionals, their active role in the clinical process is continuously developed in order to promote their self-determination and autonomy" (Flora 2015, p. 95). This recognition is thus based on a triple discrepancy: a) in relation to so-called scientific knowledge, validated by "theories" or more pragmatically acquired in degree courses; b) between so-called objective knowledge (because it comes from theories or teaching) and knowledge obtained from experience; and c) in relation to the knowledge held by those who have "power" in a field (e.g. healthcare professionals in relation to audiences that are supported and cared for). Thus, in emergency or psychiatric departments, Arborio (1996) notes this blurring of boundaries when nursing assistants, due to their close proximity to patients, have more to say than is usually recognized.

In parallel to this, and in particular within the fields of psychiatry or in relation to situations of great precariousness, peer support or peer mediator approaches are being developed (Laval and Gardien 2020). Peer support covers situations where specific audiences support individuals experiencing similar problems in their care, recovery or life *trajectory*; thus, "the definition of problems, the construction of knowledge and solutions are developed between peers from the point of view of experience" (Laval and Gardien 2020, p. 186). This movement emerged in North America at the beginning of the 20th century within groups such as Alcoholics Anonymous (Troisoeufs 2020). At the crossroads of these two fields (psychiatry and great precariousness) and of access to housing, progress has been made in France with the trial at the end of the 2000s of the "*Un chez soi d'abord*" program (Girard 2010), inspired by the Housing First policy deployed in Canada in the early 1990s and then in the USA.

The approach advocated by peer mediation, when the peer mediator is considered more as "a conflict manager, even if they aspire to be an ambassador of peace or an agent of prevention" (Laval and Gardien 2020, pp. 185) is different. The peer (patient, user) here is understood as belonging to peer community, as well as to the community of professionals who support them in their care and/or recovery journey, which can create identity tensions and delicate positions among these diverse actors.

The common feature of these different figures is the experiential knowledge that patients or users will bring to bear. For Gardien (2017), one of the first texts to define experiential knowledge is that of Borkman (1976), considered as "truth learned from personal experience with a phenomenon rather than truth acquired by discursive reasoning, observation or reflection on information provided by others" (ibid., p. 446). This general definition calls for several comments. First of all, it is the person themselves, producer of this knowledge, who recognizes its value and validity. On the other hand, experiential knowledge is not reducible to the illness or problematic situation experienced by the person; on the contrary, they encompass their life in all dimensions. Finally, they come from "long and repeated practice of an activity which allows for the emergence of the experienced individual" (Demailly and Garnoussi 2015, p. 58). Thus, "whilst experience is necessary for knowledge, it is not knowledge" (Gardien 2017, p. 32). The construction of knowledge presupposes a reflective activity on what is experienced, and not only by the person producing this knowledge; therefore, we cannot reduce this to "the sole singular experience of the individual" (Gardien 2017, p. 33). This knowledge encompasses what is experienced by others (peers). Its construction is supported or enabled by devices such as expression groups (between peers, for example, or with professionals) to promote a constructed, structured understanding of the situations experienced. It is therefore not a "pure and simple compilation of past life situations" (Godrie 2016, p. 37).

4.3. A situation to transform: the Boutique Solidarité de Marseille (BSM) of the Abbé Pierre Foundation

4.3.1. *Presentation of the BSM*

Everybody is welcomed into the Boutique, whatever their state, according to ethical orientations and strong principles such as unconditionality when welcoming, alongside non-exclusion and retention within the service. The BSM highlights the relationship with others where time is unconstrained, and choosing freely is required (see Box 4.1).

From 9 a.m. until 12 p.m., the small gate on rue Loubon (Marseille) is open and gives direct access to the shaded garden and then to the reception room*. Whoever desires to can come in and out. There is no registration (respect for anonymity), no contracting (for those welcomed), no file, no counter, no internal regulations posted. People are welcomed by staff, both volunteers and employees, and are invited to have a snack, go for a shower, call the emergency services or simply to rest, play a game of chess, or to sit at the ping-pong table and impatiently wait for an opponent to face.

Shaking hands, exchanging a smile, becomes the first gesture which will establish the encounter, the bond, the relationship. Some choose to withdraw, to remain in a corner of the garden or the reception room without saying anything, wishing to remain quiet. Indeed, it is sometimes difficult to contain themselves in the face of the violence suffered the night before, the impossibility of reaching 115[5] to find shelter for the night, and difficult to control their own psychological violence. The slightest word or look considered to be *wrong*, a spilled coffee, can trigger chain reactions, screams, conflicts. The team knows that a simple word or a kind presence can reassure, contain and allow a respite of a few hours.

Box 4.1. *Morning welcome at the BSM*
(: excluding the periods during the health crisis)*

5 Public service social emergency number in France.

The absence of internal regulations, which would define sanctionable actions, is a choice claimed by the Boutique. This position was reaffirmed in the latest version of its social project, dating from 2017, and the legal framework, which applies to everyone, those welcomed and those welcoming, is sufficient. The consumption of alcohol, legally authorized in public spaces, is not prohibited. Criminal acts (consumption of cannabis, threats, exhibition of a weapon, etc.) are subject to a reminder of the legal framework, an invitation to go out briefly, or even, when there is danger to themselves or others, to recourse to hospital emergency services or the police, but never exclusion from the service: it is indeed the actions that are banned, and not their perpetrators.

Thus, at the heart of the project is the affirmation that relationships emerge from encounters, which can lead to human accompaniment. The Boutique aims to make its reception area a space of relationship and expression open to all and where we can create meaning and commonality together. It believes that a place of reception can become the site of a political and practical experience: an attempt to "make society" by constructing a discourse and knowledge on great precariousness to influence public authorities, namely "to participate in societal responses, while also participating in constructing them as public 'problems'" (Blanc and Bresson 2019, point 8).

Approximately 100 to 200 [6]people come through the door of the Boutique. The profiles are heterogeneous: single adults, families, young people between 18 and 25 years old, elderly people, of French nationality or not, regularized or not, out of work or long-term beneficiaries of social minima, extremely marginalized, residents of a neighborhood in a situation of precariousness and/or isolation, migrants from Eastern European countries, sub-Saharan Africa or the Maghreb, low-income retirees, unaccompanied foreign minors, etc. Men represent approximately 90% of those welcomed. Reception is handled by the Boutique's salaried team (approximately 10 people) and "volunteers", who are welcomed individuals, helping the team in welcoming those who come to the BSM.

Until 2017, the method of inclusion of volunteers favored unconditionality (anyone can become a volunteer), with great flexibility: "whoever declares themselves a volunteer becomes a volunteer" (IEI). The person wishing to join the team just had to make themselves known, in order to be invited to introduce themselves during an end-of-welcome debriefing. From then on, they were a part of the team, and participated as they wished alongside the employees in setting up both reception and services, as well as in daily meeting times (debriefing) or monthly ones (plenary team meeting, supervision).

6 Figure before the Covid-19 health crisis.

Thus, at the end of the welcome, the salaried team have their meal with the morning volunteers; then, different meetings follow. Their purpose is twofold: "to account for" the morning (to provide information on those welcomed, analysis of incidents, etc.) and thus allow the activity to continue: "resilience is thanks to the capacity of the collective, to work regularity" (IEI). Some meetings are dedicated to the salaried team alone, and others open to volunteers. These types of meetings are an opportunity to share what has been observed during the welcome: "I see the problems myself" (VII). However, the purpose of afternoon meetings is not always predefined.

4.3.2. *2017: a problematic situation calling for work on the organization of the BSM*

This major organizational characteristic of fluidity and the absence of a framework (internal regulations) is considered to be essential for the Boutique, even when faced with a certain fatigue among the salaried team. This having been said, the multiplication of morning incidents caused increasingly frequent autonomous adjustments, as Martinez-Perez (2013) also observes, but with significant and persistent team exhaustion in our field as a consequence.

A climax was reached in June 2017, with the attack on members of the paid team by one of the volunteers, resulting in a prison sentence and the closure of the BSM throughout the summer.

This dramatic episode, experienced as a failure, led the salaried team to question the organization of the Boutique and the way it carries out its project, particularly with regard to volunteers: their relatively unformalized role within the organization, and the vagueness of what they can expect "in return" for their commitment (administrative assistance, procedural support, material benefits?) explains (notably) these growing tensions. The support for volunteers was then becoming invisible and was poorly defined by employees who were often unable to help volunteers in great pain, in particular those suffering from psychiatric pathologies, who put the entire team and the welcoming activity of the organization in difficulty.

With the repositioning of the BSM social project solely on the morning welcome, "visible" and "technical" activities (help with administrative procedures, etc.) had been eliminated[7] and volunteers sometimes felt helpless in relation to developing relationships with those welcomed; their place during afternoon meeting times was not always easy: "seeing as we're no longer supporting [as administrative assistants], we feel powerless"; "the new operation of the Boutique no longer made

7 The BSM wanting to solely dedicate itself to welcoming the most deprived.

sense. Before there were work tools (the photocopier) which allowed us to get in touch with the person"; or even "I feel like I'm of no use" (VII). Since then, "many volunteers [have] left, because they were no longer able to do the work that was required" (VII). Certainly, "they almost do employees' work" (VII); but "speaking out was not always easy, due to a relational style perceived as 'too top-down'" (VII).

Finally, the reasons for resorting to volunteering remained marked by ambivalence: supporting the volunteer in their recovery process, understood as an approach allowing them to "reengage in an autonomous and satisfying life, which socially gives them a place, other than status of mentally ill" (Pachoud 2012); or an " additional resource" for the employee team.

Table 4.1 describes the situation of the Boutique in 2017.

<table>
<tr><th>Weak control regulation</th><th>Autonomous regulation</th><th>Consequences</th></tr>
<tr><td rowspan="2">– Based on: a) the values of the APF and unconditionality in the welcome offered; b) respect for the laws of the Republic.
– Absence of internal regulations.
– Collective meetings, but with often unclear objectives.</td><td rowspan="2">– Aside discussion (sometimes invisible to the team) between those welcomed, between those welcomed and volunteers, between volunteers themselves.
– Permanent adjustment of activities, often without real consultation, to overcome (micro) incidents.</td><td>1) Team exhaustion → significant meeting times to "report" what happened, limiting time to devote to projects.
2) Volunteer in an uncomfortable situation.
3) Morning BSM closures, sometimes exclusion.
4) A difficult questioning of unconditionality (latent but never assumed).</td></tr>
<tr><td>An unsatisfactory joint regulation:
1) A de facto joint regulation, through analysis in meetings, but in which the volunteer had an ill-defined place.
2) A question: What did the volunteer do and say? What could they bring to the team?</td></tr>
</table>

Table 4.1. *Situation of the Boutique Solidarité in 2017*

Following this dramatic episode, the social project was rewritten during the summer of 2017, reaffirming the unconditional acceptance as volunteers of those welcomed. The activities have been rethought, namely: giving up administrative support activities in favor of welcoming. The wish of the BS was to fully reinvest its mission of supporting those welcomed by focusing on the relationship. Thus, "the objective of the Boutique has changed radically over the past two years… There was this administrative support. And overnight it no longer exists. It's a big change" (IIES). The aim of the volunteer recovery is reaffirmed; but there remained a need to orchestrate a reflection and a change in the organization and the work within the Boutique. How can volunteers take up their space during morning welcome, when their work consists of only "welcoming"? Namely a welcome made up of micro-activities that the volunteers described as invisible (speaking, listening, observing, etc.). This questioning highlighted the team's feeling that the volunteers' words were not always listened to, or that their words were not supported enough to be put into action.

4.4. The intervention-research (IR) approach

In 2017, the BS submitted a funding request to the ARS PACA[8] for an intervention-research defined as follows: "Modeling the organization and operation of the Boutique Solidarité de Marseille to create the conditions for the emergence of volunteer capacities, with a dual aim of recovery and improvement of the functioning of the service, as closely as possible to the needs of the people received". For the BSM, it is a matter of questioning an "invisible point", the organization, namely the "framework" of its activities.

The IR took place from February 2019 up until the end of 2020, aiming for the implementation of new organizational frameworks. This end-of-year objective was largely disrupted for several months by the Covid-19 health crisis, which led the BSM to temporarily close its premises and adapt its activity (marauding, then welcoming in the building's garden, without allowing those welcomed into any enclosed spaces on the premises). At the end of 2021, as health conditions improved, the activity became less tiring; and the last stage (see below) of the IR took place from January 2022. As part of this contribution, we focus the presentation of the IR approach on the volunteer and their experience as a contributing regulation factor within the Boutique.

IR aims to produce useful knowledge (theoretical and empirical) which emerges from the encounter between the researcher and a field, in response to a problem, of an also theoretical and empirical nature. The specificity of IR lies in the permanent dialogue between these two parties which, together, will build *problems*, *analysis process* (tool for collecting, analyzing and interpreting data) and *knowledge*. As a result, this (participatory) research is deemed to be effective in terms of social transformation (Fals-Borda and Rahman 1991).

8 As part of the innovative actions of ARS PACA, Agence régionale de santé de la région PACA (Provence Alpes-Côte d'Azur, sud-est de la France): Regional Health Agency of the PACA region (Provence Alpes-Côte d'Azur, south-east of France).

Therefore, IR presents the following characteristics: research that is collaborative, immersive (the researcher being "almost" an actor among those in the field that they have analyzed) and constructivist since it is together that the researcher and the field formulate and construct (continuous) knowledge for a "concrete transformation project" (David 2001, p. 205).

We conducted the IR based on the methodological framework proposed by Hatchuel and Molet (1986) (see Table 4.2 in section 4.8 detailing the process of the IR):

– the perception of a problem;

– the construction of a "rational myth"; by the transformation of perceptions into concepts and data, constitution of an (emerging, enrooted) theory of the organization associated with the problem;

– experimentation; by the deployment of what will transform the organization (tools, devices, activities, roles, functions, etc.), observation in survey on the reactions of the actors concerned (assessment of the "fit", of an appropriation of what is supposed to transform the organization), eventual adjustments;

– the definition of a set of action and organizational logics; aiming to identify learning processes at work, or counter-learning (resistance, difficulties of the transformation to unfold, etc.);

– the process of change; understood here as a new stabilization of the organization, which will have been able to respond to the problem identified at the start of the intervention.

During our research, we conducted 25 interviews: 15 with employees, 8 with volunteers and 2 with external stakeholders. We also kept a logbook when we participated in certain welcome mornings and afternoon meetings, as well as the July and August 2019 workshops aimed at designing the new framework of the Boutique. A final IR report was written in early 2020, in a largely collaborative manner. Our data was recoded with regard to the theoretical framework of this present work (regulation and experiential knowledge), and this chapter was submitted again for discussion with certain BSM employees to stabilize the analysis.

4.5. The transformation of the BSM: the establishment of the Mutual Agreement Contract (MAC) as a regulation tool

The first important transformation was the establishment of the Mutual Agreement Contract (MAC) between the volunteer and the Boutique, correlated with a second transformation concerning the general organization of the life of the BSM.

When someone welcomed expresses their wish to become a volunteer, they participate in a few trial mornings. If they confirm their wish, and after informal exchanges followed by more formal discussions with the salaried team, they sign the MAC.

The moment of signing is ritualized, the volunteer being accompanied by a referent volunteer and a referent employee. Entries into volunteering are made in three waves over the course of the year (January, May and September), so as to create a collective dynamic between volunteers.

Every four months, the volunteer is received by the term's referring employee to take stock of their commitment.

Also attached to the MAC are training for welcoming, communication in tense/crisis situations, first aid, etc., according to volunteer requests and to the possibilities of organization by the BSM.

Box 4.2. *Setting up the MAC*

4.5.1. *The MAC*

The MAC consists of a contract which is signed by the volunteer. It is presented in the form of four documents: a) the presentation of the values of the BSM; b) the contract itself, which specifies the commitments of the volunteer and the employees[9]; c) the operation and organization of the Boutique; and d) the document from the Abbé Pierre Foundation on volunteer commitment.

Its principle, content and management methods emerged from the summer 2019 workshops (see Table 4.2, section 4.8) when employees and volunteers worked on the "framework" and values of the Boutique. Around 15 volunteers[10] signed a MAC in mid-2022; and the term meetings have taken place as planned in the workshop, despite the continuation of the health crisis during this period (see Box 4.1).

The MAC is seen as a tool "to take care of the volunteer during their journey". It is considered to be a "relationship building tool", and supports the volunteer in

9 In particular, the days and time slots when the volunteer is present, their activities and their participation in different afternoon meetings.

10 This figure may seem low. It is partly explained by the departure of certain volunteers in the disrupted context of the Covid-19 crisis. However, it is important to note that new volunteers have declared themselves as such and signed the MAC.

developing skills, gaining confidence, rebuilding links, breaking out of isolation, projecting themselves. Its signature is experienced as "a moment where we exit speech and enter an official moment" (IEI). It represents something strongly symbolic and ritualistic for the volunteer who, although unpaid, for Vallerand and Bissonnette (1992), seeks some form of reward, namely some form of recognition or valorization.

4.5.2. *The general operation of the Boutique*

The implementation of the MAC led, also during the summer of 2019, to a rethinking the organization of the Boutique, which is still in progress today:

– Morning: preparation from 8 a.m. to 9 a.m.; welcome between 9 a.m. and 12 p.m.; debriefing time; employee and volunteer meals.

– Every Monday afternoon, a meeting for the benefit of volunteers:

- 1 Monday: employee and volunteer meeting;
- 1 Monday: meeting between volunteers, discussions, proposals;
- 1 Monday: so-called supervision meeting, led by a popular educational charity;
- 1 Monday: training workshop (or self-training).

– The schedule for other afternoons reserved for employees is now clearer.

– Twice a year: seminar for employed teams, and with volunteers on the last day/half-day.

– Once a month: closure of the BS and meeting to discuss the operation and projects of the BS.

4.5.3. *The experiential knowledge of volunteers*

Finally, our interviews conducted at the beginning of 2022 led us to highlight the importance of volunteers' experiential knowledge, and to identify its areas.

During the morning welcome:

– know how to spot the person who is not doing well and alert the team: "the volunteers have knowledge in observing the person [welcomed] who is not doing well, who is angry, who has OCD; They pick it up right away" (IEI);

– know how to interact with those welcomed: “the volunteers manage to calm down those welcomed who are difficult” (IEI); “for me it’s a real increase in skills… they know when to pass the baton [to the salaried team]… they know how to better accept others in their differences, those, for example, who testify to their homosexuality” (IEI); “in the boutique on a daily basis, it is easier to establish a connection with a newly welcomed person” (VII);

– know how to facilitate the relationship between employees and those welcomed: “we have volunteers who, because of their background, help us to connect more easily with those welcomed, in relation to language problems, behavioral problems, knowledge of their situation outside the Boutique” (IEI);

– mastery of language and behavior (less irritation);

– provide information (location of accommodation, etc.) that the team does not always know:

- become more comfortable with the team: “they can come and explain to us what is happening; they know how to alert us” (IEI);

- know how to better respect the functioning of the BSM: “knowledge about punctuality, regularity, even though it is not easy for them, when they often live on the street; and we see their evolution” (IEI).

Outside welcome hours:

– proposals for the operation of the BS: “they will make us exit proposals, for example, for the maintenance of the place” (IEI);

– know how to express requests for training and support in their role.

For employees, this knowledge is enabled thanks to the MAC through which the volunteer “knows who they are and what they are there for” (IEI).

In the following “analysis” section, we will consider to what extent this knowledge has contributed to new methods of regulation within the Boutique.

4.6. Analysis of the transformation: more balanced regulations

The establishment of the MAC and the organization of the BSM allow us to observe the following transformations in terms of regulation (Table 4.2).

Weak **but** ***enriched*** **control regulation**	***Justified*** **autonomous regulation**	***Calmed*** **and** ***floating*** **joint regulation**
– "We remain free-style" (IEI). – Based on the values of the APF, unconditionality. – No internal regulations. – Fairly flexible morning organization. – The MAC. – The clarified organization of work.	"On a case-by-case basis *because* …" (IEI).	– "It makes more sense"; "We always discuss but based on elements that are better established" (IEI). – Questioning the role and place of volunteers. – Questioning the boutique's project (unconditionality). – Questioning the opening of the Boutique to the outside world.

Table 4.2. *New forms of regulation within the BSM*

4.6.1. *A weak but enriched control regulation*

The BSM remains a fluid organization ("we are free-style", IEI), because it is always eager to be able to adapt to any person welcomed, and to any volunteer according to their situation and expectations. It has reaffirmed the non-necessity to adopt internal regulations.

However, the establishment of the MAC (and its consequences in terms of work organization, particularly in the agenda of meetings and the clarification of their purposes) has enriched the control regulation: "it allows us to be within a precise framework, to work well; we know that we have obligations here" (VII); "it's really a tool that allows you to provide a framework, which is legible. We have appropriated it and that is what allows us to consider it as a framework, which reassures everyone" (IEI).

It is therefore "important to sign the MAC" (VII), and this moment is voluntarily ritualized by the employed team; moment "where we leave speech and enter into an official moment" (IEI). We consider that this rite (of passage) contributes to strengthening the regulation of control, in the sense that it formally gives a place and a role to the volunteer, who belongs to the "tribe" of the BSM: "a rite requires a tribe to observe it and a myth to give it meaning" (Riveline 1993).

This enrichment of the framework, made visible and ritualized, allowed the employees and volunteers of the Boutique to discuss the founding principle of unconditionality in welcoming (and in volunteering) more calmly, which is now considered as less of a blind spot. It becomes easier to set rules for problematic situations that lead employees to decide to exclude someone who is too disruptive to those present from a morning. This basis of control regulation thus contributes to reconstructing the values of action made legitimate thanks to regulations (de Terssac 2012). It also provides a basis for the autonomy of the volunteer, assured and supported in what they can say and do, since "regulation is the capacity to take initiatives and develop rules" (de Terssac 2003, p. 103). This capacity for initiative was then observed in autonomous regulations.

4.6.2. *Autonomous regulation justified*

"While respecting the rules, we [volunteers] can take initiatives" (VII). It is with this sentence that we can appreciate a better capacity of volunteers to know how to adjust their support for those welcomed, as well as to report on it; because the MAC recognizes a place for them to do and say: "I present the volunteer to a welcomed person by saying they are my colleague, they will be able to talk to you about this, because they know" (IEI). Our interviews thus highlighted what we call "autonomous regulation *because*", since employees and volunteers are more able to account for and justify what they do. This point is important to avoid any clandestine practices or management (Bréchet 2008).

This ability to activate autonomous regulation is supported by employees when they try to get certain volunteers to "move", when they tend to stay on the same activity in the morning (distributing coffee, for example). "It's difficult but we try to work on it gently with them" (IEI); thus, "when the volunteer manages to move from one place to another, this becomes part of their knowledge" (IEI), also giving this volunteer a broader spectrum to build their knowledge for the benefit of the operations of the Boutique.

It is also supported by employees who know better when to ask for a volunteer or not, having together developed some "codes" allowing them to understand each other (wink, physical movements in the welcoming area, etc.), in particular to regulate or talk about a problematic situation: "we have developed some little communication and regulation tricks between us; when he says to me 'you want a coffee', that means he wants to go somewhere else and talk to me" (IEI). From then on, the team said they were more comfortable calling on volunteers for morning welcome: "it took me a little time but it's something I'm doing more and more"; "I try to do it, because it's very rewarding" (IEI).

4.6.3. *A peaceful but "floating" joint regulation*

Joint regulation is carried out in a variety of spaces that bring together employees and volunteers, as shown in Table 4.3.

Control regulation	Autonomous regulation	Joint floating regulation
The BS institution (values)	– During the morning welcome – Outside the Boutique	– MAC implemented – Meals taken together by employees and volunteers – Employee and volunteer meetings in the afternoon
A missing space: that of volunteers (not forming a "collective")		

Table 4.3. *Regulation spaces*

The interactions that occur here have more clearly defined objectives, making it possible to weave and report on repeated practices (Gardien 2017), as well as to exercise reflexivity on these practices, which are the two constituent elements to the construction and mobilization of experiential knowledge.

The implementation of the MAC becomes a space of joint regulation whose signature or implementation constitutes a flexible process which is adapted according to volunteer requests or attitudes. Some sign almost automatically; others require a lot of explanation, leading the team to not necessarily mention the precise days of the volunteers' morning presence; others ultimately do not sign, or will sign later, or do not wish to add their name[11], even if they take on this role in the morning. These attitudes are understood as the expression of the volunteers' anxiety or uneasiness to which employees adapt. This adaptation means that the signature does not cause "violence", in the sense that, for Riveline (1993), a good tribe is one which does not attack its members, as long as there is mutual recognition of knowledge between volunteers and employees.

The multiplicity of spaces in which volunteers participate means that they "are more comfortable with the team. They are more interested in observing how things work and this helps them build knowledge on how to do it" (IEI).

11 Some act out of caution due to their undocumented situation.

These spaces are perceived as more secure for volunteers and conducive to the expression of their experiential knowledge; and the exchanges that take place there, based on situations experienced in the morning, make it possible to stabilize the rules: "to experience something, you have to be able to draw lessons from what you experience, to capitalize on the learning offered by confronting reality" (Lemaitre 2021, p. 6). However, to date, we describe this joint regulation as "floating" for two reasons.

On the one hand, the BSM has not yet managed to support the volunteer space, provided in its new organization (once a week). Some told us in interviews that they wanted to find their way there, but without any effectiveness. The purpose of these meetings, however, was not very clearly stated. Which brings us to the second reason why we use this term "floating": the ambivalence of the scope of the volunteers' experiential knowledge: Is it for themselves, as the basis of their recovery process, or for the benefit of the operations of the BSM? The previous examples then reveal that these volunteers would not be solicited or listened to in the same way.

From then on, the experiential knowledge of volunteers is built, either in formal meetings with the BSM team, or in a very informal way, when they exchange with each other, at the Boutique, as well as outside of it.

4.7. Conclusion

We have studied a particular case, where in the terms of Droz-Mendelzweig et al. (2011), "the primary objective of regulatory work is not the conformity of the establishment to external standards [...]" (ibid., p. 47), but the implementation of the project (within the collective action (Bréchet 2008)) of the founding and militant values of the Abbé Pierre Foundation towards the most deprived, those most "shattered" by life. Among these, the volunteers from the Boutique Solidarité de Marseille, themselves welcomed, led us to understand how the construction of their experiential knowledge could participate in regulation within this SDCC. Our field allows us to highlight two contributions.

As for experiential knowledge, it is both a clarified and reinforced organization (regulation of control), through the MAC, as well as the development of knowledge of employees to solicit volunteers, which offer a peaceful and visible framework to the construction and then expression of this knowledge by volunteers. This knowledge is constructed within the framework of the MAC and various other areas of joint regulation; but it is indeed this contract, itself a source of joint regulation in its implementation, which fuels the different interactions within the Boutique. While for Bréchet (2008), it is autonomous actors who produce regulations, and our work, actors capable of constructing and expressing experiential knowledge, it is also the importance of the "place" granted to and recognized for volunteers which matter within the BSM.

Thus, contrary to the observations of Droz-Mendelzweig et al. (2011), the coordinations necessary on a daily basis in a context of weak control regulation came to nourish and flesh out a joint regulation, which is peaceful, but always floating, and ultimately as for the very reason to support the experiential knowledge of volunteers. However, this floating characteristic does not entirely allow the Boutique's salaried team to find solutions to certain "contradictions" (Molinier 2008) in its very mission of supporting volunteers, for themselves (recovery, itself considered as an experiential dynamic (Pachoud 2012)) or to support employees in their activities.

4.8. Appendix

Stage	Period	Interventions
Preliminary step **Perception of a problem**	February to June 2017	Perception of a difficulty in supporting volunteers in their recovery process: "How to create a framework and capacity while remaining unconditional in access to volunteering"? Perception of team fatigue, due to activity multiplicity, an increase in situations creating incidents during welcome hours (increase in precariousness, etc.). Major incident ("sequestration") and recurrence of incidents have made the connection between the militant principle of unconditionality and the security of all the people of the BS (people welcomed, volunteers and salaried team) sensitive. Wish to lead an IR approach to rethink support for volunteers.
Preliminary step **Construction of a rational myth**	July to December 2017	Repeated meetings between the salaried team and the researcher. Formulating a problem: supporting volunteers; rethinking the framework of activities (organization). Submission of the intervention-research project and funding agreement through the innovative actions system.
	2018	Adjustment and discussions with ARS PACA, and with the Abbé Pierre Foundation.

Stage	Period	Interventions
IR **Perception of a problem**	January to May 2019	Start of the IR itself. Explanation of the transformational aim: develop a mutual agreement contract (MAC) linking volunteers and BSM. First wave of individual and collective interviews; presence on the ground.
IR **Construction of a rational myth**	May to June 2019	Transformation of perceptions of the problematic situation by bringing up the question of organization: militant (fight against social emergency and extreme poverty, mental health), welcoming (“to welcome well”, listening, collective) and resilient (overcoming daily incidents). Contribution of volunteers to the work of the salaried team and to the life of the Boutique.
IR **Experimentation**	July to September 2019	Organization of workshops and working groups on three themes: BS values, the MAC, organization of activities and of teamwork. The team meets in a seminar, feedback on the work in the workshop during the summer allows two documents to be written: the values of the BS, the MAC. The 3rd document (organization of work) is not finalized.
	September to December 2019	Period of adjustment of the MAC, the provisional organization of activities and the work of the team.
IR **Change process**	December 2019 to March 2020	Deployment of the MAC and arrival of new volunteers. The weekly activity schedule of employees is adjusted to support this deployment. Start of structuring the four-term volunteer journey. The Covid-19 health crisis is seriously disrupting the change process.
	2020 to end of 2021	The BSM adapts its welcome in the morning, to be only outdoors (garden).
	Early 2022	Return to the field and analysis of the change process.

Table 4.4. *The progression of intervention-research (according to the model of Hatchuel and Mollet (1986))*

4.9. References

Arborio, A.-M. (1996). Savoir profane et expertise sociale. Les aides-soignantes dans l'institution hospitalière. *Genèses*, 22, 87–106.

Blanc, M. and Bresson, M. (2019). Savoirs savants, savoirs d'action et politiques publiques. *SociologieS*.

Borkman, T. (1976). Experiential knowledge: A new concept for the analysis of self-help groups. *Social Service Review*, 50(3), 446.

Bréchet, J.P. (2008). Le regard de la théorie de la régulation sociale de Jean-Daniel Reynaud. *Revue française de gestion*, 4(184), 13–34.

David, A. (2001). La recherche-intervention, cadre général pour la recherche en management ? *Les nouvelles fondations des sciences de gestion : éléments d'épistémologie de la recherche en management*, 241–264.

Demailly, L. and Garnoussi, N. (2015). Le savoir-faire des médiateurs de santé pairs en santé mentale, entre expérience, technique et style. *Sciences et action sociale*, 1, 51–72.

De Terssac, G. (2003). *La théorie de la régulation sociale de Jean-Daniel Reynaud. Débats et prolongements*. La Découverte, Paris.

De Terssac, G. (2012). La théorie de la régulation sociale : repères introductifs. *Interventions économiques*, 45.

Droz-Mendelzweig, M., Bedin, M., Chappuis, M. (2011). La régulation en institution de long séjour. Un travail de soin et d'accompagnement auprès des personnes âgées. *Sciences sociales et santé*, 29(2), 47–74.

Epstein, S. (2001). *La grande révolte des malades. Histoire du sida*. Le Seuil, Paris.

Fals-Borda, O. and Rahman, M.A. (eds) (1991). *Action and Knowledge: Breaking the Monopoly with Participatory Action Research*. Intermediate Technoloy/Apex.

Flora, L. (2015). Du patient passif au patient expert. In *Santé mentale : guérison ou rétablissement. Regards croisés*, Dechamp-Leroux, C. and Rafale, F. (eds). John Libbey, Montrouge, 95–105.

Gardien, E. (2017). Qu'apportent les savoirs expérientiels à la recherche en sciences humaines et sociales ? *Vie Sociale*, 20(4), 31–44.

Girard, V. (2010). Petite histoire du rétablissement et des médiateurs en santé mentale à Marseille. *Rizhome*, 40(9), 9–13.

Godrie, B. (2016). Vivre n'est pas (toujours) savoir. Richesse et complexité du savoir expérientiel. *Le Partenaire*, 24(3), 35–38.

Hatchuel, A. and Molet, H. (1986). Rational modelling in understanding human decision making: About two case studies. *European Journal of Operational Research*, 24, 178–186.

Laval, C. and Gardien, E. (2020). Accompagner ses pairs n'est pas une activité de médiation, pourtant ils sont appelés médiateurs de santé-pairs. *Rhizome*, 75–76, 184–192.

Lemaitre, C.N. (2021). La capitalisation et l'usage de l'expérience patient dans les pathologies de la colonne vertébrale : quels apports d'une approche par l'activité ? *9e Colloque Santé*, Marseille, June.

Martinez-Perez, C. (2013). L'usage des plans de dessin industriel et la régulation du travail ouvrier. *La nouvelle revue du travail*, 3.

Molinier, P. (2008). *Les enjeux psychiques du travail*. Petite Bibliothèque Payot, Paris.

Pachoud, B. (2012). Se rétablir de troubles psychiatriques : un changement de regard sur le devenir des personnes. *L'information psychiatrique*, 88(4), 257–266.

Rabeharisoa, V. and Callon, M. (1998). L'implication des malades dans les activités de recherche soutenues par l'Association française contre les myopathies. *Sciences Sociales et Santé*, 16(3), 41–65.

Reynaud, J.D. (1979). Conflict and social regulation: A sketch of a theory of joint regulation. *British Journal of Industrial Relations*, 17(3), 314–321.

Reynaud, J.-D. (1997). *Les règles du jeu. L'action collective et la régulation sociale*. Armand Colin, Paris.

Riveline, C. (1993). La gestion et les rites. *Annales des mines*, 82–90.

Troisoeufs, A. (2020). Patients intervenants, médiateurs de santé-pairs : quelles figures de la pair-aidance en santé ? *Rhizome*, 27–36, 75–76.

Vallerand, R. and Bissonette, R. (1992). Intrinsic, extrinsic and amotivational styles as predictors of behavior: A prospective study. *Journal of Personality*, 60(3), 599–620.

5

Professional, Team and Digital Identity: The Impact on Patient Experience

5.1. Introduction

5.1.1. *Why is identity relevant to health and social care practitioners?*

Our sense of identity is based on our membership of groups (Tajfel and Turner 1979), including those we belong to and those we do not. Groups can provide us with a sense of belonging in the worlds we inhabit. Identity is developed through three steps: social categorization, where we seek to classify people into groups (e.g. pharmacists or nurses); social identification, where we start to adopt the identity of the group that we have aligned with; and social comparison, where we can then compare ourselves with people from other groups. Once we have moved through these three (interrelated, rather than linear) stages, our identity is established. Making changes to our identity, that is, mobilizing identity, can be challenging (Best et al. 2020), but important when working with other professions. This shift in mindset provides a platform for multi-professional working (Nancarrow et al. 2013).

Health and social care professionals can identify themselves through their individual craft group (i.e. professional identity) and/or through the team they work with (i.e. team identity). More recently, we have also seen a rise in the influence of technology on identity (i.e. digital identity). Each of these conceptualizations of identity can impact the patient experience.

Chapter written by Stephanie BEST, Ann DADICH and Sharon WILLIAMS.

5.1.2. *How does identity relate to patient experience?*

Our identity can influence how we behave (Simons 2021), providing "a shared/collective representation of who one is and how one should behave" (Hogg Abrams 1988). This relationship holds particular significance for health and social care professionals because constructing their identity with one group or another influences what is valued and the care provided, thereby directly impacting the quality of patient care. Thus, exploring the connections between the identity of health and social care professionals and patient experience is paramount.

5.1.3. *Why measure patient experience?*

Having recognized the association between identity and behavior, it is essential to examine how health and social care professionals identify themselves (including identities beyond their own professional group) and how these identities impact patients. Although patient experience is closely connected to better health outcomes (Manary 2013; Doyle 2013), a consideration of patient experience (i.e. the interactions patients have with the health and social care system) is a relatively new focus in the field of health and social care (Hefner 2019). Building on these findings, many healthcare systems are now investing in measuring patient experience. Consider, for instance, the introduction of patient reported outcome measures (PROMs), patient reported experience measures (PREMs) and quality of life measures. This partly follows a growing interest in value-based healthcare (Gray 2017; Saunders 2019).

Value-based healthcare is a model to guide the delivery of healthcare. Specifically:

> providers, including hospitals and physicians, are paid based on patient health outcomes… providers are rewarded for helping patients improve their health, reduce the effects and incidence of chronic disease, and live healthier lives in an evidence-based way.
>
> Value-based care differs from a fee-for-service or capitated approach, in which providers are paid based on the amount of healthcare services they deliver. The "value" in value-based healthcare is derived from measuring health outcomes against the cost of delivering the outcomes (NEJM Catalyst 2017).

In the context of value-based healthcare, value is defined as "better patient outcomes relative to the costs of achieving them" (Porter et al. 2017). In essence, "care is organized around the patient and meeting a **defined** set of patient needs over the **full care cycle**" (Porter et al. 2013; emphasis added). Value-based healthcare appears to redress the imbalance created by a supply-driven model of healthcare, where primacy is awarded to efficient or lean healthcare, towards a greater focus on patient experience, where primacy can be equally awarded to effectiveness (Walldius et al. 2003; Feeley et al. 2010; EIU 2016). In effect, the model "recognizes patient value as a driver for improving health outcomes at the societal and individual levels" (Nordin et al. 2017). This is indicated by some governments that recognize value-based healthcare as "delivering services that improve:

– the health outcomes that **matter to patients**

– the **experience** of receiving care

– the **experience** of providing care

– the effectiveness and efficiency of care" (NSW Ministry of Health 2019; emphasis added).

Having elucidated the context in which the importance of patient experience is amplified, we examine the links between measures of patient experience and health and social care professionals' identity.

5.1.4. *What is the aim of this chapter?*

This chapter investigates the connections between health and social care professionals' identity and measures of patient experience to clarify: (i) implications for health and social care professions and their organizations and (ii) gaps in the current research.

5.2. Conceptual background

Two key concepts inform this chapter – namely: the ways that identity can be conceived (e.g. professional identity, team identity and digital identity); and measures to report patient experience (e.g. PROMs, PREMs and quality of life measures). Here, we outline each concept before investigating the relationship between these two key areas.

5.2.1. *Health and social care professionals' identity*

Investigation into health and social care professionals' identity has developed over time. There was an initial focus on individual professions' identities before a later consideration of the influence of the team on identity. More recently, attention has focused on the impact of online interactions on identity in health and social care.

Professional identity in health and social care is the "the attitudes, values, knowledge, beliefs and skills shared with others within [the same] professional group" (Adams et al. 2006). Once developed, professional identity is considered to be difficult to mobilize (Schein 1978; Best Williams 2018). Professional identity is developed iteratively, as health and social care students embark on education and progress their career by learning to act, think and behave like others in the same profession (Shulman 2005; Best et al. 2021).

Team identity is where people see themselves as part of the same group with a collective identity (Ellemers 2011). Importantly, team identity is a shared attribute (Reis Puente-Palacios 2019) and as such, can exist in tandem with professional identity. The benefits of a team identity include recognizing the value of others, alongside perceptions of greater integrity, trustworthiness and increasing support (van Dick et al. 2008). In effect, team identity brings other professions into one common group. Team identity is developed by promoting interdependence and intra-team connectedness (Homan et al. 2008; Ellemers 2011).

Digital identity emerged with the availability of digital and online platforms, including social media for professional education, communication and collaboration. Digital identity is fluid and dynamic (Ruan et al. 2020). Digital technology (e.g. social media) is an integral part of our social construct and identity, particularly during training (John et al. 2017). Concerns have also been raised about the need for health and social care professionals to retain professionalism when online, with professionals encouraged to retain their professional identity in digital scenarios (Azu et al. 2012). Digital identity is developed through socialization with others and as a result, can lead health and social care professionals to be more deeply connected (Ruan et al. 2020). A review of the role of information and communications technology in nursing practice in Sweden reported ambiguous views on the place of technology, recognizing it is a complex process that impacts on professional identity and other areas of practice such as communication and relationships with patients and working conditions (Fagerström et al. 2017).

5.2.2. *Patient experience*

Patient experience can be examined via qualitative and/or quantitative tools. The use of measures to gauge patient experience has evolved from a focus on quality of life measures (often centered on clinical symptoms, such as pain or fatigue) to now include specific measures, such as PREMs and PROMs, which capture patient perceptions of their experience with healthcare.

Quality of life measures have been around for some time to provide a quantifiable measure of a patient's perception of their health. These measures are typically quantitative. They include some well-known resources, such as the European quality of life five dimension (EQ-5D) and the assessment of quality of life (AQoL). They can also extend to measuring clinical symptoms, like pain (e.g. numeric pain rating scale; NPRS), fatigue (e.g. fatigue severity scale; FSS), depression (e.g. Kessler-10, patient health questionnaire; 2PHQ2), anxiety (e.g. general anxiety disorder-7; GAD7), self-reported health status (e.g. 36-item short form survey; SF-36) and self-efficacy (e.g. general self-efficacy scale; GSE).

PROMs allow patients to provide direct feedback on their care and drive service improvement. Many quality of life measures now align with the PROMs category. PROMs can collect qualitative and/or quantitative data via surveys, focus groups, journals of patient stories and observation.

PREMs aim to capture patient perceptions of healthcare experiences and are the most recently developed. PREMs can encompass a wide range of healthcare experiences, including access to and ability to navigate services, consumer and carer involvement in decision-making, knowledge of care planning and pathways, the quality of communication and the "friends and family test" (would they recommend this facility to others).

PROMs and PREMs have a key role in the rapidly expanding international movement of value-based healthcare, which aims to maximize the value of patient care within available resources (Withers et al. 2021). Administrators' values often align with cost; however, value here also relates to patients', carers', as well as health and social care professionals' perceptions of value. Understanding and aligning these values is essential to maximize care (Andersson et al. 2015).

5.3. Patient experience and health and social care professionals' identity

Despite interest in the identities of health and social care professionals, few empirical studies have examined the direct link between these identities and patient experience. For instance, after a systematic search of relevant academic databases, only nine publications were identified that explicitly considered the professional, team or digital identity of health and social care professionals and patient experience (see Table 5.1). The following sections summarize these.

Publication	Identity type	Participants	Methods	Key findings
Chilcutt (2009)	Team	Dentists	Qualitative – semi-structured interviews	"a set of best practices includes a participative decision-making process; fostering an environment of open communication; and collaboration and confrontation as effective methods of conflict management. These behaviors contribute positively to a team's culture"
Gregory and Austin (2019)	Professional	Pharmacists	Qualitative – semi-structured interviews	"Personal identity was more important than professional identity… professional identity formation of community pharmacists may be incomplete, separated or functional rather than existential. Pharmacists perform pharmacy work but may not have a fully developed internalized psychological sense of profession-hood"
Hudson et al. (2016)	Team	Medical students	Quantitative – extended version of the readiness for interprofessional learning scale (RIPLS)	"the first four cohorts of medical students from our graduate-entry medical school expressed more negative attitudes to teamwork and collaboration and professional identity after an early interdisciplinary clinical experience… the associated decline in students' attitudes to patient-centeredness in the four-cohort sample, although small, was unexpected… Feeling useful in the health care team was associated with a positive attitude to the experience. It is difficult to establish roles with patients when not feeling part of the patient's care team"
McAllister et al. (2009)	Professional	Emergency nurses	A pre-test post-test study – mixed methods	"The intervention program led to the development of new nursing skills, such as the ability to ask more focused questions and to communicate in more supportive and effective ways… the intervention program appears to have extended understanding and skills in nurses. Participants reported being more able to help and having a clearer sense of the nursing role in the emergency care of self-harming patients"
Missel et al. (2020)	Professional	Nurses, physician, porters and healthcare workers	Qualitative – semi- structured interviews	"The participa[nts]… presented a strong sense of professional identity and were highly oriented towards their work. They talked about how they were preparing for battle against the coronavirus despite the risk of being infected themselves… This war metaphor as a response to the pandemic might illuminate the[ir]… stoic and altruistic work identity"

Publication	Identity type	Participants	Methods	Key findings
Palladelis et al. (2005)	Professional	Pediatric nurses	Qualitative – unstructured interviews	"the pediatric nurses… believed strongly in the 'family-centered care' concept, yet they found the application in practice to be somewhat challenging. The challenges described by the participants were linked to the nurses' beliefs about their own professional role, their desire to see themselves as the 'experts' in the care of hospitalized children, and the barriers they identified that make implementation of family-centered care difficult for them. Overwhelmingly, all participants described their role as involving not only providing nursing care for the patient and family but also protecting family members from painful or unpleasant experiences. This belief seems to cause the nurses the most conflict when they discussed the practical implications of parental participation"
Prato et al. (2022)	Digital	Carers	Qualitative – discourse analysis of blogs	"The six themes… reveal the multifaceted nature of online identity for the caregiver of an adult living with dementia and the value of belonging to an online community, both for identity construction and support, particularly during pandemic conditions"
Scheele and Vrangbaek (2016)	Professional	GPs	Qualitative – semi-structured interviews	"co-location does not qualify as a driver for cross-sectoral collaboration on its own within the context of a health center"
Yu et al. (2019)	Professional	Physicians, nurses, dietitian and pharmacist	Multi-phased study – qualitative semi-structured interviews and feasibility and evaluation of toolkit	"Clinicians' approaches to decision-making were closely tied to their professional identity, ranging from that of an educator to that of a decision-maker"

Table 5.1. *Research on patient experience and health and social care professionals' identity*

5.3.1. *Professional identity*

We identified six articles that considered the link of professional identity and patient experience (Palladelis et al. 2005; McAllister et al. 2009; Scheele and Vrangbaek 2016; Gregory and Austin 2019; Yu et al. 2019; Missel et al. 2020). McAllister et al. (2009) examined the proposed link between professional identity and patient experience. Specifically, they investigated the professional identity of nurses in the emergency department. They focused on developing nurses' professional identity and clinical reasoning to manage people presenting with self-harm. The interactive "think-aloud" approach improved nurses' attitude, confidence and ability to address psychosocial needs. The authors proposed that this method can improve quality of care for patients with mental health issues presenting at emergency departments. This active development of professional identity is counter to the experience of the community pharmacists (Gregory and Austin 2019). Here, the professionals were not actively engaged in care planning and resorted to their personal identity, rather than their professional identity, when advocating for care.

Two studies examine the experiences of multiple professionals. First, Missel et al. (2020) investigated perceptions of healthcare workers including physicians, porters among others while waiting for a Covid-19 result. For these experienced health workers, a strong link was reported between professional identity and patient experience – "[they] presented a strong sense of professional identity and were highly oriented towards their work. They talked about how they were preparing for battle against the coronavirus despite the risk of being infected themselves". Second, Yu et al. (2019) also captured the views of a mixed group, including dieticians, pharmacist and people with diabetes, to investigate views on a decision-making tool for people with diabetes. The authors reported:

> Clinicians' approaches to decision-making were closely tied to their professional identity, ranging from that of an educator to that of a decision-maker. Though the approach they used was tailored to the individual patient, they recognized that the patient had the final say. While they also recognized the critical importance of SDM [shared decision-making], clinicians highlighted… the challenge of conflicting clinician and patient agendas, the resolution of which depended on an appropriate knowledge-base on the part of the patient, and active listening on the part of the clinician, all within the context of a longitudinal relationship.

Interestingly, the roles were fluid, tailored to individual patient's needs.

Palladelis et al. (2005) examined understandings of pediatric nurses' views of identity and patient experience. They reported that, although the link between the two concepts was strong, it was challenging to enact, in practice. These professionals felt they had a key role in protecting families from painful or unpleasant experiences.

Scheele et al. (2016) examined whether co-location influenced identity and collaboration. General practitioners (GPs) reported not feeling part of the health center due to the busy nature of their work and so did not have a focus on collaborative work practices. However, they recognized cross-sectoral working as beneficial to patient experience in some cases, like chronic conditions.

5.3.2. *Team identity*

Two articles discussed team identity and patient experience. Hudson et al. (2016) examined the attitudes of graduate-entry medical students, following an early interdisciplinary clinical experience. Of some concern was their negative attitudes to teamwork and the associated decline in attitudes to patient-centered care. These findings reveal a clear connection between team identity and patient experience. They also suggest the need to actively promote team identity and prioritize patient values amidst the delivery of clinical care. Although the influence of the multidisciplinary team on identity has been recognized (Best et al. 2022), few researchers have examined the link to patient experience. One exception examined the influence of leadership behaviors in the professional identity of people working in dental practice (Chilcutt 2009). Chilcutt found the importance of adopting a participative decision-making approach within the team to empower team members to communicate the practice values to patients. This inclusive team style led to pragmatic improvements, such as increased productivity; it also significantly enhanced the level of service for patients. Yet, the study fell short of measuring how the enhanced service impacted patient experience, highlighting the knowledge gaps in this field.

5.3.3. *Digital identity*

Research on health and social care professionals' digital identity is limited and by extension, so too are efforts to link professionals' digital identity with patient experience. We identified one publication that discussed online identity and patient experience. Prato et al. (2022) investigated carer identity as constructed online. Although not centered on formal health and social care professionals, the value of belonging to an online community was recognized with proposed benefits for patient experience.

5.3.4. *Lexical analysis*

To clarify how identity and patient experience were discussed in these publications, a lexical analysis was conducted using Leximancer (Gephart 2004). Leximancer is data-mining software that uses Bayesian reasoning to detect key concepts and reveal their relationships (Zuell et al. 1989). Using algorithms,

Leximancer identifies frequently occurring and co-occurring words and amalgamates these to form and visually map concepts that reflect themes within the text (Young and Denize 2008). The maps convey three types of information – "the main concepts in the text and their relative importance; the strengths of links between concepts (how often they co-occur); and similarities in contexts where links occur" (Hewett et al. 2009). Concepts represent "collections of words that generally travel together throughout the text" (Leximancer 2011). The components of these concepts are ordered within a thesaurus, comprised of relevant words and weightings to indicate relative importance. Within the map, connections between concepts that are most probable are represented by a spanning tree of gray lines or branches – specifically, "The spanning tree... shows the most-likely connections between concepts (like a road map of highways), but there are other (less-strong) connections between concepts (like backstreets)" (Leximancer 2018). Clusters of concepts within a map – known as themes – suggest contextual similarity (Hepworth and Paxton 2007). Themes are color-coded to signify those that are (not) important, whereby the "most important theme appears in red, and the next hottest in orange, and so on according to the colour wheel" (Leximancer 2011).

Leximancer was used in two steps. First, after uploading a single Word file of the content of all nine articles into Leximancer (except the abstracts, references, tables and figures), the "discovery" mode was used to "see what concepts were automatically generated by Leximancer without intervention" (Angus-Leppan et al. 2010). The map was re-clustered several times to ensure the concepts were stable.

Second, Leximancer was used to examine the intersection of select concepts, as denoted by the likelihood percentage. The likelihood percentage represents the proportion of text segments, shared by two concepts, thus providing both directions of conditional probability. Given the focus of this chapter, attention was awarded to the concept that denoted identity.

The discovery mode concept map revealed four themes – namely: "health", "identity", "nurses" and "data" (see Figure 5.1). These highlight the key clusters of concepts represented within the text. Theme position illustrates the relationships between the themes. Consider the prominence of "health", which appears in red and overlaps with the three other less-prominent themes, particularly "identity". This suggests that when the articles referred to "health" (and the concepts therein), they were inclined to refer to "identity" (and the concepts therein):

> Theme 2: Empowerment issues This theme related closely to the participants' assumptions and beliefs about their professional identity as a nurse. Each participant made comments concerning their power as health care professionals (Palladelis et al. 2005).

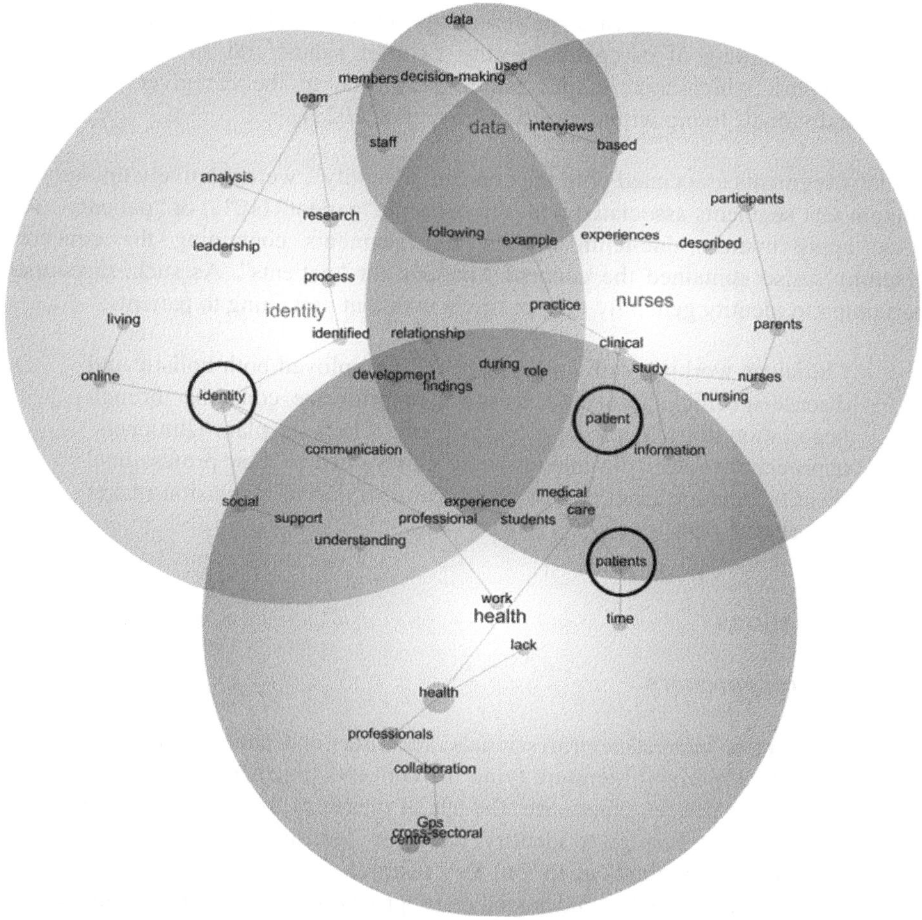

Figure 5.1. *Discovery mode concept map (visible concepts: 100%, theme size: 75%)*[1]. *For a color version of this figure, see www.iste.co.uk/flora/experience.zip*

The concept, "identity", shares the greatest likelihood percentage with the concept, "online" (94%). This means that 94% of the text segments containing the concept, "identity", also contained the concept, "online". Yet, the likelihood percentage between the concepts, "identity" and "professional", is 58%; while the likelihood percentage between the concepts, "identity" and "team", is only 16%. Collectively, these findings suggest that discourse pertaining to identity was relatively more associated with that pertaining to being online:

1 Color code: red denotes the most important theme, followed by yellow, green and purple.

> Health and social care professionals must develop a thorough understanding of caregiver identity to offer robust and appropriate support, which incorporates online resources, to the caregivers of individuals living with dementia (Prato et al. 2022).

Text segments associated with the concept, "identity", were relatively unlikely to contain text segments associated with the concept, "patient" (10%) or "patients". As such, approximately one-tenth of the text segments containing the concept, "identity", also contained the concept, "patient" or "patients". As such, discourse pertaining to identity generally did not travel with that pertaining to patients:

> Clinicians working with complex patients employed both holistic and disease-specific approaches in order to prioritize concerns through negotiation and compromise and achieve a tailored plan. Clinicians' approaches to decision-making were closely tied to their professional identity, ranging from that of an educator to that of a decision-maker (Yu et al. 2019).

5.4. Implications

5.4.1. *For researchers*

While there is interest in professionals' identities and patient experiences, this review identified minimal literature tying the concepts together. Furthermore, while there is interest in patient experience, the use of measures, such as PROMs, PREMs and quality of life, in relation to identity, were not identified. As such, there is a gap in the literature that warrants attention. Key research questions include: What is the relationship between health and social care professionals' identities and patient experience; how do professional, team and digital identity overlap, and to what effect; and how might measures, like PROMs, PREMs and quality of life, capture the relationship between professional identity and patient, particularly for people with chronic conditions who are likely to benefit from interprofessional care?

5.4.2. *For health and social care professionals and service managers*

Our findings suggest that health professionals can struggle in practice to link professional identity to patient experience. Often, patient experience teams, who obtain feedback from patients and carers, are located away from practice. Similarly, value-based activity is likely to be driven as a corporate initiative, which also requires considerable effort to reach areas of practice. Greater collaboration is required across these siloed departments and initiatives to ensure that professionals can reflect on how their professional identities impact on patients. Offering the opportunity for reflective sessions where professionals and teams can actively discuss the impact of their work on patient experience could help to establish the link between these two important concepts.

5.4.3. *For patients and carers*

The extent that patient and carer experiences are influenced by the professional identities of those providing care and support is relatively unknown. Patients and carers are frequently asked about their experiences of care, with particular attention to the different professions involved in their care. Given that many healthcare systems are moving towards a more integrated model of care, which relies on multi-professional working, this is an interesting area to pursue with patients. Calls have been made for further research to investigate more closely how teamwork contributes to a more positive experience for patients (Tremblay et al. 2017). A better understanding of how the different forms of identity discussed in this chapter impact specific aspects of patient experience (e.g. access to care, person-centered approach, patient–professional communication, etc.) would improve the interaction between professionals, patients and carers.

5.5. Conclusions

This chapter investigated the connections between health and social care professionals' identity and measures of patient experience. This served to clarify the implications for health and social care professions and their organizations; it also identified gaps in the current research.

Within the field of identity in the health and social care setting, the principal focus to date has been on professional identity, notably, the development of student professional identity (Cruess et al. 2014; Haghighat et al. 2020). The recent policy drive for integrated health and social care systems highlights the importance of team identity, but this research remains in its infancy, particularly in relation to patient experience. Covid-19 drove an increase in online activity, including video-based clinical and social care appointments. This activity, alongside the growth of social media, raised the profile of health and social care professionals' digital identity. However, this remains an understudied arena.

A range of healthcare professionals have been included in studies to date. These include GPs, nurses, dieticians and pharmacists; yet, one study examined the identity of carers (Prato et al. 2022). No studies included professionals from social care. Qualitative research was the most common approach across the studies reviewed in this chapter, with one article reporting the analysis of blogs (Prato et al. 2022). There was only one survey-based study (Hudson et al. 2016), which used the readiness for interprofessional learning scale with medical students. Two studies employed mixed methods approach (McAllister et al. 2009; Yu et al. 2019). This suggests that there are no survey instruments that measure the impact of professional identity on patient experience. Accepting that the qualitative studies identified important themes linking these two concepts, there is a need for research that uses both quantitative and qualitative approaches and more innovative methods to capture the impact of the various forms of identity on patient experience.

Patient experience, whether quality of life, outcome or experience-related, is central to day-to-day clinical and social care practice. Furthermore, it is gathering increasing attention, particularly within the sphere of value-based healthcare. However, interest in professionals' identity has yet to be well-connected with patient experiences. The limited studies investigating the relationship between health and social care professionals' identity and patient experience highlight a missing piece of the identity–experience jigsaw that requires examination. This chapter identified research priorities that require further attention by scholars.

5.6. References

Adams, K., Hean, S., Sturgis, P., Macleod Clark, J. (2006). Investigating the factors influencing professional identity of first-year health and social care students. *Learning in Health and Social Care*, 5(2), 55–68.

Andersson, A.E., Bååthe, F., Wikström, E., Nilsson, K. (2015). Understanding value-based healthcare – An interview study with project team members at a Swedish university hospital. *Journal of Hospital Administration*, 4(4), 64–72.

Angus-Leppan, T., Benn, S., Young, L. (2010). A sensemaking approach to trade-offs and synergies between human and ecological elements of corporate sustainability. *Business Strategy and the Environment*, 19(4), 230–244.

Azu, M.C., Lilley, E.J., Kolli, A.H. (2012). Social media, surgeons, and the internet: An era or an error? *American Surgeon*, 78(5), 555–558.

Best, S. and Williams, S. (2018). Integrated care: Mobilising professional identity. *Journal of Health Organization and Management*, 32(5), 726–740.

Best, S., Robbé, I., Williams, S. (2020). Mobilizing professional identity in multidisciplinary teams. *International Journal of Healthcare Management*, 15(2), 132–141.

Best, S., Beech, C., Robbé, I.J., Williams, S. (2021). Interprofessional teamwork: The role of professional identity and signature pedagogy – A mixed methods study. *Journal of Health Organization and Management*, 35(5), 561–578.

Best, S., Beech, C., Fletcher-Miles, H., Eynon-Jones, S., Robbé, I., Williams, S. (2022). Moving out of the silo: Trialing a prototype work-based education intervention to mobilise professional identity in integrated teams. *British Journal of Healthcare Management*, 28(2), 1–10.

Chilcutt, A.S. (2009). Exploring leadership and team communication within the organizational environment of a dental practice. *Journal of the American Dental Association*, 140(10), 1252–1258.

Cruess, R.L., Cruess, S.R., Boudreau, J.D., Snell, L., Steinert, Y. (2014). Reframing medical education to support professional identity formation. *Academic Medicine*, 89(11), 1446–1451.

Doyle, C., Lennox, L., Bell, D. (2013). A systematic review of evidence on the links between patient experience and clinical safety and effectiveness. *BMJ Open*, 3(1), e001570.

EIU (Economist Intelligence Unit) (2016). Value-based healthcare: A global assessment – Findings and methodology. Report, London.

Ellemers, N., Sleebos, E., Stam, D., De Gilder, D. (2011). Feeling included and valued: How perceived respect affects positive team identity and willingness to invest in the team. *British Journal of Management*, 24, 21–37.

Fagerström, C., Tuvesson, H., Axelsson, L., Nilsson, L. (2017). The role of ICT in nursing practice: An integrative literature review of the Swedish context. *Scandinavian Journal of Caring Sciences*, 31(3), 434–448.

Feeley, T.W., Fly, H.S., Albright, H., Walters, R., Burke, T.W. (2010). A method for defining value in healthcare using cancer care as a model. *Journal of Healthcare Management*, 55(6), 399–411.

Gephart, R.P. (2004). From the editors: Qualitative research and the Academy of Management Journal. *Academy of Management Journal*, 47(4), 454–462.

Gray, M. (2017). Value based healthcare. *British Medical Journal*, 356(1/2).

Gregory, P. and Austin, Z. (2019). Pharmacists' lack of profession-hood: Professional identity formation and its implications for practice. *Canadian Pharmacists Journal*, 152(4), 251–256.

Haghighat, S., Borhani, F., Ranjbar, H. (2020). Is there a relationship between moral competencies and the formation of professional identity among nursing students? *BMC Nursing*, 19(1), 49.

Hefner, J.L., McAlearney, M.A., Spatafora, N., Moffatt-Bruce, S.D. (2019). Beyond patient satisfaction: Optimizing the patient experience. *Advances in Health Care Management*, 18. doi: 10.1108/s1474-823120190000018010.

Hepworth, N. and Paxton, S.J. (2007). Pathways to help-seeking in bulimia nervosa and binge eating problems: A concept mapping approach. *International Journal of Eating Disorders*, 40(6), 493–504.

Hewett, D.G., Watson, B.M., Gallois, C., Ward, M., Leggett, B.A. (2009). Intergroup communication between hospital doctors. *Social Science & Medicine*, 69(12), 1732–1740.

Hogg, M.A. and Abrams, D. (1988). *Social Identifications: A Social Psychology of Intergroup Relations and Group Processes*. Routledge, London.

Homan, A.C., Hollenbeck, J.R., Humphrey, S.E., Knippenberg, D.V., Ilgen, D.R., Van Kleef, G.A. (2008). Facing differences with an open mind: Openness to experience, salience of intragroup differences, and performance of diverse work groups. *Academy of Management Journal*, 51(6), 1204–1222.

Hudson, J.N., Lethbridge, A., Vella, S., Caputi, P. (2016). Decline in medical students' attitudes to interprofessional learning and patient-centredness. *Medical Education*, 50(5), 550–559.

John, N.J., Shelton, P., Lang, M., Ingersoll, J. (2017). Training psychiatry residents in professionalism in the digital world. *Psychiatric Quarterly*, 88(2), 263–270.

Leximancer (2011). Leximancer manual. Report, Leximancer Pty Ltd.

Leximancer (2018). Leximancer user guide: Release 4.5. Report, Leximancer Pty Ltd.

Manary, M.P., Boulding, W., Staelin, R., Glickman, S.W. (2013). The patient experience and health outcomes. *The New England Journal of Medicine*, 368(3), 201–203.

McAllister, M., Billett, S., Moyle, W., Zimmer-Gembeck, M. (2009). Use of a think-aloud procedure to explore the relationship between clinical reasoning and solution-focused training in self-harm for emergency nurses. *Journal of Psychiatric & Mental Health Nursing*, 16(2), 121–128.

Missel, M., Bernild, C., Dagyaran, I., Christensen, S.W., Berg, S.K. (2020). A stoic and altruistic orientation towards their work: A qualitative study of healthcare professionals' experiences of awaiting a COVID-19 test result. *BMC Health Services Research*, 20(1), 1–9.

Nancarrow, S.A., Booth, A., Ariss, S., Smith, T., Enderby, P., Roots, A. (2013). Ten principles of good interdisciplinary team work. *Human Resources for Health*, 11(1), 1–11.

Nordin, P., Kork, A.A., Koskela, I. (2017). Value-based healthcare measurement as a context for organizational learning. *Leadership in Health Services*, 30(2), 159–170.

NSW Health (2019). Value based healthcare [Online]. Available at: https://www.health.nsw.gov.au/Value/Pages/default.aspx [Accessed 24 February 2019].

Palladelis, P., Cruickshank, M., Wainohu, D., Winskill, R., Stevens, H. (2005). Implementing family-centred care: An exploration of the beliefs and practices of paediatric nurses. *Australian Journal of Advanced Nursing*, 23(1), 31–36.

Porter, M.E., Pabo, E.A., Lee, T.H. (2013). Redesigning primary care: A strategic vision to improve value by organizing around patients' needs. *Health Affairs*, 32(3), 516–525.

Porter, M.E., Kaplan, R.S., Frigo, M.L. (2017). Managing healthcare costs and value. *Strategic Finance*, 98(7), 24–33.

Prato, L., Abley, C., Adamson, J. (2022). Exploring online identity construction for the caregivers of adults living with dementia and the value of interactions with health and social care professionals. *Health & Social Care in the Community*, 30(1), 295–306.

Reis, D.P.D. and Puente-Palacios, K. (2019). Team effectiveness: The predictive role of team identity. *RAUSP Management Journal*, 54(2), 141–153.

Ruan, B., Yilmaz, Y., Lu, D., Lee, M., Chan, T.M. (2020). Defining the digital self: A qualitative study to explore the digital component of professional identity in the health professions. *Journal of Medical Internet Research*, 22(9), e21416.

Saunders, C. (2019). Towards value-based healthcare – Modelling an answer for cancer care delivery. *Australian Health Review*, 43(2), 121–122.

Scheele, C.E. and Vrangbaek, K. (2016). Co-location as a driver for cross-sectoral collaboration with general practitioners as coordinators: The case of a Danish municipal health centre. *International Journal of Integrated Care*, 16(4), 1–11.

Schein, E.H. (1978). *Career Dynamics: Matching Individual and Organizational Needs.* Addison-Wesley, Reading.

Shulman, L.S. (2005). Signature pedagogies in the professions. *Daedalus*, 134(3), 52–59.

Simons, J.D. (2021). From identity to enaction: Identity behavior theory. *Frontiers in Psychology*, 12(3118).

Tajfel, H. and Turner, J.C. (1979). An integrative theory of intergroup conflict. *The Social Psychology of Intergroup Relations*, 94–109.

Tremblay, D., Roberge, D., Touati, N., Maunsell, E., Berbiche, D. (2017). Effects of interdisciplinary teamwork on patient-reported experience of cancer care. *BMC Health Services Research*, 17(218/218), 1–11.

Van Dick, R., Van Knippenberg, D., Hägele, S., Guillaume, Y.R.F., Brodbeck, F.C. (2008). Group diversity and group identification: The moderating role of diversity beliefs. *Human Relations*, 61(10), 1463–1492.

Walldius, Å., Olve, N.-G., Aminoff, H. (2003). Mapping health outcome and costs when coordinating local information system redesign. *Studies in Health Technology and Informatics*, 215, 242–253.

Waltham, M.A. (2017). What is value-based health care? [Online]. Available at: https://catalyst.nejm.org/what-is-value-based-healthcare/ [Accessed 12 May 2019].

Withers, K., Palmer, R., Lewis, S., Carolan-Rees, G. (2021). First steps in PROMs and PREMs collection in Wales as part of the prudent and value-based healthcare agenda. *Quality of Life Research*, 30(11), 3157–3170.

Young, L. and Denize, S. (2008). Competing interests: The challenge to collaboration in the public sector. *International Journal of Sociology and Social Policy*, 28(1/2), 46–58.

Yu, C.H., Ke, C., Jovicic, A., Hall, S., Straus, S.E. (2019). Beyond pros and cons – Developing a patient decision aid to cultivate dialog to build relationships: Insights from a qualitative study and decision aid development. *BMC Medical Informatics & Decision Making*, 19(186), 1–12.

Zuell, C., Weber, R.P., Mohler, P. (eds) (1989). *Computer-assisted Text Analysis for the Social Sciences*. Mannheim, Germany.

6

Mobilizing the Experience of People with Disabilities: A Necessity in the Transfer of Innovations

6.1. Introduction

A paradigm shift has taken place in recent decades, driven by a profound conceptual evolution in the representations of disability consisting of a shift from an individual and medical approach to an interactional approach integrating social and environmental factors (Ravaud and Fougeyrollas 2005). In this interactive framework, disability is then the result, in a given situation, of an interaction between a person who is different on a bodily or functional level and a specific physical and social environment (Fougeyrollas 2002). Driven by this new paradigm, the Convention on the Rights of Persons with Disabilities (CRPD) adopted in 2006 by the United Nations establishes disability as a human rights issue (Office of the High Commissioner for Human Rights (OHCHR) 2021). The convention aims "to promote, protect and ensure the full and equal enjoyment of all human rights and fundamental freedoms by all persons with disabilities, and to promote respect for their inherent dignity". The principles of this convention are:

– respect for inherent dignity, individual autonomy including the freedom to make our own choices and independence of persons;

– nondiscrimination;

– full and effective participation and inclusion in society;

– respect for difference and acceptance of people with disabilities as part of human diversity and humanity;

Chapter written by Éléonore SÉGARD and Philippe CHERVIN.

– equality of opportunity;

– accessibility;

– equality between men and women;

– respect for the evolving capacities of children with disabilities and respect for the right of children with disabilities to preserve their identities.

These developments are associated with the awareness that disabled people must be able to make their own choices, to be the actors in their own lives. Human rights, the power to act and emancipation are determining elements at the heart of the transformations underway. This new paradigm encourages us to change the way we look at people with disabilities, to give them a place as a subject and to reimagine their participation within society. *Thus, the principles set out in the Convention serve as a basis for recognizing the experience of people with disabilities and the experiential knowledge that stems from it.*

Having a disability is a lived experience, which is multidimensional and complex (WHO 2011). The interactive model of disability as defined in Article 1 of the Convention on the Rights of Persons with Disabilities leads to thinking about disability in a broad social and environmental context. The International Classification of Functioning, Disability and Health (ICF), an instrument for describing disability, adopted by the World Health Organization in 2001 (WHO 2021) describes it through activity limitations and participation restrictions. Thus, beyond functional limitation, the environmental, cultural and social barriers that limit opportunities will contribute to the experience of disability. The experience of disability therefore, in a complex manner, encompasses numerous interdisciplinary and intersectorial dimensions, which may affect living conditions, access to work, housing, care, etc., as well as representations, behaviors, social norms and feelings.

An experiential approach thus seems necessary, because it is global, so as to integrate all of the dimensions of the person with disabilities and in particular within their family, social and professional interactions, etc., and in order to avoid restricting them to only one of these aspects.

The knowledge resulting from this experience is commonly called "experiential knowledge" (Jouet et al. 2010). The recognition of people's experience and of experiential knowledge benefits the people with disabilities themselves in the context of their individual support, while it additionally aims to go beyond this scope and can also contribute to changing the entire system (as seen in the field of health (Pomey et al. 2015)).

In this chapter, it is this second axis that we will investigate. We will reflect on the place of the experience of the person with disabilities in the transformation of services and support for persons with disabilities provision, and in particular in the context of the development and transfer of social innovations.

The transfer process is in fact nowadays identified as being key in accelerating the transformation of the service provision. Different actors should advance the transformation of services and support for persons with disabilities.

First, we will briefly present what is at stake in the transfer of innovations in serving the transformation of services and the work that we have undertaken on the subject. We will present the four processes that make up the operational approach that we have developed to initiate an effective transfer.

Secondly, we will show the specificity of innovations in the field of disability: the experience of disabled people is generally already at the heart of the process of developing social innovations.

Thirdly, we will put into perspective the experience of disabled people within the transfer process. We will explore in what sense and how the experience of people with disabilities can/should be a resource for action within transfer.

Finally, we will conclude with the challenges and perspectives of placing the experience of disabled people as a lever from which to reshape the provision and delivery of services.

6.2. The transfer of innovations to accelerate the transformation of services: a new approach

The current transition in the field of disability is leading society to a turning point in supporting people with disabilities and requires new responses in line with the principles set out in the CRPD.

In response to this, many social innovations are implemented by field actors on the ground. These innovations increasingly tend to be mapped on sharing platforms such as NOV'AP, the platform of the Fédération des établissements hospitaliers et d'aide à la personne (FEHAP 2020), the Lab'AU of L'observatoire national de l'action sociale (ODAS 2020) or the initiatives of APF France Handicap and NEXEM.

There is no stabilized definition of innovation in the field of disability. We propose a definition based on generic definitions of innovation and adapted to disability: *any dynamic in supporting people with disabilities, with a transformative aim, in line with the principles supported by the CRPD (freedom of choice, nondiscrimination, full participation, equality of opportunity, accessibility, etc.).*

This definition highlights the aim of innovation more than the nature of innovation. In accordance with the interactive framework of the social model of disability in which we situate ourselves, the dynamics aiming to create an enabling environment to this objective are included in our definition of innovation.

Box 6.1. *Our definition of innovation*

The observation made by actors is that innovation too often remains local, it rarely goes beyond the borders of an organization, it is restricted to a territory, and so it does not manage to be deployed to benefit a larger number of individuals (UNIOPSS 2021). This considerably limits its transformative potential.

One of the keys to increasing the impact of these innovations and accelerating the transformation of society is transfer. Thus, an innovation that has emerged in a given territory can be implemented in other territories and benefit other people. The transfer makes it possible to multiply the innovations that are effective, and to increasingly extend an inclusive environment in order to end up covering the entire territory.

It appears increasingly obvious that the lack of strategy for changing the scale of local innovations limits their potential. Having a transfer approach, as well as methodological guidance and tools seems essential.

Today, transfer is little described and practiced in the field of disability and rarely represents the fruit of specific research work. *In order to address this issue, we carried out exploratory research in order to study both theoretical bases and transfer practices*, in two areas close to disability: the public health sector and the social and solidarity economy sector.

Based on the lessons learned from this work, a structured approach was proposed to operationally support innovators in the transfer of innovations in supporting people with disabilities (Ségard 2022). Four intertwined processes make up the approach: evaluation, capitalization, transferability and implementation.

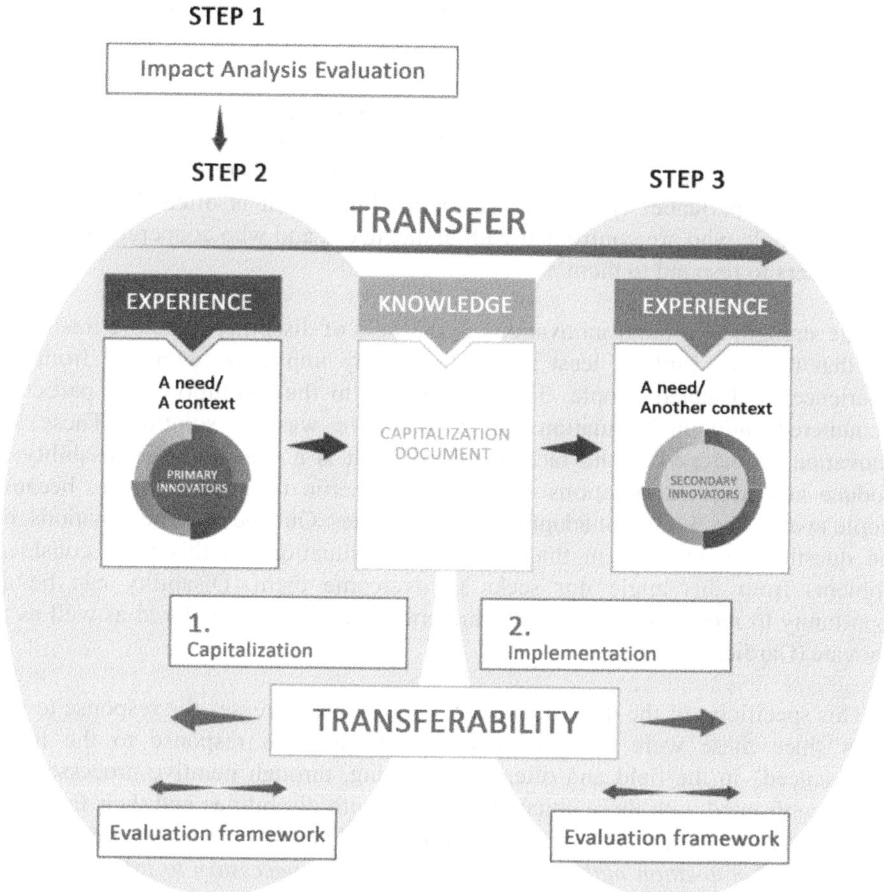

Figure 6.1. *The transfer process (figure from Ségard (2022)). For a color version of this figure, see www.iste.co.uk/flora/experience.zip*

Each of the four processes is briefly explained below and then explored with regard to the experience of people with disabilities. It is clarified that the object here is not to describe the approach itself and the way in which the processes fit together. The question asked here is: In what way and how can the experience of people with disabilities be a resource for action at the level of each of these processes?

Before beginning this reflection, we will look at the conditions for the emergence of innovations in the field of disability, and question the place of the experience of disabled people in their development.

6.3. People's experience at the heart of the development of ground innovations in the field of disability

In the field of disability, innovations emerge, to a large extent, from the impetus of actors who support them locally, or within the framework of national networks (Bertillot et al. 2018; UNIOPSS 2021). Innovative initiatives are generally motivated by personal experiences (Loubat et al. 2016). Initially, it is often the parents of disabled people who are confronted with unmet needs and who cooperate with local stakeholders to respond to them.

The strength of ground innovations in the field of disability therefore lies in the fact that they are built at least in part, generally implicitly, with and from the experience of disabled people. They correspond to the resolution of a particular encountered individual situation for which there was no solution. These are innovations developed in the face of necessity. It is a specificity of disability to produce and reiterate situations and barriers specific to certain people, because people evolve in a world not adapted to their abilities. Outside of these situations, no one questions themselves in this way, defines situations in this way, considers problems from this angle nor seeks to overcome them. Disability can be an opportunity to move forward in paths hitherto little or never explored as well as to innovate (Gardien 2012).

This specificity of the development of innovations increases the response to real needs since these were designed and manufactured in response to the needs "experienced" in the field and often by involving, through iterative processes, the people confronted with these situations (people with disabilities and their families). *The fact that the experience of people with disabilities has often directly informed the design of innovation makes it legitimate and even necessary to take their daily experience into account in the transfer of these innovations.*

This section focused on the experience of disabled people who contributed to the design of the innovation. The following section explores, for each of the four processes making up the transfer, the place of the experience of people with disabilities who benefit from, the innovation and use it.

6.4. Taking into account the experience of people with disabilities in the transfer process

6.4.1. *Evaluation*

The evaluation of an innovation is necessary to validate the relevance of the innovation to be transferred and then to ensure the success of the transfer.

The evaluation of a public health intervention is a major issue which is the subject of numerous debates, particularly in terms of the evaluative question and the level of evidence, and this can consume a lot of time and resources (Rychetnik et al. 2002; Hawe et al. 2004). In particular, methodologies tend to take into account the complexity of an intervention and to integrate the fact that context is one of the components of the result and influence it (Cambon and Alla 2019).

But the evaluation, beyond methodological issues, also reveals fundamentally ethical and political issues (Benmarhnia et al. 2019). It involves societal choices and values. This is particularly true today in the field of disability. As explained above, the place of the person with a disability, their ability to act, to decide, to participate, is today at the center of lines of questioning. Actions intended for supported people should be guided by these principles which are considered fundamental, and to which our societies are legally committed, in particular by signing the CRPD.

To be consistent with these elements, it would then be necessary to decide to primarily base the evaluation of innovations on the experience of disabled people and more precisely to *place the experience of the use of an innovation by persons with disabilities at the heart of its evaluation.*

This naturally raises the question of how to evaluate a person's experience.

In the field of disability, several instruments have been developed to measure activity limitations and participation restrictions as defined in the International Classification of Functioning, Disability and Health (ICF) (Noonan et al. 2009) or in the Quebecois model of the "disability production process" (Fougeyrollas et al. 2019).

Many issues accompany this theme: the development of validated scales, adapted to the context (language, culture, etc.), actualized with regard to international models, and meeting the criteria of scientific validity, etc. This area still requires a lot of research (seen in the field of psychological disability (Prouteau et al. 2014)). Initiatives aim to make measurement tools visible (Côte à Côte 2021).

It should be noted, however, that these tools and scales have generally been developed as part of the assessment of a person's support needs. We can question their relevance in the context of the collective evaluation of an innovation.

Furthermore, and as already stated, the experience of disability is multidimensional and quantification through indicators may appear reductive in view of the nature of the sought-out objectives. It will then certainly be necessary to propose a series of indicators which will best approximate the effect studied.

This leads to the question of prioritizing the dimensions to be measured in the context of evaluating an innovation. In line with current issues, it seems relevant to prioritize the dimensions relating to participation, autonomy, self-determination and the power to act. However, it should be noted that the evaluation of such dimensions and in particular of autonomy raises ethical and methodological questions. We must pay attention in order to ensure that the tools concerned do not adopt a "normative" but "dynamic" evaluation, that is, the person is compared to themself and especially to their own aspirations, with autonomy in mind. It cannot be a heteronomous measure.

Furthermore, the question arises of knowing from whom the experience should be collected. Should it be collected from the people concerned only or extended to those close to them, relatives, family? And what about the professionals who regularly interact with those affected? They too hold decisive knowledge drawn from their practice, from their intimate knowledge of support work. Cross-referencing opinions is certainly very valuable, but it also requires specific methodologies.

Consistent with the interactive disability framework in which we place ourselves, certain intermediate and environmental indicators are also important to take into account. Thus, it may be relevant to measure the impact of an innovation on the skills or behaviors of people with disabilities' entourage and of professionals who support them. These measures complement and enrich the measures of people's experience. This is, for example, the case in the field of inclusive education. The attitudes of mainstream teachers towards integration in schools are seen as fundamental to the successful implementation of inclusive education programs. A scale was developed to measure teachers' attitudes towards school inclusion: *teachers' attitude towards inclusion* (Cullen et al. 2010). In the field of supported employment, several studies show that variations in results depend essentially on the quality of support and more specifically on certain skills and attitudes of supported employment advisors (Drake et al. 2006). 90 skills, attitudes and kinds of knowledge are included in the latest version of the skills assessment scale for these professionals (Corbière et al. 2014).

It should be noted that some sectors have more resources than others. For example, the field of supported employment cited above has been heavily invested in. Measurement scales and indicators have been developed and validated by researchers (Pachoud et al. 2017). They are recognized and shared by those in the field, which facilitates their implementation, use and exploitation. The more a sector has produced data and developed tools and methodological expertise, the easier it will be for stakeholders to be part of an evaluation dynamic, because they will be able to benefit from pre-established work.

6.4.2. *Capitalization*

In the field of international development, capitalization was defined by Pierre de Zutter as the transition from experience to shareable knowledge (de Zutter 1994). This is a key phase in the transfer of innovations in the field of disability. As was shown in section 6.3, innovations generally emerge from the field and they have not always been formalized at the time of their design. They then do not have a solid methodological base, and their degree of formalization may be low (Gardien 2012).

This involves identifying the elements which may have led to this innovation and which will enable other actors to implement the innovation in their context. The question is how to find and organize these elements a posteriori. It is about bringing out "the unthought of action" and updating the processes at play (Pillant 2020).

Capitalization is based on the accounts of the actors, their experience and their expertise and, thus, on the objectification of their practices and strategies and on their observation of what these practices produce. Examples of capitalization techniques are given in certain works (Grenier 2017). The actors are at the center of this approach.

Here too, as in the evaluation, it is an ethical choice: to leave a central place for disabled people so that capitalization is nourished by their knowledge. The people concerned should participate and be at the heart of this investigation and cross-checking work, in the same way other actors are doing in the field. Indeed, they will pay great attention to dimensions which are peripheral to professional expertise, but essential to innovation.

Focusing on these dimensions will make it possible to rely on unique and complementary knowledge to other dimensions which will make it possible to understand innovation from new and more global angles. These criteria, less focused on functional, but more on relational and environmental limitations, are just as decisive for effective support and must be updated in the capitalization phase.

6.4.3. *Transferability*

The concept of transferability is used and widely studied, particularly in population health intervention research (PHIR), in the context of complex interventions. PIHR questions how, why and by what mechanisms the implementation of an intervention succeeds or fails (Hawe and Potvin 2008). This research underlines the crucial role of context: the effects of an intervention result both from the intervention itself and from the context (particularly the institutional environment, and implementation conditions particularly in terms of planning and partnerships, etc.) in which the intervention was developed (Hawe et al. 2009). The premise is that if we understand the mechanism of the intervention, then the intervention can be adapted to many contexts. This is what transferability aims to assess. Transferability is understood as "the extent to which the effect of an intervention in a given context can be achieved in another context" (Cambon et al. 2012).

The characteristic of population health research that consists of anchoring itself in the complexity of "real life" conditions, particularly through the study of the transferability of an intervention, meets a need in the field of support for disabled people. As such, we have identified transferability as a key step in the transfer of innovations in the field of disability.

Since experiential knowledge takes into account the contextual complexity of situations it is essential to take it into account at this stage of transferability. It is in the process of producing experiential knowledge that we can find the reasons for this proposition. Ève Gardien offers a description of the process of constructing experiential knowledge (Gardien 2020). This shows that it is constructed through experience, in given situations, through a set of criteria which combine elements relating to people and contextual elements. The semanticization of daily experience thus makes it possible to integrate the context. Experiential knowledge is therefore situated and will in this respect be key in the study of transferability. It will increase the external reliability of an innovation and facilitate the appropriation of innovations by stakeholders in the field. According to the author, this knowledge is built between peers. Indeed, they live through similar situations and experiences, which will be favorable to the work of semanticization and "typification" which occurs through cognitive and social processes constructing intersubjectivity. For example, this experiential knowledge will make it possible to collect elements and anticipate certain areas such as support accessibility or the specificities of each disability which will be useful to best adapt the deployment of innovation in other contexts.

6.5. Implementation

Implementation is the mirror stage of capitalization. This is the transfer phase that consists of moving from knowledge to experience (or practice). This involves implementing innovation in a new territory, based on capitalization work and the study of transferability. This process can be compared to a "recontextualization" of innovation.

If the upstream work has been carried out by integrating the experience of disabled people, the appropriation of the innovation in a new territory will a priori be easier. Indeed, since experiential knowledge has a collective scope, validity, relevance and legitimacy, the people "receiving" the innovation will be able to recognize themselves in the innovation that will be accessible to them. They will position themselves in a posture of peerjectivity, that is, objectivity which is limited to the community of peers (Gardien 2020). Basing themselves on their own experience, they will compare it with those of their peers, through experimentation with innovation. This way, they will be able to adopt the innovation.

The study of transferability will make it possible to best handle and combine the contextual elements to make it as appropriate as possible. However, it is likely that certain aspects will need to be adjusted in the new context. In this case, taking into account the experience of people benefiting from the innovation and experimenting with it in the new territory will also be crucial due to the same reasons as those explained in section 6.4.3: these new circumstances will lead to a new cycle of production of experiential knowledge through the work of constructing meanings and "typifications" between peers. This cycle will make it possible to best integrate these new combinations of contextual factors. This will enable innovation to evolve towards greater accuracy in the framework of the new context, and to further the construction of experiential knowledge. Innovations will be able to be increasingly refined, and be closer to the needs of disabled people.

6.6. Conclusion

Taking context into account is key in the transfer of innovations in the field of disability. Recent work highlights two essential conditions for the transition from experience to knowledge: the registration of the experience in a specific place and time, and the ability to make sense of this singular experience (Hejoaka et al. 2020). Several dimensions of experiential knowledge are identified, and in particular three relevant dimensions in the context of our reflection: a pragmatic dimension, a situated dimension and a holistic dimension. In this sense, experiential knowledge is astute, sensitive, holistic sensors of the richness and complexity of the context and must therefore be integrated into the transfer of an innovation.

Our analysis highlights that the experiences of people living with disabilities can be thought of at two levels in the transfer of innovations: 1) the experience of people who participate, upstream, in the design of the innovation and 2) the experience of people who benefit from and adopt the innovation in the original context of the innovation and then in the new context following its transfer. Regarding the first level, the challenge during the transfer will be to recognize this part of the experience which nourished the development of the innovation (generally implicitly), and to determine how this experience materializes concretely in innovation, how it is identifiable, how it is transferred. The second level questions the operationalization of taking experience into account in the different phases of the transfer. How do we mobilize people's experience in the four transfer processes? And how does this second level interact with the first level, particularly in the capitalization process? The challenge currently lies in operationalizing the consideration of experiential knowledge. We do not have all the practical keys. We must continue the research and experimentation with frameworks to work, exchange and experiment with all actors and articulate different knowledge.

Taking into account the experience of people with disabilities and experiential knowledge is therefore a major contribution to the transformation of services and support to persons with disabilities, and in particular to understand its complexity and encourage the deployment of appropriate innovations that can be adopted by people.

Beyond the richness that the experience of disabled people constitutes as a resource for action, taking their experience into account repositions people at the heart of their own lives. This dynamic contributes to promoting their power to act (Gross and Gagnayre 2017), as well as their autonomy, in accordance with the developments desired by the CRPD.

6.7. References

Benmarhnia, T., David, P.-M., Godrie, B. (eds) (2019). *Les sociétés de l'expérimentation. Enjeux épistémologiques, éthiques et politiques*, 1st edition. Presses de l'Université du Québec. doi: 10.2307/j.ctvhn0cr5.

Bertillot, H., Rapegno, N., Bloch, M.-A. (2018). Transformer l'offre médico-sociale ? Habitats "inclusifs" et établissements "hors les murs" : l'émergence d'accompagnements alternatifs pour les personnes âgées et les personnes handicapées. Research Report, CNSA, EHESP.

Cambon, L. and Alla, F. (2019). Current challenges in population health intervention research. *Journal of Epidemiology and Community Health*, 73, 990–992. doi: 10.1136/jech-2019-212225.

Cambon, L., Minary, L., Ridde, V., Alla, F. (2012). Transferability of interventions in health education: A review. *BMC Public Health*, 12, 497. doi: 10.1186/1471-2458-12-497.

Corbière, M., Brouwers, E., Lanctôt, N., van Weeghel, J. (2014). Employment specialist competencies for supported employment programs. *Journal of Occupational Rehabilitation*, 24, 484–497. doi: 10.1007/s10926-013-9482-5.

Côte à Côte (2021). Côte à Côte Inclusion [Online]. Available at: https://cote-a-cote-inclusion.com/ [Accessed 15 January 2021].

Cullen, J., Gregory, J., Lori, N. (2010). The Teacher Attitudes toward Inclusion Scale (TATIS) Technical Report.

De Zutter, P. (1994). *Des histoires, des savoirs, des hommes : l'expérience est un capital*. Charles Léopold Mayer, Paris.

Drake, R.E., Bond, G.R., Rapp, C. (2006). Explaining the variance within supported employment programs: Comment on "what predicts supported employment outcomes?". *Community Mental Health Journal*, 42, 315–318.

FEHAP (2020). L'observatoire FEHAP de l'innovation : NOV'AP [Online]. Available at: http://novap.fehap.fr/ [Accessed 14 December 2020].

Fougeyrollas, P. (2002). L'évolution conceptuelle internationale dans le champ du handicap : enjeux socio-politiques et contributions québécoises. *Perspectives interdisciplinaires sur le travail et la santé*. doi: 10.4000/pistes.3663.

Fougeyrollas, P., Boucher, N., Edwards, G., Grenier, Y., Noreau, L. (2019). The disability creation process model: A comprehensive explanation of disabling situations as a guide to developing policy and service programs. *Scandinavian Journal of Disability Research*, 21, 25–37. doi: 10.16993/sjdr.62.

Gardien, E. (2012). *Des innovations sociales par et pour les personnes en situation de handicap – A liberté égale*. Érès, Toulouse.

Gardien, E. (2020). Pairjectivité : des savoirs expérientiels ni objectifs, ni subjectifs. Éducation et socialisation. *Les Cahiers du CERFEE*. doi: 10.4000/edso.12581.

Grenier, C. (2017). Intervenir pour réduire les inégalités sociales de santé : des espaces favorables pour expérimenter, pérenniser et diffuser l'intervention – Guide IVRISS d'accompagnement méthodologique. Kedge Business School, ARS Provence-Alpes-Côte d'Azur.

Gross, O. and Gagnayre, R. (2017). Caractéristiques des savoirs des patients et liens avec leurs pouvoirs d'action : implication pour la formation médicale. *Revue francaise de pedagogie*, 201, 71–82.

Hawe, P. and Potvin, L. (2008). What is population health intervention research? *Canadian Journal of Public Health*, 100, 18–14. doi: 10.1007/BF03405503.

Hawe, P., Shiell, A., Riley, T. (2004). Complex interventions: How "out of control" can a randomised controlled trial be? *BMJ*, 328, 1561–1563. doi: 10.1136/bmj.328.7455.1561.

Hawe, P., Shiell, A., Riley, T. (2009). Theorising interventions as events in systems. *American Journal of Community Psychology*, 43, 267–276. doi: 10.1007/s10464-009-9229-9.

Hejoaka, F., Simon, E., Halloy, A., Arborio, S. (2020). État de l'art des savoirs d'expérience. In *Les savoirs expérientiels en santé : fondements épistémologiques et enjeux identitaires*, Simon, E., Arborio, S., Halloy, A., Hejoaka. F. (eds). Presses Universitaires de Lorraine, Lorraine.

Jouet, E., Flora, L.G., Las Vergnas, O. (2010). Construction et reconnaissance des savoirs expérientiels des patients : note de synthèse. *Pratiques de formation/Analyses*, 58/59, 13–94.

Loubat, J.-R., Hardy, J.-P., Bloch, M.-A. (2016). *Concevoir des plateformes de services*. Dunod, Paris.

Noonan, V.K., Kopec, J.A., Noreau, L., Singer, J., Chan, A., Mâsse, L.C., Dvorak, M.F. (2009). Comparing the content of participation instruments using the international classification of functioning, disability and health. *Health and Quality of Life Outcomes*, 7(93). doi: 10.1186/1477-7525-7-93.

ODAS (2020). Laboratoire de l'autonomie [Online]. Available at: https://odas.labau.org/ [Accessed 14 December 2020].

Office of the High Commissioner for Human Rights (OHCHR) (2021). Convention relative aux droits des personnes handicapées [Online]. Available at: https://www.ohchr.org/fr/professionalinterest/pages/conventionrightspersonswithdisabilities.aspx [Accessed 29 January 2021].

Pachoud, B., Marec, M.-G., Corbière, M. (2017). Étude évaluative de cinq dispositifs d'emploi accompagné pour des personnes en situation de handicap psychique ou mental. NEXEM.

Pillant, Y. (2020). Capitalisation d'expérience : la Coopérative d'activités et d'emploi de l'Association CCDE à Ras Jebel. IMFRTS.

Pomey, M.-P., Flora, L., Karazivan, P., Dumez, V., Lebel, P., Vanier, M.-C., Débarges, B., Clavel, N., Jouet, E. (2015). The Montreal model: The challenges of a partnership relationship between patients and healthcare professionals. *Santé publique*, 1, 41–50.

Prouteau, A., Koleck, M., Belio, C., Dayre, E., Destaillats, J.-M., Merceron, K., Mazaux, J.-M. (2014). Mesurer le handicap psychique : enjeux et méthodes. *L'information psychiatrique*, 90, 191–195.

Ravaud, J.-F. and Fougeyrollas, P. (2005). La convergence progressive des positions franco-québécoises. *Santé, société et solidarité*, 4, 13–27. doi: 10.3406/oss.2005.1047.

Rychetnik, L., Frommer, M., Hawe, P., Shiell, A. (2002). Criteria for evaluating evidence on public health interventions. *Journal of Epidemiology and Community Health*, 56, 119–127. doi: 10.1136/jech.56.2.119.

Ségard, E. (2022). *Le transfert des innovations dans le domaine du handicap – Quelles approches opérationnelles pour soutenir le transfert sur le terrain*. FIRAH, Paris.

UNIOPSS (2021). *Les associations réinventent l'innovation*. Les cahiers de l'Uniopss, Paris.

WHO (2011). World report on disability 2011. World Health Organization, World Bank.

WHO (2021). Classification internationale du fonctionnement, handicap et de la santé [Online]. Available at: https://apps.who.int/iris/bitstream/handle/10665/42418/9242545422_fre.pdf [Accessed 29 January 2021].

PART 2

Crossed Perspectives on the Impacts on Organizations and Health Systems

Introduction to Part 2

The second part of this book, *Experience in Healthcare Innovation: Fad or New Paradigm?*, consists of eight chapters that examine how and to what extent, experience (of the patient or beneficiary and of the professional) can modify the delivery of care and support for dependent or sick people.

In Chapter 7 entitled "Reorienting our Health System towards its Users thanks to Design Thinking: The Experience of Kaiser Permanente", **Inès Gravey** examines service design (or design thinking), an approach used by private companies, governments and public institutions and particularly suited to meet the challenges of healthcare organizations in meeting their challenges related to innovation (Acha 2006). The design thinking process is widely defined by practitioners and the literature as occurring in five stages: 1) empathy, 2) problem redefinition, 3) ideation, 4) prototyping and 5) experimentation and testing.

The author presents its application in practice within Kaiser Permanente, one of the world leaders in integrated systems, a nonprofit organization, based in the United States, and bringing together within it: insurance and care provision, a hospital and city offer, in the health and medico-social field. Since 2003, through a partnership with the IDEO agency (based in California), it has integrated the design discipline by massively training its staff (more than 12,000 people trained).

The feedback highlights the following few strong points: design as a lever for rebalancing powers between users and traditional experts, the importance of empathy to identify the needs of patients and professionals, the importance of forming heterogeneous teams, particularly during the ideation phase; design as a lever for cultural transformation in the bureaucratic and health context, in particular by promoting a culture of autonomy and creativity. Ines Gravey also identifies the

---

Introduction written by Corinne GRENIER, Luigi FLORA and Frédéric PONSIGNON.

barriers and facilitating factors put in place to propagate the practice of service design.

We continue in the hospital field in Chapter 8, entitled "Patient-Centered Care at Public Hospitals: A War of the Worlds?". **Marie-Eve Laporte, Patrick Gilbert** and **Karim Zinaï** examine the tensions experienced by a hospital service (orthopedics) faced with contradictory injunctions: how do we maximize health gains with limited resources and increased quality requirements, while placing the patient at the center of care? Drawing on the theoretical framework of economies of worth (Boltanski and Thévenot 1991; Boltanski and Chiapello 1999), the authors explore the tensions that are expressed and the methods deployed to reach compromises.

The notion of patient-centered care is defined as providing care while respecting the preferences, needs and values of patients, who are then considered as actors in the decisions made. It is a holistic and empowering approach (patient empowerment) but criticized (David 2006) for being an application of the customer centricity of the commercial world.

In the service under study, the "war of the worlds" was present when the approach was initiated, particularly between the domestic, industrial and civic worlds (Orvain and Angelé-Halgand 2011; Grenier and Oiry 2021). The first result is the interest in adopting a project approach outside of routine organization, to test new approaches and avoid direct confrontation between worlds on the broader spectrum of the hospital. This project approach was carried out in two care units that had recently been created. The understanding was developed in two different ways: a) around the "project" world within a unit by adopting an agile and collaborative mode to deliver care differently, while also focusing on a segment of autonomous patients, who are quite young and very connected; b) between different worlds (industrial, commercial, domestic and civic) by finding a compromise with regard to the well-being of the targeted population, as well as the elderly (and their caregivers). In both cases, the debrief room will have played an essential role in making tensions visible and being able to discuss them and in finding avenues for conciliation.

Chapter 9 is presented as an interview with **Marielle Ravot**, conducted by **Luigi Flora** and entitled "A Brief History of Changes in the Medico-Social Sector over Recent Decades. Interview with Marielle Ravot", based on Marielle Ravot's experience of more than 20 years in the evaluation of social and medico-social establishments. It puts into perspective the organizational changes of these establishments and the public services which sponsor them, the increase in skills of the personnel involved in these establishments and the different functions that it has taken on while establishing outlines. It then, in conclusion, puts into perspective the contribution that the care partnership approach with patients could make (Karazivan et al. 2015).

In Chapter 10, "EPoP: An Approach to Developing Peer Intervention", **Sabrina Sinigaglia** presents an original experiment, carried out by the French Red Cross (in partnership with other associations) and deployed to date in two regions (Hauts-de-France and Nouvelle-Aquitaine). EPoP aims to support the use of the experiential knowledge of people with disabilities (PWD), the author recalling the long journey in France and other countries, which allowed for the recognition of this knowledge (Flora 2021), in particular through peer support, "peers" being defined as "individuals engaged in the accompaniment or support of those living or having lived an experience similar to theirs, in other words their presupposed 'peer'" (Gardien 2021).

EPoP (Empowerment and Participation of Persons with Disabilities) aims to gain recognition and further mobilize the experiential knowledge of PWD, whatever their disability situation, by deploying peer intervention in all its forms and in any exercise context. It is about strengthening self-determination, people's power to act by allowing them to progress in their career in accordance with their wishes, drawing on their lived experiences and their practical expertise. EPoP promotes two new functions: the IP (*intervenant pair-accompagnement*: peer support worker) and the RP (*référent pair-accompagnement*: peer support specialist, facilitating professional and/or professional using the practical knowledge of PWD). In both regions, EPoP is led by a regional leadership, supporting the IPs and RPs who will have been specifically trained beforehand to carry out their missions. After presenting the general architecture of the experiment, Sabrina Sinigaglia reports on some projects already carried out and illustrates how EPoP enriches the life course of PWD.

In Chapter 11 on the "The Potential for Digital Health to Reframe the Role of Compassion in Patient Experience Innovation", **Lester Levy**, **Ann Dadich** and **Kevin Lowe** study the development of digital APPS in healthcare, questioning to what extent these tools can aid or hinder compassion within healthcare. Compassion is defined as "a feeling of concern for the suffering of another person that is accompanied by a motivation to help [...] [It is] a feeling for the other and not a feeling with the other person" (Singer and Klimecki 2014). It is rooted in lived experiences, understood as an intention to act to alleviate or prevent the suffering of others.

The authors carefully analyze the experience of three patients. The outcome is that while digital health can radically advance many aspects of the patient experience, it cannot provide the essential human attributes of compassion and empathy on its own (Topol 2019).

They then propose a discussion on the notion of "compassionate technologies", which could facilitate emotional awareness and attention of healthcare professionals to patients' concerns, fears and suffering.

Chapter 12 extends previous work, with "Help with Prescribing Mobile Health Applications: A Partnership Design". The authors – **Luigi Flora, David Darmon, Stephen Darmoni, Julien Grosjean, Christian Simon, Parina Hassanaly** and **Jean-Charles Dufour** – report on research funded by the French Agence nationale de la recherche (ANR) on the development of a characterization of mobile health applications, labeled in some way in order to help doctors prescribe mobile applications in the midst of the multitude of applications being created at an exponential rate. The authors describe the chosen methodology, which became participatory as the research progressed through the involvement of final users in the research process. On the one hand, with the association "Seintinelles" to understand social acceptability and uses, then through the integration into characterization of the device for helping with the prescription of an evaluation method by both doctors and patient-partners, mobilized by the centre d'innovation du partenariat (CI3P) of the University of Côte d'Azur (Flora et al. 2020) and through the integration of its patient co-director into the scientific committee. The second part of the chapter presents a new research project developed as an extension of the first research and aimed more towards patients and citizens. A project which is the result of a desire to continue their collaboration largely due to the stimulation generated by the partnership with patients.

In Chapter 13, **Yves Couturier, Marie-Ève Poitras, Marie-Dominique Poirier** and **Anaëlle Morin** present innovation research having implanted a train-the-trainer program in primary care clinics (Quebec, Canada), a system in which patient-partners surpass the usual status of witnesses to take on a full role as trainers in practice settings: "Beyond the Testimony: Patient Partners and Ongoing Training". More precisely, this research consisted of developing, implementing and evaluating a train-the-trainer strategy aimed towards supporting the use by these nurses and social workers of said practice guides. This involves questioning original training practice (that of training by patients), which is still poorly developed and studied (Fraser et al. 2017) and which encounters barriers, such as the resistance of healthcare professionals from training to full patient participation.

The authors rely on the concept of "circumdisplinarity" (Couturier and Belzile 2018) by which pragmatically interdependent and coactive actors recognize that it is legitimate that they mutually collaborate, regardless of their status (particularly as professional or patient).

The main result of the research reveals that, contrary to what the team of researchers, trainers and patients could have expected, the contribution of the latter has proven to be an important source of learning, even though it came up against practical issues (such as diary management, the "oversight" (resistance) of professionals in giving patients a voice, etc.). The authors draw some lessons on the conditions favorable to the deployment of this type of training, such as: the attention paid to the constitution of the team of patient-trainers and trainers, in order to bring about solidarity between them, as well as a rebalancing of the symbolic weight of each person's knowledge; the importance of good literacy among professionals with regard to partnership with patients before starting this type of training. Couturier and colleagues then conclude with an enrichment of the Montreal model known as the patient-partner model (Pomey et al. 2015).

After the experiences recounted in hospital and medical–social organizations, in the ordinary environment, or in a training context, **Philippe Anhorn** analyzes how to deploy the patient-partner within a regional health system, in the final chapter entitled: "The Care Partnership: Challenges and Perspectives for Healthcare Systems". This analysis is based on the theoretical model of business ecosystems, in which all stakeholders must share values, language and practices that aim to achieve a common objective, and studies the Réseau Santé Région Lausanne in particular, through intervention research on the deployment of an advance care planning project (Emanuel et al. 2000). This involves establishing and then continuously updating the care objectives between professionals, patients and caregivers, regardless of the care setting (hospital, home, retirement home, etc.). The author's hypothesis is that this project can contribute to creating a convergence of all the stakeholders concerned around the patient-partner approach (Anhorn et al. 2018).

The results showed that the patient-partner principle was very well known, accepted and valued, presenting interests for the quality, safety and economics of care in health organizations and for training. However, these results are lesser when patients are questioned, encouraging the further promotion of a common culture. On the contrary, its development requires more collaboration between organizations and/or professionals, due to its systemic dimension. Indeed, the following obstacles have been identified: a lack of a shared electronic patient files, disparate financing methods and the lack of evidence of this approach's benefits. Finally, the author noted with surprise how the Covid-19 health crisis has reinforced the interest and appeal of the care partnership, both among patients and among professionals and structures within the network.

Finally, Anhorn adapts Moore's coopetition model (1996) to promote the deployment of patient–professional partnerships within healthcare systems. It thus formulates some managerial, operational and strategic recommendations.

References

Acha, V. (2006). Open by design: The role of design in open innovation. Report, DIUS.

Anhorn, P., Chinet, M., Devaux, L. (2018). Projet anticipé des soins : un modèle pour des soins intégrés. *Bund, Kantone und Gemeinden in der integrierten Versorgung Rollenszenarien 2026.*

Boltanski, L. and Chiapello, E. (1999). *Le nouvel esprit du capitalisme*. Gallimard, Paris.

Boltanski, L. and Thévenot, L. (1991). *De la justification : les économies de la grandeur*. Gallimard, Paris.

Couturier, Y. and Belzile, L. (2018). *La collaboration interprofessionnelle en santé et services sociaux*. Presses de l'Université de Montréal, Montreal.

David, A. (2006). Quelques enjeux contemporains de la relation de service public. *Politiques et management public*, 24(3), 5–12.

Emanuel, L.L., von Gunten, C.F., Ferris, F.D. (2000). Advance care planning. *Archives of Family Medicine*, 9(10), 1181–1187.

Flora, L. (2021). Recognition of patients' experiential knowledge and co-production of care knowledge with patients and citizens in the 21st century. In *Altering Frontiers: Organizational Innovations in Healthcare*, Grenier, C. and Oiry, E. (eds). ISTE Ltd, London, and John Wiley and Sons, New York.

Flora, L., Darmon, D., Benattar, J.-M. (2020). Le Centre d'Innovation du partenariat avec les patients et le public : un moteur du développement de la culture du partenariat de soin avec le patient, avec les patients et le public en Europe. *Le partenariat de soin avec le patient : analyses*, CI3P, Université Côte d'Azur, 1, 138–163.

Fraser, C., Grundy, A., Meade, O., Callaghan, P., Lovell, K. (2017). EQUIP training the trainers: An evaluation of a training programme for service users and carers involved in training mental health professionals in user-involved care planning. *Journal of Psychiatric and Mental Health Nursing*, 24(6), 367–376.

Gardien, È. (2021). Instituer le pair-accompagnement au risque de perdre les qualités spécifiques de la relation entre pairs. In *L'accompagnement par les pairs : enjeux de participation et de professionnalisation*, Gardien, È. (ed.). PUG, Grenoble, 93–111.

Grenier, C. and Denis, J.L. (2017). S'organiser pour innover : espaces d'innovation et transformation des organisations et du champ de l'intervention publique. *Revue Politiques et Management Public*, 34(3/4), 191–206.

Grenier, C. and Oiry, E. (2021). *Altering Frontiers: Organizational Innovations in Healthcare*. ISTE Ltd, London, and John Wiley and Sons, New York.

Karazivan, P., Dumez, V., Flora, L., Pomey, M.-P., Del Grande, C., Guadiri, S., Fernandez, N., Jouet, E., Las Vergnas, O., Lebel, P. (2015). The patient as partner in care: Conceptual grounds for a necessary transition. *Academic Medicine*, 90(4), 437–441.

Moore, J.F. (1996). *The Death of Competition: Leadership and Strategy in the Age of Business Ecosystems*, 1st edition. HarperBusiness, New York.

Orvain, J. and Angelé-Halgand, N. (2011). Les manufactures de santé : l'art du compromise entre domesticité et industrie. *Sciences sociales et santé*, 29(1), 5–27.

Pomey, M., Flora, L., Karazivan, P., Dumez, V., Lebel, P., Vanier, M., Jouet, E. (2015). Le "Montreal model" : enjeux du partenariat relationnel entre patients et professionnels de la santé. *Santé publique*, 1, 41–50.

Singer, T. and Klimecki, O.M. (2014). Empathy and compassion. *Current Biology*, 24(18), R875–R878.

Topol, E. (2019). The Topol review: Preparing the healthcare workforce to deliver the digital future. Health Education England, Leeds.

7

Reorienting Our Health System towards its Users Thanks to Design Thinking: The Experience of Kaiser Permanente

7.1. Introduction

On the eve before the Covid-19 pandemic started, France had recorded almost a year of social conflict with its hospital professionals, marked by strikes and mass resignations from medical managers. For citizens, the issues of healthcare provision appeared at the forefront of the concerns of the gilets jaunes[1] and their approximately 50 weeks of marching. Today, as the pandemic crisis begins to come to an end, massive departures of staff from French establishments highlight another, no less fearsome wave, and for this, we do not yet have a vaccine.

In forms moving away from the French system, social movements of patients, caregivers and carers, demanding organizations and health systems centered on the needs of humans rather than on plans, processes and indicators defined remotely from the field, have grown throughout the world[2].

Chapter written by Inès GRAVEY.

1 The gilet jaunes movement – named after the yellow high visibility vests worn by demonstrators – is an unstructured and sporadic protest movement that appeared in France in October 2018. This spontaneous social movement finds its origins in diffusion – mainly on social media – of calls for demonstrations against the increase in the price of automobile fuels, but which was quickly expanded to the general improvement of living standards.

2 A revolution of compassion and solidarity initiated by Mayo Clinic doctor Victor Montori in the United States or a call to power launched by the British innovation foundation NESTA were just some of those calling the status quo of organizational and managerial models in health into question.

The global challenges facing the health sector, such as an aging population and the impact of chronic diseases, combined with the demand for more efficient and responsive services due to budgets being under stress, highlight the need to work and resolve problems differently within the health institutions and organizations in developed countries (insurers, providers, supervisory authorities).

However, transforming our health system and more specifically the care providers within it, as well as their supervisors, is an arduous task. Complex and highly regulated, responding particularly to the bureaucratic organizational and cultural model, they naturally resist change in exchange for stability, predictability and operational imperatives such as security and cost control. True transformation and massive commitment to innovation centered on the needs of users to overcome the problems faced would require a cultural revolution and a range of very distinct postures and methods from the toolkit available to health decision-makers and managers today.

Among these disciplines, service design, in its most accessible (and sometimes misguided) form, design thinking, benefits from unprecedented attention. Heralded as a new[3] method of problem solving based on radical collaboration with final users, it is considered to be well suited to meet the challenges our organizations face and to encourage innovation (notably Acha 2006; Hughes et al. 2010; Design Council 2014).

The design thinking process democratizes (and sometimes oversimplifies) the postures and methods of the service design discipline in five steps:

– *The phase of empathy* towards users (namely in health: patients, caregivers and carers) using tools from the human sciences (ethnographic interviews, immersions, etc.) in order to obtain an in-depth understanding of the user experience and the identification of "blind spots" traditionally not perceived by managers and decision-makers.

– *The problem redefinition phase* resulting from the previous research phase.

– *The ideation phase* so that a maximum of ideas can be generated by mobilizing techniques for deploying collective intelligence, in particular.

3 Despite the recent attention given to design thinking, its origins actually date back to the 1960s (e.g. Alexander 1964; Gregory 1966; Simon 1969). Since then, the so-called designers' way of thinking and knowing (e.g. Cross 1982, 2007) and the complex problems they tackled (e.g. Buchanan 1992; Goldschmidt 1997) have gradually shifted from the competence of classically trained designers to the field of management. The problem-solving tools and postures specific to design are now advocated as effective approaches for companies seeking to innovate and transform organizations (Brown 2008, 2009).

– Quick and low-fidelity *prototyping* to allow projection into future solutions as early as possible.

– *Experimentation and testing* according to quick iterative cycles.

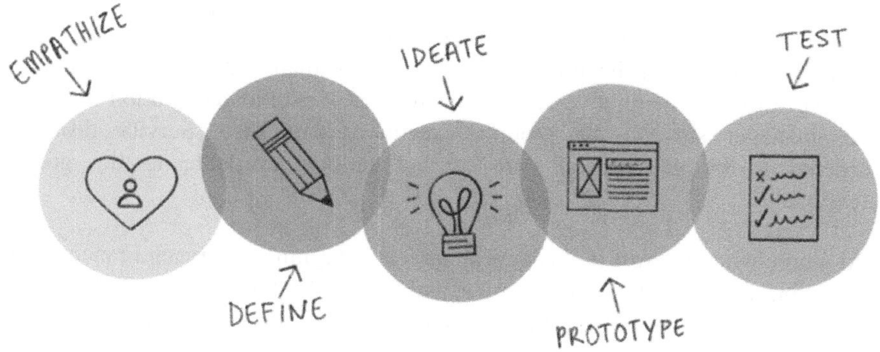

Figure 7.1. *The design thinking process (according to uxdesign.cc). For a color version of this figure, see www.iste.co.uk/flora/experience.zip*

Over the last two decades, design thinking has been used to equip innovation in both the public and private sectors: within governments (in the wake of the pioneering Danish laboratory Mindlab in 2002); large companies (one example, among the most successful on a large scale, is IBM) and the most renowned consultancy companies which have acquired design agencies in order to internalize their skills (McKinsey, Accenture or Deloitte).

The health field has not remained isolated from this craze. Major healthcare providers such as Kaiser Permanente or the Mayo Clinic have over the past 10 years developed their own internal innovation units which integrate design thinking into their daily practice, and universities have enriched their curriculum with design thinking courses, which are adapted to health professionals (Stanford Medical School, Dell Medical School, University of California at Berkeley, etc.)[4].

This chapter seeks to deepen the discussion on the value of design thinking for healthcare organizations by examining its large-scale implementation with regard to

4 Design thinking has thus been able to be applied to the organization of care (e.g. Roberts 2016 or Jun 2014), the training of health professionals and service users (Sandhu 2015; Van de Grift 2016), integration innovations such as therapeutic applications (Mordecai 2021) or health actions in developing countries (Bazzano 2017).

one of the subject's pioneers: Kaiser Permanente (KP)[5]. The American champion is in fact one of those with the greatest perspective on the discipline: since the start of an unprecedented partnership with the innovation agency IDEO (design agency based in California and which has become world famous), in 2003–2005, the group has integrated the discipline of design on a large scale via its application to various projects (administrative, clinical, etc.) and at all scales (from national to local) and while massively training health professionals (more than 12,000 people trained in the organization). A distinctive sign of the subject's level of recognition is that the design manager sits on the group's executive committee. Service design is considered to be an integral part of the toolbox available to the group's professionals.

At a time when interest in this new approach is beginning to reach France via the proliferation of innovation laboratories and related initiatives among healthcare providers and their administrative attachments which claim the use of these new tools, 15 years on average after the English speaking countries (Molloy 2018), it seems all the more necessary to look at the experience of the pioneers of the subject abroad, rich in lessons for those who try to open up the way in France.

The method is as follows (see the Appendix, section 7.6): field research, based on a one-year immersion in the heart of the innovation department at Kaiser Permanente (KP) headquarters, this research was based in particular on:

– qualitative individual interviews of 45 minutes with a diverse sample of 41 professionals practicing design or exposed to it, with varied profiles;

– case studies of a selection of projects at KP having been carried out using a methodology integrating design thinking;

5 As a world leader in integrated, non-profit health systems, the American group Kaiser Permanente (KP) has nearly 13 million members and operates in eight states. Based in California, KP is defined by a triple degree of integration by bringing together insurance and healthcare services, hospital and city services as well as health and medico-social services. The group employs nearly 220,000 employees and has 700 medical care practices in the city, 39 of its own hospitals as well as several dozen partner hospital structures. It has become one of the highest rated systems for quality and is considered to be one of the most innovative in the United States. The organization is particularly known for having been among the first to have deployed the computerized patient file (2004–2010) and having at a very early stage integrated the disciplines of the field of performance (lean) and innovation (service design and agile method), in a culture of evidence-based medicine and of care centered on service user needs. The group recently distinguished itself in the opening of its own medical school (the Bernard Tyson School of Medicine, opened in 2020) based on a training model prioritizing the managerial and organizational capacities of its future practitioners.

– observation and monitoring of teams to capture fundamental behaviors that work in conjunction with design tools and postures, likely to characterize a certain way of working at KP.

The transcribed data was coded via Nvivo (a software supporting qualitative data analysis), then manually (Excel) and analyzed thematically. The results were also mobilized using online visual facilitation tools (MURAL) to enable a collaborative approach and overcome the limits of analysis by a singular person.

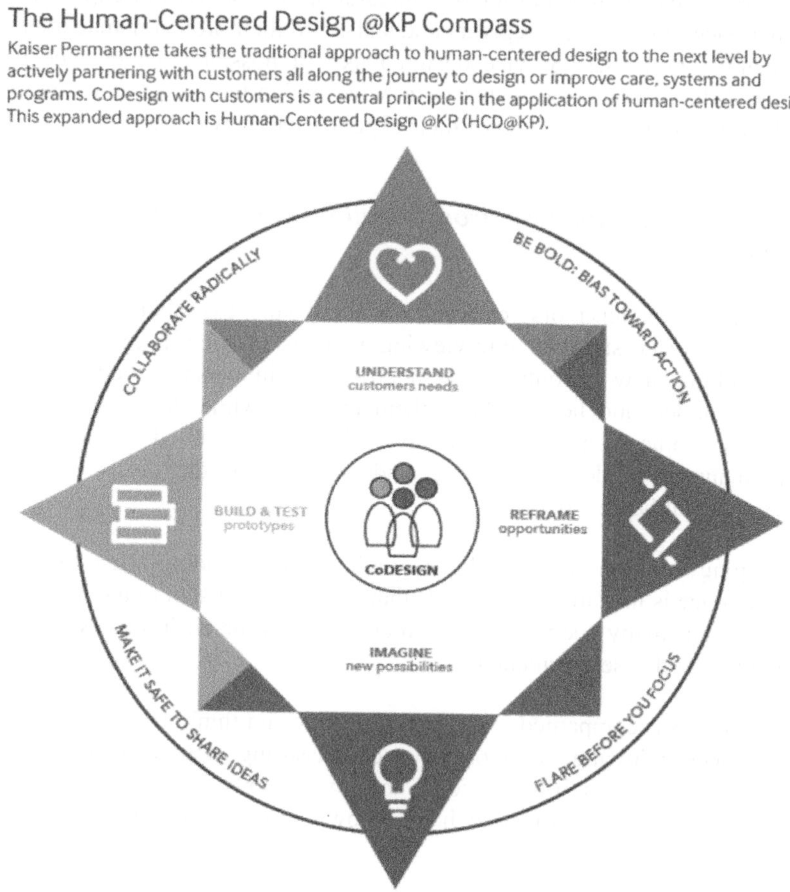

Figure 7.2. *"The compass" of co-design with users designed by Kaiser Permanente based on the postures and methods of service design (according to: Human-Centered Design @ KP Pocket Guide; NEJM Catalyst (catalyst.nejm.org)© Massachusetts Medical Society). For a color version of this figure, see www.iste.co.uk/flora/experience.zip*

7.2. A lever for rebalancing powers between users and traditional experts

In organizations falling under the bureaucratic model, solutions are classically conceived by traditional experts, drawing their authority from their level of skill or experience. In health organizations, and particularly healthcare providers, the power of expertise is mainly recognized in clinicians and administrative managers, often in decision-making positions at different levels of these organizations. Healthcare providers still have difficulty in routinely integrating new sources of expertise, such as the experience of patients, caregivers and staff, into their project management and decision-making processes. Service design makes it possible to rebalance power between the different sources of expertise at work within these organizations for the benefit of users and the recognition of their experiential knowledge.

7.2.1. *The power of empathy: from traditional experts to users in order to identify needs*

Following cancer survivors for weeks in their daily lives before defining the organization's cancer strategy, interviewing patients in their living environment before rethinking new ambulatory standards and immersing themselves with caregivers to understand how to keep them engaged while their loved ones are hospitalized are some examples of how service design has enabled different teams at Kaiser Permanente to develop a deep understanding of the needs of patients, caregivers and healthcare workers:

> Bringing the user in from the beginning, understanding what their experience is like and having tools that force you to listen to them and listen to as many people as you can and to put yourself in their shoes (Internist at Kaiser Permanente).

This posture is accompanied in the practice of design thinking by tools from the human sciences allowing a rigorous and reassuring approach: ethnographic interviews, focus groups, observations and immersions, all techniques having integrated the toolbox, on the one hand, growing with professionals, at Kaiser Permanente.

The participants in this research helped to highlight five main impacts on mobilizing user experience to acquire an in-depth understanding of their needs:

– *Direct connection with the user experience*, encompassing the full range of interactions that patients and caregivers have with their health system, from their perspective and paying attention to each point of contact.

– *Adopting a holistic approach to users*, focusing on their individual context to integrate factors such as the conditions in which people are born, grow up, live, work and age (defined as the social determinants of health).

– *Secure and directly actionable reception of user returns:*

> We were reluctant to go and talk to people directly, because we thought: what's the point of only collecting a series of complaints? No one wants to open Pandora's box. Now we have conducted so many patient interviews that everyone realizes how useful it is (Innovation manager of one of the KP medical centers (California)).

– Building an emotional engagement with users, by allowing organizational stakeholders to consider patients as human beings in their own right and not as an abstract number of service admissions:

> It was incredibly powerful. I remember sitting there with these husbands, these wives, these parents, they were crying because they had to relive all these intense moments with us (Kaiser Permanente pediatric oncologist recalling a working session with former patients to co-construct the organization's bone marrow transplant pathway).

– *Problem reformulation*: by insisting that decision-makers suspend decision-making or the choice of a solution and explore the problem in more depth, new understanding from exploratory research paves the way for redefining the problem. Thus, in so-called bureaucratic environments, service design leads to a shift from "the command", which is well known in our administrative environments, to the search for solutions to correctly identified needs.

7.2.2. The power of ideation: from managers to users in order to imagine solutions

Bringing patients and practitioners together to find new resources that could help overcome the demographic shortage of mental health workers or pairing oncologists and cancer survivors to uncover blind spots in the strategy against cancer are some examples of how KP teams have attempted to bring strategic problem solving back to the front lines of the organization.

The tools most commonly used during the ideation phases consist of facilitation and brainstorming techniques. They can be embodied in work sequences modeled in the formats of sprints or hackathons (time of intensive and collaborative work intended to generate a maximum of ideas), facilitated by professional facilitators and bringing together diversified skills to mobilize collective intelligence around the resolution of specific problems.

The data collected identifies five major impacts of using service design postures and tools in the ideation phase:

– The formation of heterogeneous teams, allowing diversified reflection around resistant problems in the organization. The "secret recipe" of these work sequences consists, according to the research participants, of bringing together users (patients, caregivers, health professionals), traditional health experts (clinicians and administrators) and also other profiles (designers, engineers, etc.) and people external to the organization in a balanced manner.

– The construction of a shared vision and will between the different stakeholders for the benefit of the generation of ideas, by focusing participants on concrete tasks and emphasizing tangibility and visualization (in particular via techniques in visual information management).

– The freeing up of a space allowing the emergence of better solutions, leaving a space for creativity and collaboration which does not exist in traditional working formats (formal bodies or committees and working groups and informal committees):

> It helps to move away from standardized solutions because one is so specialized in their field that their expertise sometimes limits their ability to think differently, to break free from what one already knows (Kaiser Permanente pediatrician).

– Mitigation of cognitive biases. Liedtka (2014) established a linked between service design and reducing cognitive bias in decision-making:

> Humans often project their own worldview onto others, limit the options considered, and ignore data that contradicts their vision. They tend to be overconfident in their predictions, regularly end the solution search process prematurely, and are overinvested in their first solutions, which harms the quality of generating and testing various hypotheses.

– The operationalization of collective decision-making processes:

> The traditional way of working leads us all to discuss a topic for an hour, only to decide on a future meeting in which we don't really make a decision either. Whereas with service design, we can do it in 30 minutes to 1 hour: here is the user experience, here are all the ideas, here are the choices, let's group them together. Look, we have a

> consensus here: more people have this idea there! We can visually see it, it is transparent for everyone. And then, we will vote … and the group agrees to co-design a concrete solution (Designer at Kaiser Permanente).

7.2.3. *The power of prototyping and testing: from the theoretical to empirical in bringing solutions to life*

Probing a new interaction between doctor and patient with a simple script, constructed and performed in front of dozens of people, all in two hours; prototyping a toolbox for patients at home including all the necessary devices in a mock-up version, in a similar time, or creating a deck of cards around teambuilding in just one hour during an end of year seminar, are some examples taken from the daily life of KP teams mobilizing service design to bring their ideas to life.

The posture associated with the prototyping phase could be summarized as follows: "Be biased towards action, always. Stop thinking, start doing".

This posture is embodied thanks to prototyping techniques. Prototypes include everything that can help a team to project itself physically and/or emotionally into a solution, without limits other than those of people's imagination. It could be Scotch tape on the floor to simulate workflow, a video to embody a new profession, a poster to imagine an event, a storyboard for a new clinical service, a paper model for a new space, a skit for a new caregiver/patient interaction, etc.

The participants in this research highlighted three impacts of using the prototyping and solution testing phases:

– Allowing projection into the solution within a shorter time period, the objective not being to achieve a high-fidelity solution, but to put the participants into action with very limited resources in terms means and time, to obtain a quick return before investing in a more sustainable solution.

– Providing a safe space to experiment and get constructive feedback:

> When our patients tell us something isn't going to work, I think about how I'm so glad I didn't spend another year trying to move things forward (Marketing manager at Kaiser Permanente).

– Enabling rapid and continuous iteration cycles, ensuring that the prototype is extensively tested and exposed to feedback, comments, suggestions, points of vigilance from users during subsequent iteration cycles, assuming from the start that many cycles will potentially be necessary until the correct prototype version is obtained.

7.3. A lever for cultural transformation in the dual bureaucratic and health context

The participants in these works described their experience of design thinking as "powerful" and "revealing". Many of them highlighted the value of design when it broadly permeates its environment, when its language, its postures and its tools infuse their host organization.

Emerging from the various interviews conducted and from the literature (Zuber 2017) is a real interest in analyzing in depth the role played by the "pioneers" of this new way of working in organizations and their power to transform uses as closely as possible to the field, far from traditional models of change management, which are more vertical and concentrated. Under different names and facets, agents of change (Battilana 2012), positive deviants or other corporate hackers (Branchet 2018) challenge the status quo in their organizations in favor of another way of working. Social movements taking place inside companies have been recognized for having enabled tangible changes in the interaction between organizations and their users. Defined as "non-bureaucratically structured groups/organizations" (e.g. Leach 2005), social movements can achieve precisely what bureaucratic organizations strive for: engaging themselves in lasting change in important cultural practices of organizations (adapted from McCarthy and Zald 1977; Weber and Soderstrom 2012). These pioneers are also actors in the integration of "meshed" design with other methodologies benefiting from more seniority among healthcare providers such as the quality method or the lean method (Kachirskaia 2018).

In response to questions relating to the redefinition of expected managerial models, the respondents to this research collectively constructed the manager/leader model profile to better support the integration of service design among care providers:

– visionary: clearly articulates what the future of healthcare should look like, fueling its vision with inspiring references and knowledge of what is happening in similar industries;

– empathetic: strongly connected to patients, caregivers and staff experience. Passionate about people and wishing to connect these different worlds;

– storyteller: capable of engaging its community with a story generating collective commitment to change;

– action-oriented: thriving by testing and experimenting to bring new ideas to the world while recognizing the risk of failure of each experiment;

– humble: inviting us to admit that they do not know and to learn from successes and failures.

Value experienced	Quote
Embedding user-centric values	"People come to work in healthcare to act towards patients, carers, caregivers, but along the way they get bogged down in processes and protocols" (Doctor at Kaiser Permanente)
	"We talk a lot amongst healthcare providers about wanting to be patient-centered, but honestly, until recently, those were just statements of intent. Service design resonates with many people because now we can say: here are some concrete tools and postures to actually take action" (Vice President of Quality at Kaiser Permanente)
Direct contact with users recognized as the right way to work	"No one asks this question anymore: why did you spend hundreds of hours immersed with patients? No one asks this question anymore" (KP vice-president in charge of design)
Distinctive work formalization modalities	"These ways of capturing our work last much longer. Everyone remembers a video, an experience map, a portrait of a caregiver. People remember a patient verbatim much more than an Excel file" (User relations manager at KP)
Promoting a culture of autonomy and creativity	"The opportunity to tap into people's passion and creativity is so exciting. I think there is unlimited potential for what we could do with it" (Organizational Development Manager at KP)
The creation of a community linked by "another way of doing things", service design at KP based on a broad socialization of the concept, the famous "snowball effect", some respondents humorously qualifying themselves as "evangelists" of this new approach	"People started calling it their side-project. I have to do my usual job, but there are other things I believe in and want to improve" (Administrative agent at Kaiser Permanente)

Table 7.1. *Values experienced in the design thinking experience*

7.4. Obstacles and facilitators to integration

Barriers	Levers
Bureaucracy, in its organization (hierarchy, strata, silos, position perimeters) **and also the ideology that accompanies it** (culture of command and permission, relationship to transparency, etc.) "For someone who doesn't come from a healthcare background, that's what struck me the most in the healthcare field. It's much more hierarchical than other organizations."	Encouraging **the logic of communities and networks** bringing together professionals with an appetite for "another way of doing things"[6], which transcends traditional divisions and allows innovators to find support. "Part of the power of design is its ability to connect people and the socialization that it brings".
Habits, "our way of doing things": "To compete with Amazon, Google, and all the other big tech companies moving into healthcare and focusing in a completely different way on the patient experience, we may have to change the way we work in order to meet people's needs."	Supporting **the audacity** of those who want to attempt to do otherwise. "What are some other solutions we haven't tried before? Let's be a little more creative and let's be a little more courageous."
Focus on solutions: "In the health sector, as soon as there is a problem people immediately think in terms of solutions. It's the nature of things." But retaining the qualification of a problem made by a leader or a manager, taking it for granted and then rushing towards making a decision on this or that solution is one of the main explanations as to why innovation approaches struggle to infiltrate healthcare providers so much.	Service design begins by trying to gain **a deeper understanding of problems in order** to redefine them in such a way that they can be resolved. It does not take more time; this only differently reallocates the time we usually spend on duplicative work or on the efforts deployed to generate the adhesion of patients/clinicians to solutions conceived in a top down manner.
Risk aversion found in both administrative and health environments due to the pervasiveness of the quality and safety culture.	Promoting the emergence of secure spaces for experimentation in healthcare environments to limit the consequences of failure.
***Evidence-based* culture** and the hierarchy of evidence.	Supporting **the progressive recognition of the value of the experience** lived by users and of experiential knowledge.
The diktat of ROI (*Return on Investment*) regardless of the evaluation of the adoption and the impact on the experience of the solutions/services financed.	**Promoting ROL** (Return on Learning) to measure the degree of "learning" of our organizations, a key determinant of innovation: what have we learned from this project? How can we avoid repeating our mistakes? How do we transmit acquired knowledge?

Table 7.2. *Obstacles and levers to the integration of design thinking in health organizations*

6 Research in management and organizational sociology highlights the major role of change agents (Battilana 2013), positive deviants (Pascale and Sternin 2010) and other corporate hackers.

7.5. Discussion

There are obviously limitations to this exploratory study. First of all, it only covers the unique experience of the Kaiser Permanente group. The choice of an exclusive research area was deliberate due to the immersive dimension sought and to the need to closely observe the practices and behaviors at work around service design over the long term, as well as to take part in the organization's projects. While the Kaiser group was precisely chosen for its precedence on this new approach and for its similarities with the administrations and providers of the French health system (bureaucratic organizational and cultural model, place of the general interest, etc.), the comparison nevertheless has its limits. Kaiser Permanente is a private (not-for-profit) provider within a privatized health system, with its headquarters in a unique innovation ecosystem: the San Francisco Bay Area. Other immersive works integrating the experience of a plurality of pioneering design care providers (e.g. the Mayo Clinic, John Hopkins or Dell Medical School in the United States, and also providers more recently positioned in relation to this subject in Europe) would deepen knowledge on the value of design in the healthcare environment and identify different integration models.

Subsequently, these projects have attempted to paint a holistic picture of the constituent elements and outcomes of design thinking and how they interact with each other. By necessity, they have sacrificed depth of analysis in specific areas of design to allow for the bigger picture. There are many opportunities for additional research that could deepen knowledge on specific topics such as the development of empathy or the variation between different methodologies employed.

Another important limitation is the difficulty of measuring the types of results presented in anything other than a qualitative form.

Another limit is that most (but not all) interview participants described themselves as practitioners convinced of the added value of service design and tended to mention initiatives considered successful within their organization. This having been said, this work also gave rise to interviews with people describing themselves as "skeptics" and projects considered as failures in order to identify the obstacles to the integration of service design. It would be useful for subsequent research efforts to include more cases of failure to assess whether the same practices leading to success can lead to failure in other contexts.

This study paints a decidedly enthusiastic picture for this new approach when properly integrated: in the context of Kaiser Permanente, many of the conditions seem to be met. The group has a recognized track record with regard to quality and innovation, and it has on a large scale integrated many of the new disciplines that have appeared in the last 20 years (notably Lean six sigma), presenting a degree of managerial maturity and change management which are favorable breeding ground for successful design experimentation. The long-term integration of design, by devoting a massive effort to training and developing the expertise of their internal community, inevitably has an impact on the results obtained. However, the current enthusiasm for innovation in general, without a precise integration strategy or specialized skills, risks leading to poorly designed and poorly implemented attempts which will have to be studied carefully.

Implementation challenges are also underdeveloped in this chapter, although other researchers have focused on them (Calgren et al. 2016), and while elements specific to Kaiser Permanente's experience could be the subject of future publications.

The study of design thinking and its effects among healthcare providers is in its infancy and opportunities for research are numerous.

7.6. Appendix: methodology

The idea for this research project emerged from my managerial experience in the French health system, marked by nearly 10 years of carrying out hospital reforms and restructuring and punctuated by more or less severe crises, as director of human resources in the field and then in central administration. Its starting point is a poorly formulated intuition, a feeling: management methods at the end of their tether resulting in particular from a certain conception of performance and within a bureaucratic organizational and cultural model very often revealing the impotence of public action to design and act based on the needs of users: whether they are patients, caregivers or health professionals. It is also the extension of several experiments to integrate design thinking in France in environments which are very unfamiliar with these approaches and of the need to find inspiration from more advanced organizations and systems on this subject.

This article is the result of qualitative research work based on a one-year immersion (from September 2019 to September 2020), as part of the Harkness Fellowship of the Commonwealth Fund with the pioneer of service design applied to health: Kaiser Permanente, an American integrated care system in the United States.

Focused on a single organization, this work is the result of the deliberate choice to join and analyze in depth the experience of one of the first two healthcare organizations in the world (along with the Mayo Clinic) to have started to integrate the field of service design in 2003 which would later be described as a pioneering exploration (Zuber 2017). This work attempted to capture Kaiser's experience, 15 years after the start of this exploration, through three distinct prisms:

– Kaiser professionals in particular via qualitative, individual, 45-minute interviews with 41 of them, based on their experience of integrating this discipline into the environment of a healthcare provider. The sample of respondents included a balanced representation of managers and non-leaders, professional designers and non-professional designers coming from different backgrounds (doctors, nurses, administrators, etc.) and working in different functions (research and development, innovation, human resources, care services) and locations of the organization (present in eight American states). The interview grids used were semi-directive and largely inspired by the principles of ethnographic interviewing (IDEO).

– Projects carried out at Kaiser in particular via case studies of a portfolio of significant projects for the organization and carried out in the application of service design methods and postures.

– Practices: observation and monitoring of the concerned teams in their daily work and their interventions to capture the fundamental postures and behaviors which work in conjunction with service design techniques and which would be characteristic of a certain way of working.

More broadly, this research is based on a year of immersion within the innovation department of Kaiser Permanente, continuous exchanges with the service design community within the organization and also in its partner networks of the Californian innovation ecosystem, participation in the life of the group and discovery of the professional paths of the many people who contributed to this research.

The interviews were recorded with the prior consent of the interviewees and transcribed by professional transcription services. Data analysis was deliberately open-ended. Interview transcripts and other data sources were reviewed for the identification of themes and patterns without a pre-established codebook. Data was coded inductively through iterative cycles of coding, first with a qualitative research software (Nvivo), then manually (Excel) as the codebook became refined. After several iterations, the themes were classified into broader categories with representative quotes collected through the interviews and illustrations identified in the case studies or observed in the field. This process was repeated until theoretical saturation was reached. The synthesis was supervised by a panel associated with the different stages of research and by my mentor during a visual facilitation exercise (MURAL).

7.7. References

Acha, V. (2006). Open by design: The role of design in open innovation. DIUS research report, 8–10.

Battilana, J. and Casciaro, T. (2012). Change agents, networks, and institutions: A contingency theory of organizational change. *Academy of Management Journal*, 55, 381–398. doi: 10.5465/amj.2009.0891.

Branchet, B., Richard, D., Bardet, F., Chabanet, D. (2018). Corporate hacking and makestorming: Toward a New Public Management able to deal with the unexpected? *34th EGOS Colloquium*, Tallinn.

Brown, T. (2008). Design thinking. *Harvard Business Review*, 86(6), 84–141.

Brown, T. (2009). *Change by Design: How Design Thinking Transforms Organizations and Inspires Innovation*. HarperCollins Publishers, New York.

Brown, T. and Wyatt, J. (2010). Design thinking and social innovation. *Stanford Social Innovation Review*, 8, 30–35. doi: 10.1596/1020-797X_12_1_29.

Buchanan, R. (1992). Wicked problems in design thinking. *Design Issues*, 8(2), 5–21.

Calgren, L., Rauth, I., Elmquist, M. (2016). Framing design thinking: The concept in idea and enactment. *Creativity and Innovation Management*, 25(1), 38–57.

Clark, K. and Smith, R. (2008). Unleashing the power of design thinking. *Design Management Review*, 19, 8–15.

Design Council (2014). Innovation by design [Online]. Available at: https://www.designcouncil.org.uk/sites/default/files/asset/document/innovation-by-design.pdf.

Dining Zuber, C. and Moody, L. (2016). Learning from the best: Unpacking the journey of organizational design thinking leaders. *20th International Design Management Research Conference*, Boston [Online]. Available at: http://www.dmi.org/?ADMC2016Overview.

Dunne, D. (2018). Implementing design thinking in organizations: An exploratory study. *Journal of Organization Design*, 7(16). doi: 10.1186/s41469-018-0040-7.

Elsbach, K.D. and Stigliani, I. (2018). Design thinking and organizational culture: A review and framework for future research. *Journal of Management*, 44(6), 2274–2306. doi: 10.1177/0149206317744252.

Forrester Research Inc. (2018). The total economic impact™ of IBM's design thinking practice [Online]. Available at: https://www.ibm.com/design/thinking/static/Enterprise-Design-Thinking-Report-8ab1e9e1622899654844a5fe1d760ed5.pdf.

Hughes, A., Moore, K., Kataria, N. (2010). Innovation in public sector organisations. NESTA [Online]. Available at: https://media.nesta.org.uk/documents/innovation_in_public_sector_orgs.pdf.

IIT Institute of Design (2020). Lead with purpose: Design's central role in realizing executive vision [Online]. Available at: https://id.iit.edu/lead-with-purpose/.

InVision (2019). The new design frontier [Online]. Available at: https://www.invisionapp.com/design-better/design-maturity-model/.

Kachirskaia, I., Mate, K.S., Neuwirth, E. (2018). Human-centered design and performance improvement: Better together. *NEJM Catalyst Innovations in Care Delivery*, 4(3) [Online]. Available at: https://catalyst.nejm.org/doi/abs/10.1056/CAT.18.0144 [Accessed 24 April 2021].

Kolko, J. (2015). Design thinking comes of age. *Harvard Business Review* [Online]. Available at: https://hbr.org/2015/09/design-thinking-comes-of-age [Accessed 3 December 2019].

Leach, D.K. (2005). The iron law of what again? Conceptualizing oligarchy across organizational forms. *Sociological Theory*, 23, 312–337.

Leavy, B. (2012). Collaborative innovation as the new imperative – design thinking, value co-creation and the power of "pull". *Strategy & Leadership*, 40, 25–34.

Liedtka, J. (2014). Perspective: Linking design thinking with innovation outcomes through cognitive bias reduction. *Journal of Product Innovation Management*, 32. doi: 10.1111/jpim.12163.

Liedtka, J. (2017). Evaluating the impact of design thinking in action. *Proceedings*, Academy of Management Annual Meeting. doi: 10.5465/AMBPP.2017.177.

Martin, R. (2009). *The Design of Business: Why Design Thinking is the Next Competitive Advantage*. Harvard Business Review Press, Brighton, MA.

McCarthy J.D. and Zald M.N. (1977). Resource mobilization and social movements. *American Journal of Sociology*, 82(6), 1212–1241.

Molloy, S. (2018). Innovation labs in healthcare – A review of design labs as a model for healthcare innovation [Online]. Available at: http://openresearch.ocadu.ca/id/eprint/2364/ [Accessed 24 April 2021].

Mordecai, D., Histon, T., Neuwirth, E., Heisler, S., Kraft, A., MSDI, Bang, Y., Franchino, K., Taillac, C., Nixon, P. (2021). How Kaiser Permanente created a mental health and wellness digital ecosystem. *New England Journal of Medicine Catalyst*. doi: 10.1056/CAT.20.0295.

Neuwirth, E.B., Bellows, J., Jackson, A.H., Price, P.M. (2012). How Kaiser Permanente uses video ethnography of patients for quality improvement, such as in shaping better care transitions. *Health Affairs*, 31(6), 1244–1250.

Service Design Network (2017). Service design impact report: Health sector [Online]. Available at: https://www.service-design-network.org/books-and-reports/service-design-impact-report-health-sector-en.

Sheppard, B., Sarrazin, H., Kouyoumjian, K., Dore, F. (2018). Business value of design. Report, McKinsey Quarterly [Online]. Available at: https://www.mckinsey.com/business-functions/mckinsey-design/our-insights/the-business-value-of-design.

Weber, K. and Soderstrom, S. (2012). Social movements, business, and the environment. In *The Oxford Handbook of Business and the Natural Environment*, Bansal, P. and Hoffman, A.J. (eds). Oxford Academic, Oxford.

Zald, M. and Berger, M. (1978). Social movements in organizations: Coup d'Etat, insurgency, and mass movements. *American Journal of Sociology*, 83(4), 823–861 [Online]. Available at: http://www.jstor.org/stable/2777718 [Accessed 24 April 2021].

Zuber, C.D. and Moody, L. (2016). Learning from the best: Unpacking the journey of organizational design thinking leaders. In *20th International Design Management Research Conference*, Boston, 28–29 July.

Zuber, C.D., Alterescu, V., Chow, M.P. (2009). Fail often to succeed sooner: Adventures in innovation. *Permanente Journal*, 9(4), 44–49.

8

Patient-Centered Care at Public Hospitals: A War of the Worlds?

8.1. Introduction

Patient-centered care (PCC) was developed under pressure from public authorities, keen to preserve health systems whose financial balance is weakened by the aging of the population and the increase in chronic diseases (Royal College of General Practitioners 2014). This approach also corresponds to the expectations of individuals, who intend to become actors in health and now have access to information and personalized services thanks to the rise of digital technology (Grewal et al. 1994; Crié and Chebat 2013; Agarwal et al. 2020).

France is no exception to this trend. Thus, the French President Emmanuel Macron, in his presentation on the healthcare system transformation strategy in 2018, called for "*putting the patient at the center and guaranteeing all French people better prevention and access to quality healthcare*". However, PCC constitutes a challenge for French public hospitals, whose budgets are constrained. How can health gains be maximized with limited resources and increased quality demands, while placing the patient at the center of care?

Faced with what at first glance appears to them as a "contradictory injunction" (Watzlawick et al. 1972, p. 218), healthcare workers hesitate or even oppose it. In such a context, what could be more normal than experiencing the establishment of the PCC as a source of tension. The surprising fact, which is the starting point for

---

Chapter written by Marie-Eve LAPORTE, Patrick GILBERT and Karim ZINAÏ.

qualitative research (Dumez 2016), lies elsewhere: while in many cases people resist it, they nevertheless generally end up accommodating this orientation. This is, in any case, the observation that we made in the orthopedics department of a large Parisian hospital. Despite the tensions, those involved in healthcare services are able to adjust. Based on the theoretical framework of economies of worth (Boltanski and Thévenot 1991; Boltanski and Chiapello 1999), particularly adapted to the hospital context according to Denis et al. (2007), the objective of this research is to clarify this mystery. More precisely, it aims to explore the tensions that are expressed and to identify the methods that lead the actors of a public hospital to find compromises.

8.2. Patient-centered care

8.2.1. *Definition of patient-centered care*

The United States National Academy of Medicine (Institute of Medicine 2001, p. 6) defines PCC as "providing care that is respectful of and responsive to individual patient preferences, needs, and values and ensuring that patient values guide all clinical decisions". In the United Kingdom, the Royal College of General Practitioners (2014, p. 4) refers to "care that is holistic, empowering [patient empowerment], and that tailors support according to the individual's priorities and needs". The PCC approach therefore assumes that patients are stakeholders in their health and have a say in the decision (Levinson et al. 2010).

There are numerous works on PCC in the academic literature, particularly in nursing. Thus, articles have reviewed the state of the art of what constitutes PCC (Robinson et al. 2008; Hobbs 2009; Morgan and Yoder 2011; Lusk and Fater 2013; Rathert et al. 2013; Constand et al. 2014).

8.2.2. *An international enthusiasm for patient-centered care*

Renowned hospital institutions are promoting their patient-centered approach around the world, as the examples presented in Box 8.1 show.

> The Mayo Clinic in the United States is considered a pioneer of PCC in the world. Its co-founder, Doctor William Mayo, affirmed in 1910 that the best interest of the patient is the only interest to take into account, and that joining forces is necessary to enable patients to benefit from advances in knowledge. The model of care is based on a central principle that the needs of the patient come first. Patient experience management occupies a recognized position. The values are expressed in an acronym known to all staff, rich ties, meaning respect, integrity, compassion, healing, teamwork, innovation, excellence and stewardship. These values are engraved in the stone of Heritage Hall, the museum

within the clinic, and developed on its website and in a 117-page book, *The Little Book of Mayo Clinic Value*[1].

In one of the most renowned hospitals in Latin America, the Albert Einstein Hospital in São Paulo, Brazil, everything is done to demedicalize the environment and provide a pleasant living environment for patients, their families and staff. The hospital contains a mini-market, restaurants and numerous shops (clothing, sports, home decoration, hairdressing and a beauty institute, etc.). A grand piano is available to everyone. The numerous indoor and outdoor relaxation spaces are carefully designed, decorated with trees (even indoors), pools, fountains and works of art. The goal is to offer patients and their families a safe and comforting experience, based on their individual preferences and needs, not just their pathologies. Interestingly, PCC includes families, as evidenced by the name of the Patient and Family Experience Service (*Experiência do paciente e familia*)[2].

In a much smaller country at the crossroads of African and Asian influences, one of the main private health players in Mauritius, C-Care, has a mission to provide medical services and attentive care that everyone can be proud of and who systematically put the patient first. The president of the group is committed to a holistic approach and a patient-centered culture, in order to continue to innovate and best meet the needs of patients. In this country lacking medical infrastructure, the objective is also to empower patients, by providing them with knowledge allowing them to become actors in their care in complete safety and under the control of caregivers[3].

Box 8.1. *PCC around the world*

8.2.3. *A counter-nature approach for the French public hospital*

In France, the implementation of PCC is not without raising questions, particularly in public hospitals. Some see it as an application of customer centricity from the commercial world. Thus, according to David (2006, p. 6), the customer would be a detour to face the challenges of public service transformation: "The use

1 Sources: "Strong Organizational Culture in a Crisis: Mayo Clinic's Values Driven Response to the Covid-19 Global Pandemic", communication by Melody White at the ARAMOS 2021 study day on her MBA thesis completed at IAE Paris-Sorbonne under the direction of M-E Laporte: www.mayoclinic.org.

2 Sources: ongoing research by one of the authors, observations and interviews carried out on site in April 2022.

3 Sources: MBA dissertation by Philippe Journade, IAE Paris-Sorbonne and University of Paris Dauphine, under the supervision of M-E. Laporte: c-care.com/mu/.

of the concept of 'customer' is a historically dated means of provoking changes in the way public service organizations operate".

The approach also encounters limits. As Gummesson (2008, p. 316) notes, "the border between customer and citizen is fuzzy. Since customer centricity reached the public sector in the 1980s it is claimed that patients are customers, students and parents are customers of the school, and so on". For this author, the extension of the concept to the public sphere poses difficulties:

> "As a citizen, you have needs that are partly different and more fundamental than those that can be satisfied by commercial means. Citizens have obligations and rights, they pay for social service mainly through taxes and do so according to their abilities and not their individual needs. When we talk about competition and the fact that we live in a society of abundance, the most basic services such as humane care for the elderly, an efficient emergency service, legal security, good schools and good housing is left behind. This should not prevent a doctor from being partially client-centered, for example when communicating with patients". (Gummesson 2008, p. 316).

The public hospital as an area of application of customer centricity is therefore by no means self-evident, because the stakeholders are not on the same line. In practice, points of view clash but nevertheless often manage to agree with one another.

Economies of worth offer a relevant theoretical framework for understanding this phenomenon in the pluralistic organizational context of the hospital, that is, "characterized by [...] multiple objectives, diffuse power and knowledge-based work processes" (Denis et al. 2007, pp. 179–180).

8.3. The theory of economies of worth – a key for understanding tensions

The theory of economies of worth refers to seven "higher principles" corresponding to what actors consider legitimate and which fuel their expectations of others. This results in worlds colliding. Boltanski and Thévenot (1991) identified six worlds (the inspired world, the domestic world, the world of fame, the civic world, the market world and the industrial world), to which Boltanski and Chiapello (1999) added a seventh world, that of projects (Table 8.1).

World	State of worth	"Great being"
Inspired	The one who creates, escapes the certainties of technology as well as the reason of common sense and habits and primes singularity.	The artist
Domestic	The one who respects history, customs and contributes to the establishment and maintenance of hierarchies.	The leader
Fame	The one who is recognized, renowned: "Fame makes greatness".	The star
Civic	The one who represents the collective, who subordinates their particular and immediate interests to the general will.	The elected entity
Market	The one who, driven by desire (their own and that of others), faces competition, seizes opportunities, to increase their possessions.	The seller
Industrial	Someone who, qualified and competent, pursues a quest for performance and masters their own environment in which they are effective.	The expert
Projects	The one who commits and trains by relying on a network that they know how to mobilize.	The project manager

Table 8.1. *The seven worlds of economies of worth (inspired by Boltanski and Thévenot (1991); Boltanski and Chiapello (1999); cited in Gilbert and Laporte (2023))*

This can lead to a real "war of the worlds" when people refer to distinct worlds and settle on positions that may seem irreconcilable. However, the public hospital provides a rich example of cohabitation between seemingly rival worlds.

8.4. Study of the orthopedics department of a Parisian hospital[4]

We studied PCC-labeled orthopedics department of a Parisian hospital, by combining participant and nonparticipant observation during three weeks of immersion in the department, individual and collective interviews with around 50 people (medical, paramedical and administrative staff at all hierarchical levels and patients) and the analysis of documents obtained in the department (around 300 pages of leaflets for the patient, internal procedures, etc.). The use of the theory

4 The study of this service gave rise to three articles (Gilbert and Laporte 2022, 2023; Gilbert et al. 2022) and communications at conferences (in particular, Gilbert and Laporte 2021). This chapter draws on this work.

of worth as a reading grid made it possible to bring the war of the worlds around PCC and conflict resolution mechanisms to light.

8.4.1. *War of the worlds*

The public hospital offers a context conducive to the confrontation of different worlds. For a long time, the medical profession was able to claim a preponderant place for itself in the system of power of the public hospital to the detriment of management. Gradually, the balance of power was reversed, which the head of the orthopedics department deplores:

> When I was an intern, the department heads had enormous power and the administration did not bother them. Now, we are under the thumb of the administration and they sometimes make completely stupid decisions. And we follow, unfortunately.

Simultaneously, a socially stratified order, highly divided, vertically organizes status groups (doctors, nurses, nursing assistants, etc.) and horizontally arranges professions (pharmacist, anesthesiologist, surgeon, etc.) based on their prestige. These orders themselves are part of different entities (weekly hospital, geriatric postoperative unit, multidisciplinary outpatient surgery unit) with a specific mode of organization and social culture.

This leads to different representations of the role of the patient and the behavior to adopt towards them. As noted by other authors, the domestic and industrial worlds (Grenier and Oiry 2021) and the civic world (Orvain and Angelé-Halgand 2011) are prominent in the service studied. Thus, the domestic world advocates kindness towards the patient, provided that they respect their "rights but also their duties", as expressed primarily by paramedical staff and anesthetists. The industrial world, notably represented by surgeons, celebrates the performance of the technical gesture and its effectiveness in "putting the patient back on their feet, literally and figuratively" (medical intern), and also the economic efficiency for management. The civic world is very often mobilized, in the constant reminder of the values of the public hospital "which treats everyone the same way, regardless of their income, even homeless people" (the secretary). The other worlds are also present, but to a lesser extent. The inspired world is heard when patients and caregivers rave about the beauty and inventiveness of certain gestures performed by surgeons, who are seen as true artists. The market world expresses itself in opposition to the supposed values of private clinics. The world of fame is reflected in the mention of the international reputation of certain surgeons in the service, to which caregivers and patients refer with respect. Finally, the world of projects is at work behind the implementation of innovations, such as enhanced recovery after surgery (ERAS), which allows patients to significantly reduce the length of stays, or even to be operated on, as an outpatient, with a hip or knee prosthesis.

All seven worlds are therefore present in the service, which generates misunderstandings about the place the patient should be given.

8.4.2. *Responses segmented by patient profile*

As we were able to observe and as the staff unanimously noted, two types of populations immediately stand out among the patients: on the one hand, autonomous patients, rather young and very connected, and on the other hand, fragile people, often elderly, who do not have access to online information. As one anethesist notes, "these people, often elderly, were satisfied with a speech made by a person carrying hierarchical and moral authority. Conversely, young, informed patients have more access to contradictory discourse. They ask a lot more questions. They indisputably benefit [from patient empowerment], on the psychological level and in adherence to the therapeutic project".

In response, the service is trying to adapt its discourse and practices by experimenting with new care spaces. Let us study two recently created care units that embody this dichotomy more precisely: on the one hand, the outpatient surgery unit (UCA, in French) common to several departments including that of orthopedics, and on the other hand, the geriatric postoperative unit (Upog, in French) within the orthopedics department.

8.4.2.1. *The outpatient surgery unit: agility serving emancipated patients*

This recent unit, located on an annexed site, accommodates several disciplines including orthopedics, in operating rooms dedicated to specialties, but which can be reallocated according to needs. On the patient side, everything is done in order to forget the hospital setting. The waiting room is like a living room, with soft tones, light wood, softened lights and relaxing music. As most operations are scheduled, patients are reassured in advance by nurses who contact them by SMS two days before the operation and then the next day to check that they are well. The UCA also accommodates delayed (non-vital) emergencies, which require both agility and coordination with other services. Thus, after each "emergency staff meeting" (daily meeting at 7:30 a.m.), the orthopedics department sends out a table with the list of patients who arrived during the night and the medical decision taken with regard to them. Patients who are candidates for outpatient surgery (autonomous patients with limited fractures) are in green and the UCA adapts its operating program accordingly.

UCA, through its agile and collaborative mode, falls into the world of projects. For the health executive behind its creation, this requires a network, because "without a network, we cannot do anything". This person encourages everyone to collaborate: "The staff is in the post-intervention care room, within day hospitalizations and at reception. [...] They distribute themselves as they see fit, they make their own schedule. [...] I don't intervene unless it doesn't make sense." Everyone is consulted, particularly during monthly meetings. Thus, it is caregivers who chose operating timetables since they place the patients on them. Meeting reports, activity figures, congratulatory messages from doctors or patients are posted in the corridor for staff, in a desire for transparency and involvement.

For surgeons, the UCA is an ideal response to the expectations of busy patients, and effective for the hospital, within the logic of the industrial world to which they tend to belong. "It's the perfect organizational model [...] a beautiful tool that works well" (the department head). "The patients love it, because they're not really hospitalized. [...] And what's more, it's quite efficient in terms of patient flow. It makes it easy to operate on five, six, seven patients in a room, over a day" (a surgeon). However, we only discovered the existence of the UCA late. Many non-medical personnel in the orthopedic department are unaware of its existence, and when they have heard of it, they often do not know how to locate it. It must be said that the UCA aroused jealousy and rivalries during its creation. The person who initiated it remains very cautious, first refusing to answer our question to find out how the UCA is perceived in the hospital, then minimizing its particularities and successes, because as the head of the orthopedics department explained, "at the beginning, no one gave her justice and she had a hard time". Indeed, the UCA embodied a logic of productivity, rupturing, for some, from the mission of the public hospital, in leaving those most fragile aside. This is illustrated by the words of this caregiver, anchored in the civic and domestic world:

> Outpatient units may be important, but for me they are not beds, it's not the same. [...] I wonder about the future of the public hospital, about patient care, about the psychological and physical aspect. [...] As we are in a society that promotes youthfulness, we tend to get rid of everything that is old.

Aware of these reluctances, the UCA focuses on patients from the first population segment identified, that is, the "autonomous, rather young and very connected patients" mentioned above. The creation of this distinct unit, both by its principle and by its location, institutionalizes a compromise around the well-being of the emancipated patient, in response to the war of the worlds (Boltanski and Thévenot 1991). But this resolution remains fragile, because the UCA retains opponents, which explains internal discretion, at odds with the world of fame.

8.4.2.2. *The geriatric postoperative unit: a conciliation between several worlds for the most fragile elderly patients*

Upog is aimed at the opposite segment to that of the UCA, that of people with low autonomy over the age of 75 suffering from multiple pathologies, and therefore requiring a holistic approach. As the geriatrician in charge of the Upog explains, "geriatrics has no organ specialty; our organ is the whole human body". It was the head of department who took the initiative for the creation of the Upog: "I knew it existed elsewhere. I saw that elderly patients were not being treated well. We don't know how to treat them, we're not doctors, we're surgeons!". Faced with reluctance ("I was told: 'Very complicated, it is really expensive'"), he justified the investment through clinical research with geriatricians, which demonstrated the faster recovery of patients and ultimately, a shortened average length of stay: "We show that patients are doing much better. This brings more money to the hospital. There, in terms of coding [of procedures], it makes stays much more expensive and the hospital earns more money." (head of the service)

The Upog also includes psychological, social and emotional components. We were able to verify this at length during the observation phases. For example, a patient living alone, visibly happy in the ward, tried by all means to convince the nurse to keep him in the ward:

> I don't see the progress … – But yes, look, you managed to go to the toilet in a walker, that's really very good! You will be very comfortable in the rehabilitation center. – But I don't have enough clothes to go there, I arrived with almost nothing after my accident. – Don't worry, we will ask the chaplaincy or social assistance to help you out, tell us what clothes you need. – Clearly, you have the answer to everything! [After a short reflection] Or, I could act like a dying person, drool a little [he does so] and then you would keep me! [Patient bursts out laughing] Do you know what my job was? A comedian!.

The Upog cannot keep patients for too long, but as soon as they arrive in the department, it organizes reception in a follow-up and rehabilitation center. It also involves family caregivers. So, in the department, a room was designed for them. In this comfortable, carefully decorated living room, the patient can spend time with their loved ones "like at home" (a nurse). At the same time, the Upog monitors its indicators to demonstrate the effectiveness of such an approach. It was able to highlight a drop in the average length of stay for this type of patient, from 13 days when they were hospitalized in the service, to 9 days at the Upog. In this, it reconciles the logics of the industrial (good medical performance), market (competitive economic results), domestic (respect for elders) and civic (taking into account the fragility of patients) worlds. Here too, it institutionalizes a compromise around the well-being of the elderly patient.

8.4.3. *The debrief room, a place for conciliation and the establishment of arrangements*

We were able to observe another conciliation strategy, that of arrangements (Boltanski and Thévenot 1991). Alongside the UCA and the Upog, which respond to the war of the worlds through the specialization of spaces and the targeting of patients, institutionalizing compromises in the sense given in Boltanski and Thévenot (1991), the debrief room allows for the in situ manifestation of worlds and arrangements. This room houses "the staffs", medical meetings wherein patient files are studied collectively. Some "staffs" take place daily and review nighttime emergencies early in the morning. Others are organized by theme (e.g. tumors) and are taken place weekly. The "staffs" mainly welcomes surgeons, anesthetists and students (medical interns and externs). The head of department emphasizes the importance of these moments for team communication and the quality of care: "We talk. For teaching, it is essential; even for relationships; and to properly care for patients". The team comments on patient files while medical images are projected. It discusses options, taking medical constraints into account and collectively making the decision. This is reported on a large whiteboard where the notes are taken in full view of everyone, and then recorded on a computer file which is then distributed. It is a moment of reflexivity, of "companionship" for the interns, and of exchanges of good practices between experienced surgeons: "Which way would you go? – I would go ventral or lateral. Definitely not through the posterior route."

Alongside these medical discussions, the logistical constraints linked to the occupancy of beds give rise to arbitrations. A person plays a key role here to allocate beds and reduce average lengths of stay. This is a patient pathway manager whose status as a caregiver poses no problem. They sit in the front row alongside the most "senior" people, they speak to the doctors in a familiar manner and they all speak back with respect. Using their colorful T-cards, they reallocate beds during shifts, finding real-time solutions to logistical problems. As a healthcare executive notes, none of the software tested to date has matched their management of complexity. In addition, the patient pathway manager constitutes an informal relay between the medical staff and the paramedical teams when they circulate to place their cardboard T-cards in the planning boards located in each care unit.

The debrief room thus appears as a place of conciliation, where everyone makes their point of view heard, and where arrangements are established between the worlds to which the protagonists claim to belong.

8.5. Conclusion

Our research identifies the presence of the seven worlds of economies of worth in hospitals. It shows the importance of the domestic and civic worlds in the field of health, and the various conventions to which the different actors subscribe. Beyond the classic aversion of public hospitals to the market world, there is a multiplicity of conventions, varying depending on the situation, which fuel the war of the worlds observed in hospitals.

Our research also highlights different strategies for reconciling worlds, through compromises or arrangements. While PCC does not immediately reach a consensus as such, it is undeniable that the patient is at the center of care situations within it, for all actors regardless of convention references. Thus, taking into account the different expectations of patients, depending on whether they are in a process of emancipation or on the contrary in a situation of fragility requiring support, builds different social relationships. It pacifies criticism by reflecting on the organizational framework, delimiting adapted permanent times and places which institutionalize compromises (the UCA, the Upog) or periodic ones leading to arrangements (debrief room).

Our research also highlights the opportunity to adopt a project approach to avoid direct confrontation between worlds. By carrying out experiments alongside traditional organization, it makes it possible to test and learn, without questioning the fundamentals (at least in the short term), and through associating people whose higher principles are compatible, before a possible wider deployment, or a renunciation if the results are not conclusive. This research therefore proposes solutions to implement PCC in public hospitals in an appeased manner.

8.6. References

Agarwal, R., Dugas, M., Gao, G., Kannan, P.K. (2020). Emerging technologies and analytics for a new era of value-centered marketing in healthcare. *Journal of the Academy of Marketing Science*, 48(1), 9–23.

Boltanski, L. and Chiapello, E. (1999). *Le nouvel esprit du capitalisme*. Gallimard, Paris.

Boltanski, L. and Thévenot, L. (1991). *De la justification : les économies de la grandeur*. Gallimard, Paris.

Constand, M.K., MacDermid, J.C., Dal Bello-Haas, V., Law, M. (2014). Scoping review of patient-centered care approaches in healthcare. *BMC Health Services Research*, 14(1), 271.

Crié, D. and Chebat, J.-C. (2013). Health marketing: Toward an integrative perspective. *Journal of Business Research*, 66(1), 123–126.

David, A. (2006). Quelques enjeux contemporains de la relation de service public. *Politiques et Management Public*, 24(3), 5–12.

Denis, J.-L., Langley, A., Rouleau, L. (2007). Strategizing in pluralistic contexts: Rethinking theoretical frames. *Human Relations*, 60(1), 179–215.

Dumez, H. (2016). *Méthodologie de la recherche qualitative*, 2nd edition. Vuibert, Paris.

Gilbert, P. and Laporte, M.-E. (2021). Patient centricity, a "war of the worlds"? *9e colloque santé*, Marseille.

Gilbert, P. and Laporte, M.-E. (2022). War and peace in hospitals: Humans, objects and paradoxes. *Journal of Business Research*, 141, 253–263.

Gilbert, P. and Laporte, M.-E. (2023). L'orientation patient à l'hôpital public : un dispositif marketing comme compromis entre mondes. *Recherche et applications en marketing*, 38(1), 40–60.

Gilbert, P., Laporte, M.-E., Raulet-Croset, N. (2022). Le "dispositif de gestion" : un cadre méthodologique pour l'analyse psychosociale du "Patient-centered care" dans un hôpital parisien. *Psychologie du travail et des organisations*, 28(4), 281–292.

Grenier, C. and Denis, J.L. (2017). S'organiser pour innover : espaces d'innovation et transformation des organisations et du champ de l'intervention publique. *Revue Politiques et Management Public*, 34(3/4), 191–206.

Grenier, C. and Oiry, E. (2021). *Altering Frontiers: Organizational Innovations in Healthcare*. ISTE Ltd, London, and John Wiley and Sons, New York.

Grewal, D., Gotlieb, J., Marmorstein, H. (1994). The moderating effects of message framing and source credibility on the price-perceived risk relationship. *Journal of Consumer Research*, 21(1), 145–153.

Gummesson, E. (2008). Customer centricity: Reality or a wild goose chase? *European Business Review*, 20(4), 315–330.

Hobbs, J.L. (2009). A dimensional analysis of patient-centered care. *Nursing Research*, 58(1), 52–62.

Institute of Medicine (2001). *Crossing the Quality Chasm: A New Health System for the 21st Century*. National Academies Press, Washington.

Levinson, W., Lesser, C.S., Epstein, R.M. (2010). Developing physician communication skills for patient-centered care. *Health Affairs*, 29(7), 1310–1318.

Lusk, J.M. and Fater, K. (2013). A concept analysis of patient-centered care. *Nursing Forum*, 48(2), 89–98.

Morgan, S. and Yoder, L. (2011). A concept analysis of person-centered care. *Journal of Holistic Nursing: Official Journal of the American Holistic Nurses' Association*, 30, 6–15.

Orvain, J. and Angelé-Halgand, N. (2011). Les manufactures de santé : l'art du compromis entre domesticité et industrie. *Sciences sociales et santé*, 29(1), 5–27.

Rathert, C., Wyrwich, M.D., Boren, S.A. (2013). Patient-centered care and outcomes: A systematic review of the literature. *Medical Care Research and Review*, 70(4), 351–379.

Robinson, J.H., Callister, L.C., Berry, J.A., Dearing, K.A. (2008). Patient-centered care and adherence: Definitions and applications to improve outcomes. *Journal of the American Academy of Nurse Practitioners*, 20(12), 600–607.

Royal College of General Practitioners (2014). Inquiry into Patient Centred Care in the 21st Century: Implications for general practice and primary care. Report of an independent inquiry commissioned by the Royal College of General Practitioners.

Watzlawick, P., Beavin, J.H., Jackson, D.D., Morche, J. (1972). *Une logique de la communication*. Le Seuil, Paris.

9

A Brief History of Changes in the Medico-Social Sector over Recent Decades. Interview with Marielle Ravot

9.1. Introduction

Marielle Ravot has 20 years of experience in the management and evaluation of social and medico-social establishments. Whether it concerns accommodation establishments for elderly people (*établissements d'hébergement pour personnes âgées dépendantes*[1,2]: EHPAD2 (accommodation establishments for elderly people, in English) or other structures in the field of solidarity (disability and social action), she has been a participating observer, and at times a pioneer, of the changes in this area.

Beyond this long experience, she wanted to provide herself with the means to put things into perspective in recent years. She thus studied as part of a Master's degree in public health – a course in prevention, health education, therapeutic education – at Aix-Marseille University (AMU) and has two university diplomas: "Training in patient–family caregiver partnerships" at the Faculty of Medicine of the University of Montpellier and "The art of care in partnership with the patient" offered by the

---

Chapter written by Luigi FLORA and Marielle RAVOT following an interview conducted by the co-author.

1 An accommodation establishment for dependent elderly people (EHPAD) has been the new name for nursing homes since Law no. 2002-2 of January 2, 2002. This law substantially modifies the previous Law no. 75-535 related to social and medico-social institutions that came into force on June 30, 1975.

2 The acronyms used in this chapter are explained when they are first used in the text, then indicated by an asterisk (*). They all appear in the appendix at the end of the chapter, section 9.4.

Faculty of Medicine of the University of Côte d'Azur (UCA). This was a final training course during which she allowed herself to live and accept living with her illness as part of her identity, a form of existential transformation.

It is therefore with this dual professional perspective of management and auditing of medico-social organizations, put into perspective through the prism of the public health and patient partner dimension, that she delivers, during an interview, her point of view on the dynamics of transformation and innovation in this field which aims to protect health – in the global sense given to it by the World Health Organization (WHO)[3] – elderly people and/or people with disabilities and then, dependency.

9.2. Interview

Interviewer (I): Thank you for sharing your experiences and your analysis of the field with us. Could you first introduce yourself?

Marielle Ravot (M.R.): I arrived in this field a bit by chance. While I was working in the IT world, which I realized did not suit me, I invested in training, in the midst of hospitalization reform, and at the time when contractualization processes and accreditation of health establishments were being organized[4].

This reorientation interested me on two counts: because of the implementation of a quality approach (which I had already experienced in the IT sector, in the form of an ISO 900x certification), and for the concerned sector that had always attracted me, that of health. As a teenager, I dreamt of being a doctor.

I therefore enrolled in a Master's degree course, entitled "Master of Arts in management of establishments in the health and medico-social sector" (class of 1998), in which the qualitative dimensions particularly motivated me. Training carried out in a business school of which Kedge is the successor[5], the École Supérieure de Commerce Marseille-Provence, located on the Luminy campus, thus named before becoming Euromed Management and then Kedge Business School. My goal was then to move into the health sector, into a quality manager role.

3 Definition of health by the World Health Organization in the preamble to its constitution: https://www.who.int/about/accountability/governance/constitution.

4 This reform was initiated by the promulgation of the orders from April 1996. For more information, see: https://www.legifrance.gouv.fr/loda/id/LEGITEXT000005620817/ and https://www.cairn.info/revue-gerontologie-et-societe1-1997-1-page-17.htm?contenu=resume.

5 Read about the history of the Kedge business and management school at: https://kedge.edu/l-ecole/groupe/l-histoire-de-kedge.

Having obtained my Master's degree, I started working in the health sector, at the time when the first *contrats d'objectifs et de moyens* (COMs)[6] were appearing. As I had trained to develop this type of contract, I was contacted by directors of private clinics who did not, at the time, have all the means to carry out this reform within their establishments. I therefore began by co-designing COMs*, before considering getting involved in the preparation for the accreditation[7] of these establishments.

9.3. The experience

It was therefore in health establishments and not medico-social establishments, and more specifically medium-stay establishments – in this case *soins de suite et de réadaptation*[8] (SSR) – that I was initially mobilized. At that time, I did not at all envisage a progression towards the medico-social sector.

It turns out that the establishment of the last director that I accompanied in the development of his COM* was "targeted" by the *Agence régionale de l'hospitalisation* (ARH)[9]. He was the subject of a review procedure of classification of its different disciplines[10] in the sense of a downgrading, notified to the manager at

6 Objectives and means contracts, in English. The hospitalization reform (1996 orders) notably established the obligation, for all health establishments, to conclude a multi-year contract of objectives and means (COM) with their regional hospitalization connection agency. For more information on the COM, see: https://www.presses.ehesp.fr/produit/le-contrat-dobjectifs-et-de-moyens/.

7 "Introduced within the French health system by order no. 96-346 of April 24th 1996 on hospital reform and specified by Decree no. 97-311 of April 7, 1997, the accreditation procedure aims to ensure that health establishments develop a process of continuous improvement in the quality and safety of care delivered to patients" (Matillon 2001).

8 Follow-up care and rehabilitation, in English.

9 Regional Hospitalization Agency, in English. ARH is the former public administrative body responsible, in France, for regional management of the health system. Since Law no. 2009-879 of July 21, 2009, the ARHs gave way to Agences régionales de santé (ARS), from April 2010, by a merger of different organizations (ARH*, DRASS* and DDASS*, and URCAM*).

10 At that time, the classification procedure concerned private hospital establishments and services. It is specified in the decree of December 15th, 1977 setting the criteria and procedures for classification applicable to private establishments mentioned in article L275 of the code de sécurité sociale (social security code) and provided for by article 2 of Decree no. 73-183 of February 22, 1973. Depending on the number of points obtained on each of the criteria of the classification grid (premises, hotel installations and equipment, technical installations and equipment, personnel, medical operation, etc.), the establishment is classified in a category (A to E, the letter A representing the "best grade") on which its financing then depends.

the time of negotiation of its COM*. I therefore had to successively and almost simultaneously constitute several files: a request for the review of classification of an establishment; a request for the transformation of this establishment into a long-stay unit (*unité de soins de longue durée*[11] or USLD) dedicated to the elderly (a specificity at the time) and for relocation with a view to the reconstruction of a dilapidated structure and, finally, a COM* (initial file, progress reports then request for renewal). At that time, I was by no means an expert in the field and I learned through practice, with the support of competent authorities. This short period (two to three years) certainly constituted an extraordinary opportunity to position myself in this environment, which was new to me and rich in encounters and lessons, and which contributed, without me fully realizing it, to the evolution of my professional career.

Indeed, even before its realization, the USLD* project was transformed into an EHPAD* project, at the joint request of the administrative authorities (ARH* and the *Conseil général*[12]). This is how I discovered the medico-social sector through the development of one of the very first tripartite multi-annual agreements that appeared as part of the reform of EHPAD* pricing (1997) and experienced the first version of the famous TarifEHPAD software package[13], allowing the development of the structure's five-year forecasted budget. This work was carried out in collaboration with those responsible for the DDASS*[14] and especially the Conseil général.

It seems as though I can say that I was incredibly lucky to have entered this sector "at the right time", when it was undergoing profound change and important reforms, and this was very formative for me.

From this experience, things accelerated: I was first hired to develop the application for the creation of a new EPHAD* by a private sector professional, with a for-profit aim, and in a municipality with a structural deficit. I was then offered the management position of an EHPAD*. I thus, for four years, managed this establishment relatively autonomously and ceased to practice at the time when the EHPAD* sector began to experience strong concentration leading to the structuring

11 Long-term care unit, in English.

12 General Council, in English. The Conseil Général is today called Conseil Départmental (Departmental Council, in English) (Law no. 2013-403 of May 17th, 2013).

13 TarifEHPAD is the software to help calculate prices and present the budget for EHPAD. In 2022, version 6 came into force.

14 The DDASS was replaced by the territorial (or departmental) delegation (or unit) of the ARS*. It is important to note that the hôpital, patients, santé, territoires (hospitals, patients, health, territories) law of July 21st, 2009 known as "HPST" has considerably reshaped the organization of healthcare in France by grouping in particular the health and medico-social sectors under the single authority of the ARS*.

of the sector as we know it today (with the predominance of few "mega-groups"). The establishment that I managed was in fact sold to one of the largest private groups. The impact on the missions devolved to the director of the establishment being of high importance, and given what I had experienced, the position very quickly became too "formatted" for me. I therefore decided to change course and applied for a position as manager of a sector including several EHPAD*, in order to regain this ability to act upstream on the organization, a position which I held until 2009.

(I): Can you illustrate to us some of the transformations that you have witnessed during this decade?

(MR): I must first specify that in 2009, I definitively exchanged my status as an employee with that of a business manager and I have since worked as an independent consultant. In this capacity, I mainly carried out external evaluations and transition management missions[15] within *établissements et services sociaux et médico-sociaux* (ESSMS)[16]. I will go come to it eventually. My vision of the sector, as an operational person in the field (director then sector manager of EHPAD*), therefore dates back to a more than a decade ago.

This vision nevertheless remains generally consistent with current reality, which I have continued to understand within the framework of my transition management missions.

Initially, I was very motivated by the encouraging prospects of the reform of the EHPAD* sector: the medicalization of establishments, the redesign of financing and the establishment of contractualization initiated with tripartite conventions, the implementation of the tools of Law no. 2002-2[17] and the deployment of an evaluation approach. This reform aimed in particular at the better supervision of the activity, the provision of additional human and financial resources and the professionalization of teams accompanied by a rate of supervision more favorable to quality reception and care, which is also evaluated.

15 La Fédération des acteurs du management de transition (the Federation of Interim Management Actors, in English) defines transition management as "the use by an organization (private, public, charity) of external operational managerial skills with the aim of accomplishing a specific mission over a limited period of time. Thus, a transition management mission always has a precise objective, and by definition a beginning and an end": https://www.francetransition.org/.

16 Social and medico-social establishments and services, in English.

17 The seven tools of Law no. 2002-2 of January 2nd, 2002 are the establishment (or service) project, the residence contract or DIPC*, the operating regulations, the welcome booklet, the CVS*, the qualified person and the charter of rights and freedoms.

The tripartite agreement[18] signed by the establishment that I then directed thus made it possible to foresee major changes.

9.3.1. *In terms of human resources*

The majority of the "care" staff employed by the establishment were non-qualified when I took the role on, the establishment back then also calling on private nurses[19]. The agreement process led to an obligation to recruit qualified staff.

To do this, all partners (the ANPE*, professional training organizations specializing in (medico-)social professions, the OPCA*, the URSSAF*, etc.)[20] have mobilized to facilitate the qualification of existing volunteers and/or the training of those to be recruited through qualification contracts. This professionalization approach has enabled a considerable recovery from the lack of qualified personnel, mainly concerning nursing assistants (ASD) and medico-psychological assistants (AMP) and has continued over time with, for example, the emergence of the specialization of care assistants in gerontology (ASG)[21]. Internal promotion, through the qualification of people who have been in their position for many years, has led to superb successes, in which I have at times been personally involved.

18 The (multi-annual) tripartite agreement in force in the ESSMS* at that time was already provided in article 5-1 of Law no. 75-535 of June 30th, 1975 and was clarified some 20 years later by Appendix 1 of the decree of April 26th, 1999 establishing the content of its specifications. It was signed between the ARS*, the Conseil général/départemental and the ESSMS* (art. L. 313-12 of the CASF*). It was replaced by the contrat pluriannuel d'objectifs et de moyens (CPOM), multi-year contract of objectives and means, introduced by order no. 2005-1477 of December 1st, 2005 (art. L.313-11 of the CASF*) and the laws of adaptation of society to aging known as "ASV" of December 28th, 2015 (Law no. 2015-1776) and financing of the sécurité sociale (social security in France) for 2016. For more information on CPOM, see the summary sheet available on: https://solidarites-sante.gouv.fr/IMG/pdf/Presentation_CPOM.pdf.

19 Clarification: the choice was made not to use inclusive writing in the transcription of this interview so as not to weigh down the text.

20 The ANPE (Agence nationale pour l'emploi or National Employment Agency) is the ancestor of the current Pôle Emploi; the OPCA is the joint collection body, approved by the state and responsible for managing the financing of ongoing professional training in the private sector; URSSAF is the union for the recovery of social security contributions and family allowances.

21 ASG (gerontology care assistant) training is a specialization reserved for ASD* and AMP* graduates working with people suffering from a type of Alzheimer's disease. For more information on this specialization, see: https://solidarites-sante.gouv.fr/metiers-et-concours/les-metiers-de-la-sante/les-fiches-metiers/article/assistant-de-soins-en-gerontologie#:~:text=Dans%20ce%20cadre%20l'assistant,au%20domicile%20de%20la%20personne.

Even though things improved significantly subsequently, the deficit in qualified personnel in EHPAD* persists for other reasons which have been added on since (the sharp increase in needs following the opening of numerous EHPAD*, the lack of recognition and disinterest in professions working with the elderly, etc.).

Another significant point in the transformations that I observed concerns the profile of directors, with, at the same time, a rejuvenation of the profession partly linked to the qualification requirement[22], an accelerated turnover and a reduction in the professional lifespan.

9.3.2. *Concerning the reform of EHPAD pricing**

The reform led to the establishment of so-called ternary pricing and financing based on three distinct sources: the "care" budget (financing of nursing staff and medical equipment), fully taken on by Health Insurance; the "dependency" budget (assistance and monitoring services for the elderly), financed mainly by departments and partly by the residents themselves; the "accommodation" budget (administration, entertainment, hotels, catering, etc.), payable by residents who can benefit from public aid depending on their financial situation. I will, if necessary, further address the subject of this assistance.

This reform gave a glimpse of the implementation of promising means, which were sufficient if not substantial. The reality was sometimes quite different. The major institutional problem, already at that time, resided in an under-evaluation of needs and therefore the under-sizing of allocated resources. This turned out to be particularly tangible with a sometimes "arbitrary" reduction, of the average real-weighted GIR[23] (GMP) of an establishment conditioning the allocation of part of its resources ("dependency" and "care" budgets). The first negotiations of tripartite agreements were not easy and were relatively disparate, depending on departments.

9.3.3. *About the implementation of a quality approach within EHPAD**

While this undoubtedly constitutes a major step forward, it has not only presented positive points. Preparing and then monitoring the evaluations required

22 The qualification requirements for professionals responsible for managing ESSMS* are specified in a circular: https://solidarites-sante.gouv.fr/fichiers/bo/2007/07-06/a0060143.htm.

23 The GIR (iso-resources group) corresponds to the level of loss of autonomy of an elderly person. There are six of these, with GIR 1 corresponding to the level of the most dependent person. It is evaluated based on a national grid called AGGIR (*autonomie-gérontologie-groupe iso-ressources*). The GMP represents the average level of dependency of all residents of a structure.

considerable investment and proved to be time-consuming. They were able to lead to the development of procedures and the production of writing not always followed by concrete effects on practices. As an external evaluator, for example, I noted a strong disparity in the state of progress of the structures and I still wonder, above all, about the follow-up given to the first waves of external evaluations, the outcome of which was to be a management and steering tool, conditioning the renewal of the authorization!

To conclude, I will cite two other areas in which I saw a clear improvement that I would like to highlight. These are those of catering and entertainment.

(I): And during this period, have you noticed any changes in the hosted population?

(MR): Oh yes! My first observation is the increase in the average age of entry into EHPAD*, linked to the aging of the French population. Even though one of the residents welcomed in my establishment joined the "circle" of centenarians shortly after I took office, their number has continued to grow since.

Furthermore, the number of people living with Alzheimer's disease, a related disease or another neurodegenerative disease[24] (*maladie neurodégénérative*: MND) has also increased, due to both the sharp increase in their prevalence and the increase in the number of dedicated places and units reserved for these people: with the various successive national Alzheimer's plans[25], dedicated ADJs, adapted activity and care centers (*poles d'activités et de soins adaptés*: PASA) and even reinforced accommodation units (*unités d'hébergement renforcées*: UHR)[26] appeared in EHPAD*.

As far as my experience is concerned, I have been led, since that time, to welcome people living with disabilities and/or with psychiatric problems.

---

24 A definition that the patients' association "DingDingDong" (which was organized for Huntington's disease patients) denounce as a qualifier for its impact at the time of diagnosis, preferring the term maladies neuro-évolutives (neuro-progressive diseases). MND mainly includes the diseases of Alzheimer's, Parkinson's and multiple sclerosis (MS).

25 The three national Alzheimer's plans were followed, for the period ranging from 2014 to 2019, by the neurodegenerative diseases plan (PMND).

26 For more information on PASA*, see: https://www.pour-les-personnes-agees.gouv.fr/vivre-dans-un-ehpad/prevention-accompagnement-et-soins/les-pasa-des-espaces-amenages-au-sein-des-ehpad; and for the UHR*: https://www.pour-les-personnes-agees.gouv.fr/vivre-dans-un-ehpad/prevention-accompagnement-et-soins/les-uhr-des-lieux-dhebergement-amenages-dans-les-ehpad.

Nothing specific was planned for the latter and I was, for example, asked by the Conseil Général, due to a lack of suitable structures, to accommodate an elderly person with psychiatric experience as well as another person under 60, living with MS*.

(I): And at the team level?

(MR): At the team level, it's quite similar. In my opinion, this is a sector that remains under tension. Although I have no longer worked there since the pandemic, during the last replacement missions that I carried out, I was faced with difficulties, the shortage of staff having become a structural problem. I sometimes had to spend the night in establishments, in conjunction with the coordinating doctor and with the help of involved and dedicated full-time professionals, because replacement staff had canceled at the last minute.

For this reason, for example, I was pushed to alert the representatives of the ARS* in certain regions: the recruitment of nursing staff on permanent contracts (*contrats à durée indéterminée*: CDI) was becoming a real challenge.

Due to insufficient remuneration, certain professionals preferred to accumulate fixed-term contracts (*contrats à durée déterminée*: CDD), over the same time period, sometimes being very short in duration, on both day and night shifts. This is an operation that has proven to be detrimental both for the organization and the management of schedules, and above all for the well-being and safety of those welcomed. This could also have caused a real "disengagement" of professionals, who were not involved in the various establishments where they worked, as well as an increase in the number of complaints made, or even in complaints filed by service users.

(I): Were the complaints from relatives or residents?

(MR): Mainly from the families, I personally received very few complaints from the residents themselves during my career, except for few rare cases when I started, because the residents were younger and more autonomous, whereas today they are much older and often very weak, and it is the family caregivers who take on a stronger position. This is another form of tripartite relationship, where internal conflicts within families often play out. In this case, the elderly resident is often put in the background.

(I): And did you also carry out audits?

(MR): Yes, between 2012 and 2015, after founding my company and following training to do so. I carried out various external evaluations of ESSMS*, in partnership with another professional specialist in quality and audit: I brought my field knowledge and my experience as an establishment director. This is what allowed me to discover other parts of the medico-social sector, by first carrying out assessments in EHPAD*, and then in establishments welcoming people with disabilities or supporting people in precarious situations. It was also on this occasion that I discovered the charity world, since I mainly carried out evaluations of establishments managed by large associations or foundations. An opening which brought me a lot and which I found fascinating.

In fact, I have experienced and accompanied all of the major organizational transformations of the sector over the last few decades, and I have had – which I consider a privilege – the opportunity to work on them locally, within establishments where I was stationed. While they have been the vector of numerous and undeniable improvements, they have also, and sometimes paradoxically, given rise – as we see today in the health sector and in the medical field – to a certain dehumanization of care.

(I): In fact, if I rephrase – and correct my remarks if necessary – you have witnessed a strong technicalization, whether it be in terms of acquired skills or at the organizational level, which has ultimately evolved to the detriment of the relationship?

(MR): To a certain extent yes, and yet, at the same time, we have seen the emergence and multiplication of approaches favoring the quality of the relationship, such as, for example, the Humanitude® approach, developed according to the principles of Gineste-Marescotti® treatment methodology. This is an approach that I was not familiar with when I was myself involved on a daily basis in establishments, but which I discovered as part of my missions as an evaluator and/or director of transition.

(I): Do you believe that this approach is a good thing and that it allows us to reorient the bias that appeared with the high technicization that you have shed light on?

(MR): If this doesn't remain a label, then yes. This gave healthcare professionals the opportunity to ask themselves questions and the teams I met were motivated by these proposals and open to their adoption. Everything then depends on the resources allocated, both for training and for the implementation of the corresponding framework, and this is where it can become complicated. The challenge lies in the adequacy between the means and the objectives.

The concept of humanitude is based on a definition of humans as communicating animals endowed with capacities and living in a particular environment, which implies needs which are specific to the human species. This concept was popularized and adapted to the care of the elderly by **Yves Gineste** and **Rosette Marescotti** 30 years ago. The method thus developed has shown its effectiveness for people suffering from neurodegenerative diseases of the Alzheimer's type and those related to it. It aims to restore the person's dignity as a human being and is thus part of an approach to **well-treatment**.

This new approach to care for the elderly is based on **four pillars**.

Speech remains our main means of communication and contact with others. It is thanks to this that we possess discursive thought, because "it is in words that we think". Whilst Man has been defined ever since ancient philosophy as a rational animal, it is through the existence of speech that we adopt this status. Thus, speech remains important in care since it allows patients and family caregivers to define themselves as human beings.

In cases of dementia, the impossibility of speech does not signify the death knell of communication. In fact, **sight** remains, and this is our primary communication tool. From our earliest days, when speech could yet be mobilized, looking is a non-discursive means of communication which remains extremely expressive. While words are not yet possible, are no longer possible, are unsuitable, the look still allows us to say something. To do this, the gaze must fix the person's face, hold on to it, stop there and not flee. These are the practical principles that humanitude puts forward.

Touch is still a form of communication, even though it remains more restricted than the two previous cases. We can nevertheless distinguish two types of touch in care. Touch in service of technique, such as palpation, allowing the doctor or family caregiver to obtain information relating to the person's state of health. The second form is more a way of caring, a way of making contact. Within care, this touch brings comfort and promotes self-esteem in the patient.

Finally, while bipedalism is not a trait unique to humanity, it remains essential to our motor functions. Three weeks of immobility are enough to make an able-bodied person bedridden. In addition to motor skills, **verticality** allows for good spatial perception. It thus promotes good cognitive functioning[27].

Box 9.1. *The concept of "humanitude"*

(I): If I'm to analyze your words, we are facing a problem that requires a systemic response? Would it be necessary to train all parties in this type of

27 See: http://www.bientraitance.fr/qu%E2%80%99est-ce-que-l%E2%80%99humanitude/.

approach? The professionals in the field but also the decision-makers and among them the shareholders who, in the end, are the decision-makers or guide decisions?

(MR): This is one of the reasons as to why I left the private for-profit sector. All of my evaluation and management replacement missions were then carried out within associative structures. During this period, I had the opportunity to work throughout the metropolitan territory, thus discovering very different modes of operation and environments, and it was extremely interesting that I was thus able to note, for example, a very varied involvement of relatives and families depending on the region, in both qualitative and quantitative terms. This choice to carry out transition management missions, limited in time, perfectly met my expectations, and contributed to a considerable opening up of my field of experience. Apart from the restrictive impact of travel and distance, I have excellent memories of this period.

(I): If you allow me, I proposed a hypothesis regarding the necessities for a favorable impact of "Humanitude®" type approaches, but according to you, what would be necessary for a positive impact over time?

(MR): As I have already said, I have not personally experimented with an establishment that has managed to take on such an approach. On the other hand, I participated in the ISO 9001, the 2000 version certification of the group with which I began my career as director, and then carried out assessments in the various types of establishments mentioned. To sustain the positive impact of a "Humanitude" type approach, it seems to me that it is important to train all of the establishment's staff and not just the family caregivers, which is increasingly the case in the medio-social field. The approach must be monitored and evaluated over time, even if it means organizing additional training sessions, as well as, of course guaranteed by appropriate funding. It would perhaps even be appropriate to involve families and loved ones, the implications of which are very diverse. In all cases, the approach requires collaborative reflection, construction and implementation.

(I): Can family behaviors be the result of differences in monthly care costs?

(MR): I would not speak of "monthly care costs". As I indicated previously, only the costs relating to accommodation and dependency are, entirely or partially, the responsibility of the person accommodated in the EHPAD*. For these two elements of the monthly cost, aid from the Conseil départemental (departmental Council) is possible, without being obligatory or systematic: social assistance for accommodation and/or *allocation personnalisée d'autonomie* (APA)[28]. It is also worth mentioning housing assistance such as *aide personnalisée au logement*

28 Personalized, autonomy allocation, in English.

(APL)[29] or *allocation de logement sociale*[30] (ALS) which can be granted by the *caisse d'allocations familiales* (CAF)[31] or the *mutualité sociale agricole* (MSA). This aid makes it possible to substantially reduce or limit bills[32].

To return to the question asked, when I was working in the private for-profit sector, the subject of cost was indeed very sensitive and a source of complaints, even conflicts.

During the period that I describe next, on the contrary, I carried out replacements in associative establishments, which were therefore all eligible for social assistance (AS)[33] and for their overall capacity, that is, all of their beds (total authorization). As such, these establishments were likely to accommodate beneficiaries of social assistance and therefore offered relatively low "accommodation" rates to all of the people accommodated, whether or not they were beneficiaries of assistance. In any case, accommodation rates were lower than those of private for-profit establishments. I, however, experienced the period when total authorization for social assistance was questioned and when attempts were made to partially discredit, meaning that the authorization to accommodate beneficiaries of social assistance does not apply to the entire capacity of the establishment, and only to part of it, certain establishments.

---

29 Personalized housing assistance, in English.

30 Social housing allowance, in English.

31 Family allowance fund, in English.

32 To find out more about APA, see: https://www.pour-les-personnes-agees.gouv.fr/preserver-son-autonomie-s-informer-et-anticiper/perte-d-autonomieevaluation-et-droits/lallocation-personnalisee-dautonomie-apa. Social assistance for accommodation in France is a relatively complex specificity. For more information, see: https://www.service-public.fr/particuliers/vosdroits/F2444 or the easy to read and understand sheet (fiche facile à lire et à comprendre: FALC) offered on the portal dedicated to elderly people: https://www.pour-les-personnes-agees.gouv.fr/annuaires-et-services/facile-a-lire-et-acomprendre/tout-savoir-sur-laide-sociale-a-lhebergement. For an overview of all financial aid dedicated to elderly people and their loved ones, in EHPAD*, see: https://www.pour-les-personnes-agees.gouv.fr/vivre-dans-un-ehpad/aides-financieres-en-ehpad; at home: https://www.pour-les-personnes-agees.gouv.fr/vivre-a-domicile/aides-financieres.

33 The social assistance authorization of an EHPAD*, like any other establishment, is the authorization issued to it by the Departmental Council to accommodate beneficiaries of social assistance for accommodation, that is,, people with limited resources. In this case, payment of the "accommodation" service is provided, in whole or in part, by the Departmental Council, according to rules set by the CASF* and the social assistance regulations of the department concerned: the Departmental Council establishes the difference between the accommodation rate of the establishment, which it has set itself, and the contribution of the beneficiary, or even of their dependents. Each department has its own social assistance regulations.

The paradox of EHPAD* holding full authorization to AS* was that the same rate, set by the Departmental Council, had to be applied to all residents of the establishment, whether or not they were beneficiaries of AS*[34]. It is a principle that has led to certain excesses. In a tight budgetary context, it seemed appropriate to consider alternative solutions, such as "differentiated rents"[35].

This period was already very different from the one during which I started working in this sector. At the time, the request to create an establishment came from the project leader who had to submit a file to the competent administrative authorities, which was then submitted for approval to the Regional Committee for Health and Social Organization (*Comité régional de l'organisation sanitaire et sociale*: CROSS): being part of a network, having support and/or knowing the right people was very facilitating. Since 2010, the approach has been completely reversed with the implementation of the call for projects procedure (*appels à projets*, known as AAP*): it is thus the ARS* which are now launching AAP*, based on identified needs, and this approach is part of an evolution of the sector's planning approach.

The rates practiced, including in the private for-profit sector, are now regulated, which was not at all the case when I started, when prices were very diverse and sometimes, for some, very high, even exorbitant. Today, everything is organized around the AAP*, hence the emergence of an institutional desire to encourage and favor the grouping of establishments, as long as they allow the pooling of certain functions and/or several services.

(I): During your last years of activity, have you observed any technological innovations likely to improve care, for both professionals and residents, or even for organizations?

(MR): I have not really benefited from the latest technological advances or artificial intelligence-based tools, such as the intelligent medicine dispenser. They appeared later. However, for example, I experienced the establishment of the first

---

34 I insist on this: the fact for an EHPAD* to be eligible for social assistance for its entire capacity does not in any way mean that it must exclusively accommodate beneficiaries of social assistance, but simply that it is authorized to accommodate up to 100% of social assistance recipients, which is not the same thing. Some of its residents are therefore likely not to be beneficiaries of social assistance.

35 The principle of "differentiated rents" consists of basing the "rent" or the amount due for accommodation purposes, on the income of residents, that is, maintaining the social assistance rate for those most in need, including social assistance recipients for whom it is an obligation, and to apply a solidarity "surcharge" to those who have the means.

sensory simulation spaces, known as Snoezelen[36]: when I was sector manager, we were asked to integrate such spaces into EPHAD* creation projects. However, I was subsequently very disappointed, during my external evaluation missions, to note that these spaces, which had been financed and designed, were too often closed due to a lack of dedicated and/or trained staff.

I also experienced the implementation of animal mediation, with, on the other hand, some very beautiful things.

What I was especially able to see were the overall assistance tools to ensure the safety of residents and in particular the prevention of falls and runaways: I thus witnessed the equipping of certain structures and/or the implementation of individual devices such as connected anti-runaway watches or fall detection bracelets.

I thus experienced these first technological innovations, which consist of security measures rather than measures for the comfort of residents' lives, apart from the Snoezelen spaces.

(I): And so now that you have encountered the paradigm of a care partnership with the patient, the art of care in partnership with patients, relatives and citizens, do you think that this approach would be of interest and could be organized and established in this context?

(MR): I have questioned this a lot since my training. I wondered how the partnership could be applied in EHPAD*, with people who are sometimes very old, increasingly ill, presenting polypathologies, suffering from disorientation, and therefore in a situation of dependence.

---

36 Link from the Ministry of Solidarity and Health (*Ministère des Solidarités et de la Santé*) on this system: https://solidarites-sante.gouv.fr/systeme-de-sante-et-medico-social/parcours-de-sante-vos-droits/bonnes-pratiques-en-region/ile-de-france/article/l-espace-snoezelen. "The origin: 'the snoezelen' is a method recognized in France for around ten years, which makes it possible to improve the psyche of residents suffering mainly from Alzheimer's disease or dementia. Designed on basic multisensory principles, this method is conducive to relaxation, the awakening of the senses and emotions and based on the search for pleasure with the aim of soothing the residents' minds and providing them with wellbeing. The purpose of the project is: to improve the wellbeing of very anxious residents, to create privileged relationships within this space allowing the accompanied person to exist and live through the eyes of the other, of their availability, their attentions and their way of taking care of themselves, bringing on a certain inner serenity, even if the changes in behavior are slow and fluctuate from one session to the next, knowing that over time the changes can be sustainable and beneficial".

The ideal would be to consider this partnership with residents and their families. However, it is clear that even today the partnership, when it exists, is essentially established with the members of the resident's family and the habitus, in my lived experience, leaves little room, on both sides, to the elderly person themselves. The interlocutors are generally accompanying persons, who are also not always members of the family. That being said, it would already be appropriate to develop the partnership with family caregivers, which could be considered within the social life advice (*conseils de (la) vie sociale*: CVS) framework.

From my experience, CVSs* do not always take place in a very friendly atmosphere, but sometimes transform into a place and time for expressing fears and also discontent, even anger, against the backdrop of a transfer of guilt generating contradictory feelings and inner conflicts among those close to the residents, which are at times expressed loudly during these meetings. It is perhaps from these meeting spaces that something could be done, by integrating the partnership approach and involving representatives of all stakeholders: families, relatives and residents, caregiving and non-caregiving professionals, management or even invited external partners. It seems to me that this is what directors should be prepared for as a priority, and training such as the *DU l'art du soin en partenariat avec le patient* (university diploma in the art of care in partnership with the patient) could contribute to this and would take on its full meaning. And it is in this sense that the training did me some good, for example, with what was worked on from the film Flore[37], which constitutes a model that everyone would dream of being able to benefit from. But, as director of EHPAD*, I have more often witnessed family conflicts or been confronted with very disconcerting situations, even if I have also witnessed very beautiful stories, with families present and very involved on a daily basis.

(I): And then you mentioned the film Flore, do you think it would be beneficial and possible to prepare partnership teams likely to participate in organizing such contexts?

(MR): Certainly, I think that this could be very beneficial and that professionals today are asking for innovative solutions and new approaches, including the integration of art into structures. I, for example, experienced this, when I went to meet the director of an EHPAD*, following on from my DU*, who seemed very favorable towards our interest in the animation projects that develop around art there.

37 *Flore*, a documentary by Jean Albert Lelièvre, Happiness distribution, awarded best documentary in 2014 at the Los Angeles Festival, USA.

Teams often feel very alone and far from what they would like to offer in terms of human time. When a new resident arrives, for example, in order to promote their integration, a welcome period could be offered and organized with professionals and other residents already present in the structure. Even though the length of stays in EHPAD* has decreased considerably over time, it would be desirable to do something at this very particular, and often delicate, even painful, moment of welcoming, both for the residents themselves and for family caregivers. Dedicated shared information times could be considered, relying on cultural and/or artistic intermediation.

And it is upstream, through information and/or training, that it should be prepared. It would therefore be appropriate to act before entries or placements (which most often unfortunately corresponds to the state of things) within structures. Intervention with authorities and/or people responsible for referral to EHPAD*, such as communal social action centers (*Centres communaux d'action sociale*: CCAS), hospital social services or local information and coordination centers (*Centres locaux d'information et de coordination*: CLIC)[38], aimed at raising awareness of this approach, would be very useful.

In fact, I believe that the approach proposed by the Center for innovation in partnership with patients and the public (*Centre d'innovation du partenariat avec les patients et le public*: CI3P[39]) and the way in which it is mobilized among all stakeholders (professionals, patients, relatives and citizens), through different mechanisms, is interesting, in that it contributes to raising awareness among all citizens about societal issues that concern us all, in one way or another. With regard to our subject more specifically, it is an undeniable fact that we are all going to age and that many of us have elders who are concerned.

I also think that there is a lot of work to be done with doctors treating the elderly, with general practitioners, because they are, if not at the origin, at least co-decision makers in the orientation of the elderly towards an establishment.

(I): And having yourself followed this training in the art of care in partnership with the patient[40]*, do you think it is suitable for professionals in this environment?*

38 For more details on information points dedicated to elderly people, see: https://www.pour-les-personnes-agees.gouv.fr/preserver-son-autonomie-s-informer-et-anticiper/a-qui-s-adresser/les-points-dinformation-locaux-dedies-aux-personnes-agees.

39 CI3P: Internet address accessible from the link: https://ci3p.univ-cotedazur.fr/.

40 This training was given an award by the Ministry of Higher Education and Research when it was launched as an educational innovation for lifelong training (2018 PEPS Prize: Internet access at: https://www.youtube.com/watch?v=WK5cncBW1Ao).

(MR): I do indeed think so and this applies just as much to the medical and paramedical professions working in EHPAD* as to people working in elderly homes. Staff working in all of the information centers already mentioned would benefit from training in this approach. If we consider care in the broad sense of the term, it would also be beneficial to extend this awareness-raising approach to all professionals, including EPHAD coordinating doctors*[41] so that they can set the tone: I personally had the chance to meet some who were very driven towards teams, as well as with city doctors who had patients in these establishments.

In conclusion, I think that there are things to do and possibilities to consider.

9.4. Appendix: list of acronyms

The following is a list of acronyms used in this chapter as marked by an asterisk (see footnotes for definitions in English).

ADVF: assistant de vie aux familles

ALS: allocation de logement sociale

AMP: aide médico-psychologique

AMU: Aix-Marseille Université

APL: aide personnalisée au logement

ARH: Agence régionale de l'hospitalisation

ARS: Agence régionale de santé

AS: aide sociale

ASD: aide-soignant diplômé

ASG: assistant de soins en gérontologie

---

41 The role of coordinating doctor in EHPAD was established by Annex II and the decree of April 26th, 1999 setting the content of the specifications of the multi-year tripartite agreement. Its status and missions were clarified by Decree no. 2005-550 and no. 2011-1047. They are in particular responsible for the medical supervision of the healthcare team with whom they develop and monitor the establishment's care plan, assess the level of dependency of residents and give an opinion on admissions. They are not the general practitioner of residents housed in the establishment.

AVS: auxiliaire de vie sociale

CAF: caisse d'allocations familiales

CASF: Code de l'action sociale et des familles

CCAS: Centre communal d'action sociale

CDD: contrat à durée déterminée

CDI: contrat à durée indéterminée

CLIC: Centre local d'information et de coordination

COM: contrat d'objectifs et de moyens

CROSS: Comité régional de l'organisation sanitaire et sociale

CVS: Conseil de (la) vie sociale

DDASS: Direction départementale des affaires sanitaires et sociales

DIPC: document individuel de prise en charge

DRASS: Direction régionale des affaires sanitaires et sociales

DU: diplôme universitaire

EHPAD: établissements d'hébergement pour personnes âgées dépendantes

ESSMS: établissements et services sociaux et médico-sociaux

GIR: groupe iso-ressources

GMP: GIR moyen pondéré

IA: intelligence artificielle

MND: maladie neurodégénérative

MS: multiple sclerosis

MSA: mutualité sociale agricole

OMS: Organisation mondiale de la Santé

PASA: pôle d'activité et de soins adaptés

PMND: plan maladies neurodégénératives

SSR: soins de suite et de réadaptation

UCA: Université Côte d'Azur, Côte d'Azur University

UHR: unité d'hébergement renforcée

URCAM: Union régionale des caisses d'assurance maladie

USLD: unité de soins de longue durée

9.5. References

Castanet, V. (2022). *Les fossoyeurs*. Fayard, Paris.

Flore (2014) Directed by J.-A. Lièvre [Film]. France: Wargny Lièvre Production.

Gineste, Y. and Pellissier, J. (2007). *Humanitude – Comprendre la vieillesse, prendre soin des Hommes vieux*. Armand Colin, Paris.

Hermant, É. and Pihet, V. (2017). *Le chemin des possibles*. Dingdingdong Editions, Paris.

Joing, J.-L. (2008). *Guide de l'évaluation des pratiques médico-sociales*. Afnor Editions, Paris.

Matillon, Y. (2001). L'accréditation en France. *Actualité et dossier en santé publique*, 35, 44–55 [Online]. Available at: https://www.hcsp.fr/Explore.cgi/Telecharger?NomFichier=ad354455.pdf.

Oppert, C. (2020). *Le pansement Schubert*, Denoël, Paris.

10

EPoP: An Approach to Developing Peer Intervention

10.1. Introduction

The participation of those with disabilities in issues that concern them through mobilizing their expertise has been a significant issue in recent decades in France and internationally. Several factors have given rise to this.

During the 1970s, Disability Studies contributed to fundamental conceptual developments in the definition of disability. In opposition to the "medical model", it allowed for the emergence of the "social model" of disability by laying the foundations for the definition of disability as a situation. Thus, disability is no longer reduced to deficiency and illness, but is acknowledged to be "due in large part to society's treatment of people who function differently from the norm" (Albrecht et al. 2001).

These conceptual developments of disability were initially reflected in the International Classification of Impairments, Disability and Handicaps (ICIDH)[1], adopted by the World Health Organization (WHO) in 1980. They were then supported in 2002 by the WHO in the International Classification of Functioning, Disability and Health (ICF)[2]. This introduces the classification of environmental factors into the concept of disability allowing the identification of environmental obstacles and facilitators both for the effective realization of daily life activities, as well as social life participation.

Chapter written by Sabrina SINIGAGLIA.

1 See: https://apps.who.int/iris/handle/10665/41005 (Accessed August 5, 2022).

2 See: https://apps.who.int/iris/handle/10665/42418 (Accessed August 5, 2022).

The Disability Studies current emerged in the context of the movements for disabled people's rights which developed at the end of the 1970s in the United States and Great Britain. Older movements influenced it: those of self-help, consumerism, as well as the civil rights movement (Winance and Ravaud 2010). Disability rights movements share characteristics with other social movements such as those of feminists and cultural or ethnic minorities. These characteristics include the development of "identity politics" (Anspach (1979) in Winance and Ravaud (2010)) and linking political action and scientific research (Rabeharisoa et al. (2000a, 2000b) in Winance and Ravaud (2010)).

Similarly to the other social movements mentioned above, the people concerned, actors of their future and of their emancipation, are recognized as having their own knowledge that external researchers do not hold (Albrecht et al. 2001). Knowledge that we will call: "experiential knowledge ".

DEFINITION.– Experiential knowledge.

In her research on self-help groups, Thomasina Borkman defined experiential knowledge for the first time as "a truth learned through personal experience of a phenomenon rather than a truth acquired through discursive reasoning, observation or reflections on information provided by others" (Borkman 1976). This is knowledge derived from the experience of living with a disability[3]. It should be considered as knowledge complementary to the scientific and technical knowledge of professionals. It is an experience transformed into expertise that can be passed on to others (other people with disabilities, families, caregivers, professionals in the medico-social world, businesses, etc.).

Thus, the knowledge of persons with disabilities was mobilized in the writing of the United Nations Convention on the Rights of Persons with Disabilities (UNCRPD)[4], which came into force on May 3rd, 2008 and was ratified by France in 2010. These persons participated in its implementation by local actors and in the establishment of monitoring mechanisms (Burca et al. (2013) in Eyraud et al. (2018)).

3 We limit ourselves here to experiential knowledge linked to experience arising from situations of disability. It is important to specify that it also concerns experiences resulting from illness, mental health disorders, social insecurity, etc.

4 See: https://www.ohchr.org/fr/instruments-mechanisms/instruments/convention-rights-persons-disabilities (Accessed August 5, 2022).

In France, recognition of the rights and participation of persons with disabilities found its way into legislation and regulations[5]. Thus, the logic of placing individuals (Law no. 75-534 of June 30th, 1975 in favor of disabled persons) has been replaced by that of the "life project", of the "life path" and of participation of the supported person (Law no. 2002-2 renovating social and medico-social action, Law no. 2005-102 for equal rights and opportunities, participation and citizenship of disabled people, Law no. 2009-879 on hospital reform relating to patients, health and territories, Decree no. 2017-137 of February 7th, 2017 relating to the necessary information for the development of global support plans for disabled persons, etc.).

With the impetus of these new theoretical and regulatory frameworks, professionals supporting persons with disabilities must now rethink their practices in order to promote and support the participation and self-determination of those they support as much as possible.

This evolution of support practices must also be based on the recognition and taking into account of the experiential knowledge of the people concerned as expert knowledge.

In this perspective, the latter is highlighted in Decree no. 2017-877 of May 6th, 2017 relating to the definition of social work, specifying that it:

> [...] is based on ethical and deontological principles, on university knowledge in the social and human sciences, on the practical and theoretical knowledge of social work professionals and the knowledge resulting from the experience of people benefiting from social support, these being associated with the construction of responses to their needs (Article 1)[6].

In the "Zéro sans solutions" (2014) report, Piveteau emphasizes the role of *maisons départmentales pour les personnes handicapées* (MDPHs)[7] in the construction of a form of personalized support for people with disabilities which specifically gives an important place to peer support. Based on this, axis 3: "participation et accompagnement par les pairs" (peer participation and support) of

5 The legal and regulatory texts mentioned below can be found online: https://www.legifrance.gouv.fr/ (Accessed August 5, 2022).

6 See: https://www.legifrance.gouv.fr/jorf/id/JORFTEXT000034633906#:~:text=Notice%20%3A%20le%20d%C3%A9cret%20pr%C3%A9cise%20la,travail%20social%20en%20f%C3%A9vrier%202017 (Accessed August 5, 2022).

7 Departmental homes for disabled persons.

the "une réponse accompagnée pour tous" (a supported response for all) approach[8] (2018) aims to strengthen the participation of persons with disabilities in all things that concerns them, the recognition of their experiential knowledge and the development of peer support. In addition, recommendation no. 10 of the Gillot report (2019) highlights the importance of recognizing and promoting peer support by relying on associations and the people concerned. This is defined as user expertise.

This promotion of peer support and support practices through public policies[9], which has accelerated since the 2010s, has contributed to the emergence of categories such as those of expert-patients, resource-patients, peer health mediators in the health sector, peer-helpers, peer-emulators and peer-workers in the social and medico-social sectors. These are "individuals engaged in accompanying or supporting those living or having had an experience similar to theirs, in other words their presumed 'peer'" (Gardien 2021).

With regard to these peer intervention practices called peer support[10], testimonies from persons directly concerned and scientific work carried out in particular in Anglo-Saxon countries and in Canada show their effectiveness and added value. This includes positive effects on self-esteem or self-confidence, on the quality of life of those concerned as well as less recourse to hospitalization and better support for the effects of the illness or situation of disability are reported[11].

The first experiments with systems promoting the recruitment and training of paid peer helpers within hospital mental health services and in the social insecurity domain are being carried out in the United States. In 1989, the National Association of State Mental Health Program Directors officially recognized peer supporters and funded programs to hire mental health service users (Solidarity Users Psynd).

---

8 See: https://handicap.gouv.fr/une-reponse-accompagnee-pour-tous (Accessed August 5, 2022).

9 Law no. 2005-102 lays the legal foundations for mutual aid groups (*groupes d'entraide mutuelle*: GEM), article 84 of Law no. 2009-879 introduces therapeutic patient education (*éducation thérapeutique du patient*: ETP), a practice that supports exchanges between peers, etc.

10 This is a person with a disability who helps, advises or supports one or more persons with a disability. There are several other names for peer support: peer-aid, peer-emulation®, peer-work, peer health mediator (*médiateur de santé pair*: MSP).

11 See the contributions of the literature review carried out by Ève Gardien in the chapter "Instituer le pair-accompagnement au risque de perdre les qualités de la relation entre pairs", in *L'accompagnement par les pairs: enjeux de participation et de professionnalisation*, PUG, 93–111.

During the same period, the first *housing first* program was built in New York. It is aimed at homeless people with one or more severe psychological disorders, both with and without addictive behavior. The program aims to offer them housing without the conditions of treatment or psychoactive substance consumption cessation, alongside home support by a multidisciplinary team which includes peer-helpers (Fraszczak 2019).

Canada is the other country that followed the United States in formalizing the hiring of paid peer-helpers. These different programs were then diffused in the United Kingdom and later in several European countries. However, in the latter, peer-support initiatives are not deployed on a national scale and the status of peer-helper is not always officially recognized (Sizaret 2020).

In France, with the impetus of these foreign experiences, the first salaried recognitions of peer-helpers' contribution in the domains of mental health and social insecurity is also taking place. Thus, the MARSS team[12] in Marseille has included peer-workers since 2005 and two experimental programs also welcome them: the "Un chez-soi d'abord" (Housing first) program[13] (2011) and the peer health mediators program[14] (2012) (Gesmond et al. 2016).

12 MARSS (*Mouvement et action pour le rétablissement social et sanitaire*: Movement and action for social and health recovery) is today both a team of *Assistance publique-Hôpitaux de Marseille* (Public Assistance-Hospitals of Marseille), is made up of around 15 employees and is a movement which includes many citizen volunteers who participate in different actions, all sharing the ultimate objective of greater social justice. MARSS was born in 2005 from an encounter between two practices: that of street community psychiatry, developed in the United States as part of a research project linked to Yale University, and that of risk reduction in Marseille, also in the streets, set up by Médecins du monde, a French medical NGO. See: http://www.marssmarseille.eu/qui-sommes-nous/marss-en-quelques-mots.

13 This is an experimental program inspired by the *housing first model* that which emerged in the United States at the end of the 1980s. It was deployed in Lille, Marseille, Toulouse and Paris between 2011 and 2016. The evaluation of the program reported an improvement in the quality of life and recovery of those concerned as well as a reduction in costs for public authorities thanks to the reduction in inappropriate recourse to the healthcare system and to social-monitoring structures. These positive results led to the sustainability of the program via Decree no. 2016-1940 of December 28th, 2016 relating to therapeutic coordination apartment systems "Un chez-soi d'abord" (Estecahandy 2020).

14 This is a program combining training in mental health mediation and the promotion of experiential knowledge. It has been supported and deployed since 2012 by the WHO Collaborating Center for Research and Training in Mental Health (WHOCC). It draws inspiration from foreign experiences, particularly from Quebec, England and Scotland. This program trains persons affected by psychological disorders, who have recovered or are in the process of recovery, and supports their hiring within hospital teams and medico-social mental health structures (Staedel and Hude 2020).

At the same time, several training courses in peer-support practice are offered with the aim of training future peer-workers or professionals in peer intervention. These are short (from a few hours to several weeks) or long (1 year) training courses. A document developed in 2020 and updated in 2021 by a partnership working group coordinated by the Secretary-General of the Comité interministériel du handicap (Interministerial Disability Committee) lists a little more than ten[15]. Among these training courses, we find those which train for roles particularly highlighted in the field of peer-support: on the one hand, since 2018, within mental health, the peer health mediator degree (an evolution of the university diploma for peer health mediators which has existed since 2012) as well as the peer-aid university diploma in mental health, and on the other hand, in the field of chronic physical illnesses, training and diplomas which highlight the figure of the "patient–participant (PP)/expert" proposed since 2009 by "Université des patients" (The Patient University) (Troisoeufs 2020)[16].

However, despite the promotion of peer intervention practices by public policies, the results of the introduction of these practices in health, social and medico-social establishments and services remain unimportant (Gardien 2021). Indeed, the recognition of experiential knowledge in France remains an ongoing process (Flora 2021).

In an article published in November 2021, the number of professionals providing peer-support is estimated at barely 200–300 people across the entire national territory. To date, no national census provides us with the precise number of employees (Bacle 2021).

In addition, peer intervention is of course carried out when persons with disabilities use their experiential knowledge and their unique skills to serve others with disabilities, their peers, and also caregivers and professionals or future professionals (social, medico-social, public service, business, etc.) as well as political decision-makers.

15 See: https://www.gouvernement.fr/sites/default/files/contenu/piece-jointe/2022/01/20200902_cih_formation_des_pairs_v20_21_formations.pdf (Accessed August 5, 2022).

16 In France, the first patient university was founded in 2009 at the Faculty of Medicine of Pierre and Marie Curie University. It is inspired by a German "patient university" system created in Hanover in 2006. The validation of acquired knowledge from the experience of illness is at the origin of the creation of this university. In particular, training and diplomas are offered to health and medico-social professionals and patients wishing to train in therapeutic patient education (*éducation thérapeutique du patient*: TPE) (Tourette-Turgis 2013; Flora 2021).

These other forms of peer intervention which do not relate to peer support remain little known and mobilized. These are interventions using the experiential knowledge of persons with disabilities with a view towards:

– representation[17];

– participation in the design, implementation and evaluation of public policies;

– universal design of services and goods;

– design and evaluation of support offers dedicated to persons with disabilities;

– awareness raising and training for environments and professionals.

In this context, by capitalizing on the advances made in the fields of health, mental health and precarity, the EPoP (Empowerment and Participation of Persons with Disabilities) approach wishes to highlight, recognize and further mobilize the experiential knowledge of those concerned, whatever their situation of disability, by deploying peer intervention in all its forms and in any exercise context.

10.2. The EPoP approach: a necessary framework for action

In 2021, the French Red Cross, FISAF[18], GAPAS[19], LADAPT[20] and Trisomie 21 France nationally launched the EPoP approach. Its ambition is to make it more accessible to all and to systematize the use of peer interventions by mobilizing the experiential knowledge of persons with disabilities, regardless of the environment they live and express themselves in.

The objective of this approach is to strengthen the self-determination and the Empowerment of those concerned by allowing them to progress in their journey according to their wishes, drawing on their lived experiences and their user expertise.

---

17 This is a person with a disability appointed or elected to represent the point of view of their peers to public or private structures and bodies. For example: a person with a disability involved in an association is elected to their department's *Commission des droits et de l'autonomie des personnes handicapées* (Commission on the Rights and Autonomy of Disabled People).

18 National federation for the inclusion of people with sensory or cognitive disabilities.

19 Group of social action partner associations.

20 Association for social and professional integration of disabled people.

EPoP is currently being tested in Hauts-de-France (the carrier is the CREAI[21] Hauts-de-France) and in Nouvelle-Aquitaine (the carriers are LADAPT, FISAF and the French Red Cross with the support of CREAI Nouvelle-Aquitaine).

Until 2023, EPoP will make it possible to experiment and structure the development of interventions by persons with disabilities through five complementary areas of work:

– Two territorial experiments which aim to structure, lead and coordinate a dynamic of recourse to peer intervention.

– The deployment of training for peer-workers, enabling them to transform their experience of living with a disability into transferable experiential knowledge.

– The deployment of training for peer intervention professionals of reference, responsible for developing peer intervention within their organization (company, public service, medico-social establishment, social establishment, hospital, school, etc.).

– The creation of an online resource space on a dedicated website, which will offer a geolocated trained peer-worker directory, accessible legal analyzes on various possible practice statuses, a toolbox to support the peer-intervener journey, a discussion forum reserved for peer-interveners, etc.

– Research and evaluation to study, measure the impact of the approach, draw lessons from the first experimental phase and submit a deployment kit to future territories wishing to take on the EPoP approach.

The EPoP approach is aimed at:

– All persons with disabilities wishing to become future peer-interveners and/or to have a mission complementing their initial profession by mobilizing their experiential knowledge.

– Professionals from medical–social establishments and services, businesses, public service organizations, hospitals, schools, etc., wishing to become references for peer intervention in their respective structure.

– Any actor who can benefit from peer intervention (persons with disabilities, family caregivers, professionals, common law actors, etc.).

EPoP wishes to contribute to the creation of a society where the use of peer interventions will be commonplace and a massive change in practices in medico-social establishments and services (*établissements et services*

21 Regional center for studies, actions and information for people in vulnerable situations.

médico-sociaux: ESMS) will occur in favor of self-determination and full participation of those supported in the co-construction of their life journeys.

In order to achieve this, a multitude of partners participate in the process: the French Red Cross, LADAPT, FISAF, Trisomie 21 France, ANCREAI[22], UNAPEI[23], GAPAS, HandiVoice, La Fédé 100% HANDINAMIQUE, APF[24] France Handicap, SG CIH[25], CNSA[26], ARS[27] Nouvelle-Aquitaine, ARS Hauts-de-France, AGEFIPH[28], OETH[29], Caisse des Dépôts, UNIOPSS[30]/URIOPSS[31], Nexem, Fehap[32], Fiphfp[33],

22 *Fédération nationale des centres régionaux d'études, d'actions et d'informations, en faveur des personnes en situation de vulnérabilité* (National federation of regional centers for studies, actions and information, for people in vulnerable situations).

23 *Union nationale des associations de parents et amis de personnes handicapées mentales* (National Union of Associations of Parents and Friends of People with Mental Disabilities).

24 *Association des paralysés de France* (Association for paralyzed persons of France).

25 *Secrétariat général du Comité interministériel du handicap* (General Secretariat of the Interministerial Disability Committee).

26 *Caisse nationale de solidarité pour l'autonomie* (National solidarity fund for autonomy). This fund helps to finance independent support for elderly and disabled people. It guarantees equal treatment throughout the territory regardless of age or disability type. It ensures a mission of expertise, information and facilitation (between departments, in order to support state services in the identification of priorities and adaptation of their offer, etc.) as well as an information mission for elderly people, disabled people and their loved ones. It has an expert and research role on all issues related to access and autonomy, regardless of age and disability origin. See: https://www.cnsa.fr/; https://solidarites-sante.gouv.fr/ministere/acteurs/agences-et-operateurs/article/cnsa-caisse-nationale-de-solidarite-pour-l-autonomie (Accessed August 5, 2022).

27 *Agence régionale de santé* (Regional health agency).

28 *Association nationale de gestion du fonds pour l'insertion professionnelle des personnes handicapées* (National fund management association for the professional integration of disabled persons).

29 *Obligation d'emploi de travailleur handicapé* (Obligation to employ disabled workers).

30 *Union nationale interfédérale des œuvres et organismes privés sanitaires et sociaux* (National interfederal union of private health and social works and organizations).

31 *Union régionale interfédérale des œuvres et organismes privés sanitaires et sociaux* (Interfederal regional union of private health and social works and organizations).

32 *Fédération des établissements hospitaliers et d'aide à la personne privés* (Federation of private hospitals and personal assistance establishments).

33 *Fonds pour l'insertion des personnes handicapées dans la fonction publique* (Fund for the integration of disabled people into public service).

Nous Aussi, GEM[34], CRA[35], CREHPSY[36], France Assos Santé, WHOCC[37], GCSMS[38], C360[39], etc.

10.3. The choice of a territorial approach

EPoP is organized at two interdependent levels: a national level and a local level. The choice was made to territorialize the approach, because it is at the local scale that the identification of needs and the co-construction of responses to them can be carried out in detail. Thus, a steering committee initiates the EPoP dynamic which is then co-constructed and led at the local level with all partners by regional regional team[40]. This is made up of two professionals, one of whom is a peer-intervener. The national resource team also presents with the same composition[41]. This is supplemented by a regional EPoP deployment manager, a professional who participates in deployments in the two experimental regions and prepares those in new regions.

34 Mutual support groups (*groupes d'entraide mutuelle*: GEM) are dedicated to people with a disability that resulted from psychological disorders, head trauma or any other brain injury, autism spectrum disorders or other neurodevelopment disorders. These associations are run by and for mental health service users offering a space to support each other in the difficulties encountered, particularly in terms of social, professional and citizen integration. See: https://www.cnsa.fr/actualites-agenda/actualites/tout-savoir-sur-les-groupes-dentraide-mutuelle (Accessed August 5, 2022).

35 *Centres* de *ressources autisme* (Autism Resource Centers).

36 *Centre de ressources sur le handicap psychique* (Mental disability resource center).

37 WHO Collaborating Center for Research and Training in Mental Health.

38 *Groupement de coopération sociale et médico-sociale* (Social and medico-social cooperation group).

39 *Communautés 360:* "They were created in order to respond in a more coordinated and systemic way to all persons with disabilities as well as their caregivers, close to where they live. They aim to bring together specialized and common law stakeholders in order to offer global and inclusive support to all persons with disabilities. Communautés 360 will also help to prevent the risks of route disruption by developing a "going towards" approach in the territory as a whole". See: https://www.cnsa.fr/grands-chantiers/communautes-360.

40 Composition of the two EPoP regional chieftancies: in Hauts-de-France, Pauline Tursi, EPoP regional coordinator, and Arthur Aumoite, EPoP regional peer coordinator within CREAI Hauts-de-France; in Nouvelle-Aquitaine, Fathia Vranckx, EPoP regional coordinator, and Margaux Alloucherie, EPoP regional peer coordinator within LADAPT.

41 Composition of the national EPoP resource team: Aysegul Turna, EPoP project manager, and Mustapha Sallali, national EPoP peer coordinator within the French Red Cross with Sabrina Sinigaglia, responsible for EPoP deployment in the region within ANCREAI.

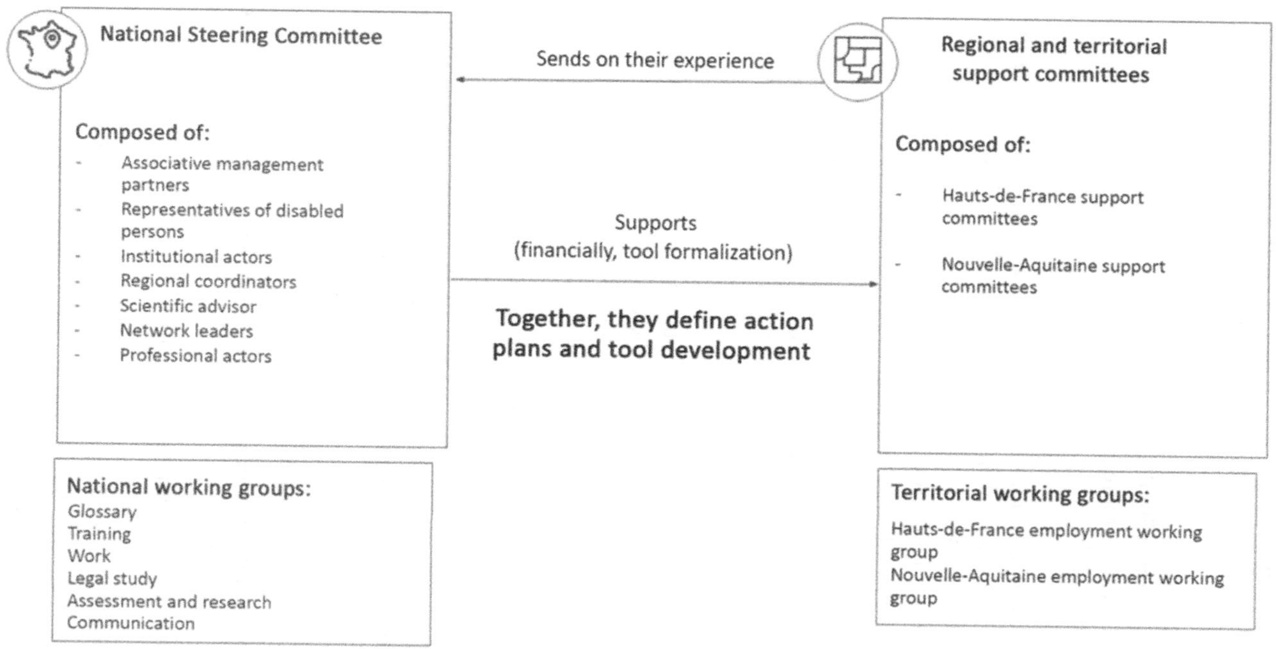

Figure 10.1. *Schematization of the organization and interdependence of the two levels of the EPoP approach: national and territorial. For a color version of this figure, see www.iste.co.uk/flora/experience.zip*

National actions focus on the coordination and facilitation of the partner and national working group network, who reflect on and work on the formalization of tools in response to needs identified at the local level.

Six working groups are being led at the national level. Regional chieftaincies participate, as do persons with disabilities who have practical expertise regarding the themes covered, as well as representatives of the different partners depending on the skills needing to be mobilized.

The glossary working group led a collective reflection regarding the choice of terms and concepts to be used throughout the process. This is in order to stabilize them and share a common language amongst different EPoP stakeholders. The working sessions of this group made it possible to produce an infographic representing the different forms of peer intervention. The "peer intervention" denomination was taken from the work of a national working group coordinated by the general secretariat of the Interministerial Disability Committee (*secrétariat général du Comité interministériel du handicap*: SGCIH). It applies to peer-to-peer interventions as well as those that mobilize the expertise of persons with disabilities in general.

This infographic is an external communication tool shared with the partner network. It served as a working basis for the design of the questionnaire, making it possible to carry out an inventory local actor level in order to identify and choose the focus in order to begin territorial experiments.

The **employment working group** is concerned with the question of the employment of persons with disabilities in connection to the valorization of experiential knowledge in different sectors of activity (company, type of public service, medical–social establishment, social establishment, hospital, school, etc.). Sessions are dedicated to the specificities of the use of peer-interveners in different contexts.

Two work areas are identified:

– the creation of a **map of missions and professions linked to the mobilization of experiential knowledge**;

– the analysis **of peer-stakeholders' journeys**.

There are multiple objectives for this **mapping**:

– to identify inspiring initiatives via a questionnaire distributed across the national territory, to contact stakeholders, to question points of blockage and the solutions put in place to overcome them, the success factors, in order to model and enable their development;

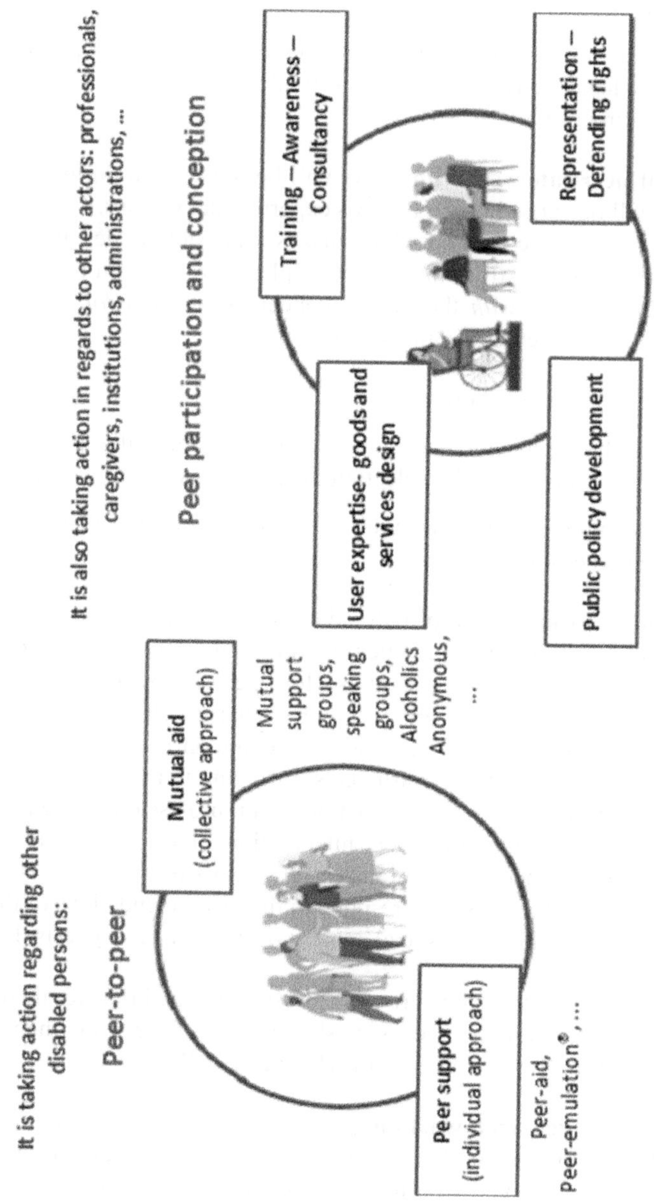

Figure 10.2. *Extract from the infographic developed by the EPoP team presenting the different forms of peer intervention*

– to identify the different forms of existing peer interventions (peer-trainers, peer-helpers, etc.) and establish a skills framework, to consider the construction of job, employment and role cards;

– to identify needs and wishes for peer interventions. To plan in particular for needs in terms of the legal study of intervention statutes (this work will be continued within the legal working group).

The **analysis of peer-intervener journeys** will be undertaken during co-design workshops which will be carried out in the two experimental regions. Co-design is a participatory and collaborative method which makes it possible to design tools, and to include all the stakeholders, from the reflection phase onwards, in the project. In this way, the project is built *with* the people concerned and not *for* them, which makes it possible to fully meet the people's expectations.

The objectives of these workshops are:

– to understand the peer-intervener journey by revealing the problems and blockage points of this journey and by selecting the priority areas for work;

– to explore and build solutions (= tools) together, to the problems identified during the peer-intervener journey.

The **legal study working group** will address the legal issues identified in conjunction with the work of the employment working group. It will conduct a legal analysis of the possible practice statuses for persons with disabilities as peer-interveners. The value of this working group is that it will make it possible to integrate the new functions of peer-intervener into common law. Indeed, the EPoP approach aims to integrate the instruments of long-term autonomy policy (mainstreaming), with the creation of functions and professions based on user expertise (e.g. the integration of peer intervention into initial training for professionals in the social, medico-social and health sectors or professions related to receiving the public, etc.). These aspects respond to the recommendations of the latest Piveteau report on social and medico-social support professions. It suggests that:

> Similarly, in order to train "expert users" to structure and transfer their expertise, funded training courses should be offered to them, particularly within social work schools (Piveteau 2022)[42].

The **evaluation and research working group** is concerned with monitoring the actions of the EPoP evaluation service provider and in the work required to produce the two monographies conceived within the framework of a research collaboration

42 See: https://www.gouvernement.fr/sites/default/files/document/document/2022/02/experts_acteurs_ensemble_rapport_final_modif.pdf (Accessed August 5, 2022).

contract with the EXPAIRs program. ESO – Rennes 2 University, whose scientific responsibility is carried by Ève Gardien[43]. The first monograph studies the deployment of a Recovery *Training* Center (*Centre de formation au rétablissement*: COFOR) carried out by a collective of affected people in partnership with a Regional *Institute* of Social Work (*Institut régional du travail social*: IRTS) in Hauts-de-France, and the latter reports on a caregiver–patient partnership device initiated by a breast cancer service, including a patient-partner position which has been funded by ARS Nouvelle-Aquitaine for three years.

The **training working group** refined the specifications for the training of peer-interveners based on the work carried out on this subject by the working group of the general secretariat of the Interministerial Disability Committee (*Secrétariat général du Comité interministériel du handicap*: SGCIH) and developed specifications for the training of peer intervention representatives. This will allow for readjustments of ongoing training and the acculturation of specifications by new regions wishing to develop EPoP.

The **communications working group** developed a communications plan to disseminate EPoP actions and the deliverables produced. A communication kit has been designed for social networks to address not only professionals, but also persons with disabilities and their families. The design of a visual identity specific to EPoP was carried out. Finally, a specific site will present:

– legal studies on intervention statutes so as to be understood by non-lawyers thanks to legal design[44];

– a directory of peer-interveners;

– a frequently asked questions (FAQ) fair and a space for exchanges between peer-interveners;

– a kit for deploying the EPoP approach in new regions;

– an EPoP approach communication kit.

43 Ève Gardien participates in the EPoP approach as a scientific advisor. She is a lecturer in the sociology department of Rennes 2 University and a researcher in the ESO laboratory (UMR 6590). She is the scientific manager of the EXPAIRs research program (see: https://expairs.hypotheses.org). Her research has shed light on various themes, including: learning about the body after an accident; disabilities within professional life; social innovations by and for persons with disabilities; accompaniment and peer support; experiential knowledge; etc. To find out more, see: https://perso.univ-rennes2.fr/eve.gardien (Accessed September 19, 2022).

44 Legal design is a set of methods for creating intelligible legal documents and services, using schemata, diagrams, etc.

On the scale of the two experimental territories, the regional chieftaincies drive a **local dynamic** aimed at promoting and supporting the development of peer interventions, both in the medico-social sector and in society in general. A **process of identification and choice, with local stakeholders, of themes** for starting the experiments was carried out. Examples of themes identified during the steering committees to develop intervention opportunities by peers trained by EPoP are the followimg:

– Access to rights and citizenship (exercising the right to vote): peer-interveners could lead awareness-raising activities aimed at electoral service agents in town halls and polling station presidents.

– Civic engagement, volunteering: peer-interveners could present their volunteer work to people supported by ESMS; peer-interveners could lead awareness-raising actions regarding welcoming volunteers with disabilities, with local associations.

– Transitions in career paths: peer-interveners could share their retirement experience with future ESAT[45] retirees, peer-interveners could present their professional integration path to young people from IMPro[46].

– Participation in the decision-making process: peer-interveners could integrate call for projects commissions from *Regional Health Agencies (Agences régionales de santé: ARS)*; peer-interveners could participate in the recruitment of ESMS professionals.

Local experiments are underway, in Hauts-de-France, in the local areas of Amiens-Montdidier-Péronne and Roubaix-Tourcoing and in Nouvelle-Aquitaine in the departments of Gironde, Vienne and Lot-et-Garonne. These experiments include carrying out a part of **basic training for 64 peer-interveners** with disabilities and of training **60 peer intervention representatives** within structures/organizations/companies. These training courses are followed for two years by **territorial activity** comprising of three work areas:

– supporting the implementation of intervention projects by peer-interveners;

– supporting the action plans of peer intervention representatives;

– the impetus of a dynamic going beyond experimentation territories, at the service of regional actors in order to bring out spaces of intervention for peer-interveners, on the basis of different topics, both new and already identified.

45 *Établissement et service d'aide par le travail* (Establishment and work assistance service).

46 *Institut médico-professionnel* (Medico-professional institute). This is a medico-educational institute (*institut médico-éducatif* or IME), which provides general and pre-professional and professional teaching to disabled teenagers aged 14–20 years with an intellectual disability and/or with sensory and/or cognitive disorders, which may be accompanied by other associated disorders.

Another area of work concerns the **promotion of initiatives using peer intervention that exist in France**. To do this, a collaborative site[47] has been launched to promote actions mobilizing peer-interveners or the experiential knowledge of persons with disabilities as well as to discover regional resources.

Complementing the national employment working group, **two employment working groups** are organized in the form of co-design workshops in order to build tools according to identified needs and priorities **in the two experimental regions**.

10.4. The stabilization of a new function, peer-intervener and of a new mission, peer intervention representatives

As explained at the opening of this chapter, EPoP is a national approach that aims to develop the use of peer-interveners. A **peer-intervener** is a person who transforms their experience of living with a disability into expertise that can be passed on to:

– other persons with disabilities with the aim of peer support or mutual aid;

– the medico-social sector, and to institutions and administrations to participate in the development of public policies, the adaptation of support offers, the training of professionals, etc.;

– common law actors in order to support universal accessibility.

These peer-interveners follow training to formalize and acquire new kinds of knowledge. This will allow them to work with other persons affected by a disability and with professionals in various fields. For two years, the regional chieftaincies will support the trained peer-interveners in carrying out their intervention projects.

A legal study will promote the stabilization of this new function by developing possible exercise statuses and the conditions for carrying out peer intervention projects while taking into account the connection between professional activity and allowances for disabled adults (*allocation aux adultes handicapés*: AAH).

Peer intervention representatives are also trained with the aim of developing and promoting recognition of this expertise within the different practice contexts of future peer-interveners (company, type of public service, medico-social establishment, social establishment, hospital, school, etc.).

47 See: https://pair-initiative.fr/.

Peer intervention representatives	Peer-interveners
Types of positions held: mutual support group facilitator, mutual support group coordinator, specialized educator, specialized instructor, social and family economic advisor, ESMS director, ESMS head of service, ESSMS social worker, journey coordinator, inclusive project support worker, caregiver, occupational therapist, *communauté 360* project manager, MDPH head of access to rights, locomotion instructor tasked with integration manager, town hall disability and accessibility project manager, town hall inclusive pathways representative, ARS territorial representative, ARS autism and TND representative, director of an adult protection center.	**Profile types**: mutual support group members, association members, presidents of social life councils, unemployed people or people looking for work or starting a business, FAM residents, workers in ordinary settings.
Support for all disability types (visual, mental, auditory, psychological, motor), autism spectrum disorders	
Action plan examples: Welcome and living space visit to for new residents by FAM residents. Integration within the *communauté 360* team of a peer-intervener in order to provide concrete solutions meeting the aspirations of persons with disabilities.	**Intervention project examples**: Facilitating writing workshops on the theme of mental health recovery. Raising awareness among future professionals about autism spectrum disorders. Awareness-raising actions through testimony. Representing peers as an elected official. Road safety awareness.

Table 10.1. *Global presentation of the characteristics of peer-interveners and peer intervention representatives trained by EPoP*

This is a new mission that professionals will find in the form of a peer intervention resource person. To achieve this, EPoP training, on the one hand, will allow them to deepen their knowledge concerning different knowledge types, and, in particular, how to recognize and support the experiential knowledge of persons with disabilities.

On the other hand, it will promote knowledge of the different dimensions of peer intervention and the operational missions linked to the role of peer intervention representative within each organization. At the same time, support from regional chieftaincies will be provided in order to design and implement action plans specific to each exercise context.

10.5. Presentation of a panel of peer-intervener projects supported by EPoP

In order to reflect the richness and transversality of the intervention projects envisaged by the EPoP approach participants, a project panel is here presented.

10.5.1. *Presentation of Mr. B's project*

As a member of a regional brain injury resource center and president of the *Conseil de la vie sociale* (CVS)[48] of a medico-social support service for disabled adults (*service d'accompagnement médico-social pour adultes handicapés*: SAMSAH), Mr. B. wishes to act as a peer-helper within a structure or a system that supports people with brain injuries following an accident, as well as their loved ones. His project is to intervene at the start of their journey, when a person first discovers their disability. He wishes to be a facilitator in order to support this period of transition and to encourage people's self-determination. Simultaneously, he also has the idea of raising awareness among able-bodied people. The goal is to break down the barriers that separate persons with disabilities from able-bodied people:

> Mr. B.: I was already doing peer-help without realizing it. It was someone from the outside who told me that I was doing peer-help.
>
> It took me 15 years to assign the word disability to myself …
>
> EPoP training gave me a different perspective on disability. […] It is important to accept your disability to have another vision of life. If we are in denial, we cannot project ourselves into the future.
>
> My need and desire are for people with disabilities to move forward […] it's being able to share my experience with newly supported people in order for them to advance more quickly […] being able to turn their weaknesses into a strength. […] By being a peer-helper, I will try to make people understand not to waste time with after-effects, because I took time, a lot of time …
>
> What is also needed is for the people supporting them (professionals and families) to understand that a different life is starting and how to start it on the right foundations.

48 Social Life Council, in English. This is a body that aims to involve service users in the operations of social and medico-social establishments.

> EPoP for me, is also the possibility of raising awareness among able-bodied people: what is disability ? How should one behave? [...] I have an invisible disability. It is complicated. When you have an invisible disability, people don't understand certain words, certain reactions [...] it can be poorly perceived. We don't want to go into details [...] even we are uncomfortable with how we reacted. [...] At first, I had anxiety attacks facing this outlook from able-bodied people [...] then, I started to tell myself that if they look at me it means that I am beautiful [...] it is important to break down the barriers that separate us.
>
> Everyone can have a disability situation in their life and we don't necessarily put up barriers [...] Being able to make people think: "he's different, but he's like me" will be able to break down these barriers ...

10.5.2. *Presentation of Mr. A's project*

A member of a mutual support group for several years, Mr. A. wishes to defend and act in favor of recovery for all. He chose writing as an educational and creative tool. He encourages the expression of his peers by organizing writing workshops. Today, in partnership with EPoP, he offers workshops on the theme of testimony and experiential knowledge to network members.

His goal is to lead and create writing workshops focused on the power to act and on recovery which are open to all:

> Mr. A.: I like to write [...] writing is a facilitator for me to identify my skills and to see how to use them.
>
> I found myself in a mutual support, then in the Board of Directors as a secretary. [...] I lead writing workshops at the mutual support group.
>
> It was the mutual support group facilitator who told me about EPoP. I said no and then after a few weeks I applied ...
>
> I want to improve my skills in terms of what I already know how to do. Understanding what peer intervention is [...] having a more theoretical contribution to gain more legitimacy [...] knowing how to open my writing workshops to all types of disabilities without exception. Add to that the fact that I've never done any facilitating before ...

> I want people to talk about disability, it's not a bad word, and above all that they express themselves with writing games, from very simple ones to the most complicated. It sets things in motion.
>
> I like seeing people face to face. I feel like I'm creating value, social connection. That's what drives me.
>
> EPoP allowed me to carry out my first writing workshops outside of my mutual support group [...] Without the EPoP training, I would never have started. It's my first salary, symbolically, it's important [...] a field of possibilities has opened up for me.

10.5.3. *Presentation of Mrs. S's project*

Mrs. S. wishes to develop a professional activity around making the touristic offer accessible. She is exploring two possibilities: creating her own consulting business or joining a company in the sector. She wishes to use her expertise to encourage inclusive tourism:

> Mrs. S.: I have a Master's degree in Italian studies, but my first professional experience was in tourism. I then worked in an ARS. I advised the ARS for the greater involvement of persons with disabilities in the implementation of public health policies. This is where I discovered EPoP. It's an interesting project, because it's there to allow people to express themselves, to give them confidence, to value them. [...] I have experienced infantilization, devaluation, and mistreatment in establishments [...] People must be supported, valued and encouraged to claim and exercise their rights. Otherwise dehumanization spikes and the result is dramatic for the person's future.
>
> I signed up for training to follow the project from the inside [at the time, Mrs. S. was still working at the ARS] and for my professional project. [...] Currently, I am unemployed. I am following the EPoP training in parallel to my reflection on my professional project. I want to return to tourism. [...] Tourism is a leisure and I tell myself that if efforts are made within this area it can bear fruit elsewhere. I want to move away from the vision of disability through the prism of health. I'm tired of going through the law and through obligation in ensuring respect for the fundamental rights of a population. I'm not interested in putting quotas in place or anything. What I want is to teach people, work with them, learn from them so that we can evolve together and

> so that they realize that inclusion is not necessarily complicated or expensive. It is often a simple question of common sense, respect, consideration and will. I want to make people's representations evolve, without reverting to the law or obligation.
>
> I would like to work with tourism stakeholders to facilitate travel for persons with disabilities. I have traveled a lot and when you live with any disability, it is far from easy. I have experience and I would like to share it with stakeholders who are interested in changing things, developing their offering, as well as their customers. I wish to work with common law actors in order to avoid establishing the same specialized sector time and time again, at all costs, since it amounts to accepting a certain segregation and the exclusion of persons living with a disability.
>
> I would like to work as a freelancer with all kinds of stakeholders (airports, travel agencies, town hall services, etc.) or as an employee of a travel agency. But I still have to explore all of the possibilities.

10.5.4. *Presentation of Mr. J's project*

Mr. J. is a psychiatric nurse and member of a mutual support group. By joining EPoP, Mr. J. wishes to develop his skills as a mental health peer-helper. With his management's support, his experience with EPoP allows him to think about an evolution of his nursing position and to equip him in his journey:

> Mr. J.: The diagnosis of my disability came quite late, I was 37 years old [...] the post-diagnosis was very complicated, I had a major phase of depression [...] I felt relief and at the same time I couldn't believe it ... After 2 years, I accepted it, because the psychologist who had diagnosed me and who followed me [...] helped me with day-to-day tools.
>
> I got to know EPoP after this diagnosis ... I thought that if I got closer to other people with the same disability as me, I would be less isolated. I approached a mutual support group and tried to set up workshops with the president of the mutual support group with a focus on autonomy (hygiene, administration skills, health, sexuality) for those in more difficult situations ... This is when the facilitator told me that there was a way to formalize this type of workshop via peer-support training. I also spoke about it at the hospital where I work and my manager accepted that I take part.

> Today I have a project on two fronts: to continue to offer workshops in my mutual support group by structuring them and setting up a peer-help project for people with autism spectrum disorders in the CMP [*centre médico-psychologique* or medico-psychological center] where I work as a nurse. I want to propose solutions that I have implemented since I was little and others that psychologists have presented to me and that I have been able to experiment with.
>
> I think that at the CMP the differentiation between the role of nurse and peer-helper will be difficult [...] I hope that the support from EPoP will help me to better define it [...] I am thinking about it ...

10.5.5. *Presentation of Mr. JB's project*

For several years, Mr. JB. has been carrying out disability awareness activities. He carried out awareness-raising interventions in the social sector and traveled across France in a wheelchair, stopping in several cities to carry out awareness-raising actions. He will soon be publishing his biography. He wishes to use this written testimony to continue to raising awareness of disability in all environments and among all audiences. Participation in EPoP allows him to consolidate his skills and to open up to new intervention methods:

> Mr. JB.: During the Covid crisis, I thought a lot and decided to write my biography. It will be published in the coming months. Based on this biography, I want to continue to raise awareness about disability.
>
> The EPoP project was presented in my nursing home and bingo, I decided to register.
>
> The training introduces me to other disabilities which do not have the same difficulties as mine. It allows me to make a lot of contacts, it makes me more credible, because I will be able to say that I also have some training experience. Perhaps EPoP will lead me to other training courses to intervene with the general public and to develop experiential knowledge.
>
> I wish to carry out public awareness interventions in order to testify about my illness, my disability and to say that despite the difficulties encountered, with willpower nothing is forbidden, many things are possible. Interventions with professionals who are going to work in the social sector. Interventions with people with motor disabilities, their families and those around them.

> During EPoP support, they offered me possible interventions: intervening with medical–social professionals by speaking on well-treatment/mistreatment of young people leaving IME and their parents to talk about life after IME.

10.5.6. *Presentation of Mrs. D's project*

Mrs. D. created her microenterprise with great perseverance in 2021, which offers parenting support for parents with visual impairments. She has not yet carried out any interventions. The training and support for carrying out peer intervention projects offered by EPoP will equip her in the implementation of her intervention projects:

> Mrs. D.: I have training in secretarial work, but with my disability and my lack of experience, I have not had any work opportunities [...] there have been many closed doors.
>
> I was supported by a parenting support service with my first child [Mrs. D. has three children] and I thought: "Why not help other people with disabilities?" [...] I created my microenterprise in 2021 to provide parenting support for parents with visual impairments. I searched the Internet to find out how to do it, I did it myself [...] but I haven't practiced any interventions yet. Well, it wasn't really the ideal time to propose that either [Mrs. D. refers to the Covid health crisis].
>
> A friend told me about EPoP and I went to an introductory meeting. I felt like I needed to get involved. The training reinforced my idea that even if we have a disability, we can intervene. Several times I was told: "You are not a professional". I regained my self-confidence. I hope this will open doors for me and that it can be a success. That we can create a network that will legitimize us.
>
> I would like to work with parents or future parents with a visual impairment and with nursing and paramedical staff (maternity care, PMI, nursery, etc.). I do not want to take on their roles. I want to show, the right actions in a different breath, because parents with a visual impairment can take care of their children differently. I want to stop hearing: "Are you sure you can take care of your child?". We

want to be considered just like everyone else, we are parents first and foremost, disability comes in later[49].

10.6. Conclusion

At the time of writing this chapter, the EPoP deployment is halfway through its course. Some training sessions have been completed and others are still taking place, the first support for peer-intervener projects of and peer intervention representatives are commencing. Parallel to this, a peer intervention action map is being constructed at the national level and a legal working group will soon be underway.

Indeed, work to formalize and stabilize activities linked to the mobilization of experiential knowledge remains necessary. To do this, a legal analysis will be carried out of the different modes of exercise of peer-interveners (volunteering, salaried work, coaching, consultancy, training, general availability, etc.) and the structures that can provide the service (sole trader, establishment and work assistance service: ESAT (*établissement et service d'aide par le travail*) outside of cities, adapted company, supported employment, classic company exploring different status types (i.e. *solidarity social utility company)*; ESUS (*entreprise solidaire d'utilité sociale*), simplified joint stock company; SAS (*société par actions simplifiée*), limited liability company; SARL (*société à responsabilité limité*), cooperative, etc.).

Tools will be developed and made accessible by a legal design service provider, such as a guide for peer-interveners, for entities wishing to provide this service and for clients/employers; a mapping of statuses with their advantages and disadvantages, the drafting/correction of legal tools necessary for the exercise of missions (employment contracts, service agreements, insurance, general sale conditions, etc.). A number of hours of legal consultation with regard to concrete issues will also be offered.

The early stages of reflection concerning the formalization and sustainability of the network driven by the EPoP approach in the two experimental regions are also beginning. The aim is to anchor these new practices in the territories and to continue to support peer intervention initiatives.

The evaluation of the current experiment underway in the first two territories will make it possible to make adjustments and analyze blockages and success points in order to transfer the lessons to future EPoP carriers and its beneficiaries.

---

49 PMI: *Protection maternelle et infantile*. Maternal and child protection, in English.

The spread and deployment of EPoP in other regions will over time continuously fuel the use of peer interventions in all settings.

Today, various actors from other territories engaged in work and initiatives wishing to promote and develop the power to act as well as the social and civic participation of people with disabilities wish to develop EPoP.

In order to support and coordinate these new deployments, the Fédération des CREAI[50] will participate in expanding into new EPoP regions alongside its other partners. The territorial anchoring of CREAIs and the quality of hybrid places (*lieux tiers*) at the intersection of the views of managers and support structures professionals, of the people concerned and of public authorities, represent resources for the spread of EPoPs.

10.7. References

Albrecht, G.L., Ravaud, J.-F., Stiker, H.-J. (2001). L'émergence des disability studies : état des lieux et perspectives. *Sciences sociales et santé*, 19(4), 43–73.

Anspach, R.R. (1979). From stigma to identity politics: Political activism among the physically disabled and former mental patients. *Social Science & Medicine*, 13A, 765–773.

Bacle, P. (2021). De l'aidé à l'aidant, un métier en devenir paru dans. *Actualités sociales hebdomadaires (ASH)*, 3233.

Borkman, T. (1976). Experiential knowledge: A new concept for the analysis of self-help groups. *Social Service Review*, 50(3), 445–456.

De Burca, G., Keohane, R.O., Sabel, C. (2013). New modes of pluralist global governance. *New York University Journal of International Law and Politics*, 45(1), 723–786.

Estecahandy, P. (2020). Un chez-soi d'abord : accompagner les personnes sans abri vers et dans leur logement. *La santé en action*, 451, 46–49.

Eyraud, B., Saetta, S., Taran, I., Cobbaut, J. (2018). La participation des personnes en situation de handicap au débat démocratique : retours sur une démarche collaborative autour de la CDPH. *Participations*, 22, 109–138.

Flora, L. (2021). Recognition of patients' experiential knowledge and co-production of care knowledge with patients and citizens in the 21st century. In *Altering Frontiers: Organizational Innovations in Healthcare*, Grenier, C. and Oiry, E. (eds). ISTE Ltd, London, and John Wiley and Sons, New York.

---

50 A national framework partnership agreement was signed between the French Red Cross and the Fédération des CREAI (ANCREAI) in Autumn 2021.

Fraszczak, L. (2019). Le "logement d'abord" : concept, état des lieux, enjeux pour l'applicabilité aux centres d'hébergement. *Mémoire de fin d'études DESSMS*, École des hautes études en santé publique, Rennes.

Gardien, È. (2021). Instituer le pair-accompagnement au risque de perdre les qualités spécifiques de la relation entre pairs. In *L'accompagnement par les pairs : enjeux de participation et de professionnalisation*, Gardien, È. (ed.). PUG, Grenoble, 93–111.

Gesmond, T., Cinget, A., Estecahandy, P. (2016). La pair-aidance. Working paper, Ministère du Logement et de l'Habitat durable, Délégation interministérielle à l'hébergement et à l'accès au logement, Paris [Online]. Available at: https://www.gouvernement.fr/sites/default/files/contenu/piece-jointe/2016/09/note_pair_aidance.pdf [Accessed 5 August 2022].

Gillot, D. (2019). Sécuriser les parcours, cultiver les compétences. Report, Ministère des Solidarités et de la Santé, Ministère du Travail, Secrétariat d'Etat chargé des personnes handicapées, Paris [Online]. Available at: http://www.cometefrance.com/wp-content/uploads/2019/07/Securiser-les-parcours-cultiver-les-competences-Preserver-nos-aidants-TOMES-1-2-CNCPH-Juin-2018.pdf [Accessed 5 August 2022].

Piveteau, D. (2022). Experts, acteurs, ensemble... pour une société qui change. Report, Direction générale de la cohésion sociale, Paris [Online]. Available at: https://www.gouvernement.fr/sites/default/files/document/document/2022/02/experts_acteurs_ensemble_rapport_final_modif.pdf [Accessed 5 August 2022].

Piveteau, D., Saïd, A., Debrabant, F.-X., Jaffre, D., Perrin, A. (2014). Zéro sans solution : le devoir collectif de permettre un parcours de vie sans rupture, pour les personnes en situation de handicap et pour leurs proches. Report, Ministère des Solidarités et de la Santé, Paris [Online]. Available at: https://solidarites-sante.gouv.fr/IMG/pdf/rapport_zero_sans_solution_pdf [Accessed 5 August 2022].

Rabeharisoa, V., Callon, M., Demonty, B. (2000a). Les associations de malades et la recherche. I. Des self-help groups aux associations de malades. *Médecine/sciences*, 16, 945–949.

Rabeharisoa, V., Callon, M., Demonty, B. (2000b). Les associations de malades et la recherche. II. Les formes d'engagement des associations de malades dans la recherche en France. *Médecine/sciences*, 17, 1225–1231.

Secrétariat général du comité interministériel du handicap (2020–2021). Formation d'intervenants-pairs en situation de handicap, Paris [Online]. Available at: https://www.gouvernement.fr/sites/default/files/contenu/piece-jointe/2022/01/20200902_cih_formation_des_pairs_v20_21_formations.pdf [Accessed 5 August 2022].

Sizaret, A. (2020). Dossier documentaire sur la pair-aidance. Ireps Bourgogne Franche-Comté.

Solidarités usagers psy (n.d.). Les pairs aidants à l'étranger [Online]. Available at: https://www.solidarites-usagerspsy.fr/s-engager/les-pairs-aidants/les-pair-aidants-a-l-etranger/ [Accessed 5 August 2022].

Staedel, B. and Hude, W. (2020). Programme médiateurs de santé-pairs. *Actualité et dossier en santé publique*, 110, 8–9.

Tourette-Turgis, C. (2013). L'université des patients : une reconnaissance institutionnelle des savoirs des malades. *Le sujet dans la cité*, 4, 173–185.

Troisoeufs, A. (2020). Patients intervenants, médiateurs de santé-pairs : quelles figures de la pair-aidance en santé ? *Rhizome*, 27(36), 75–76.

Winance, M. and Ravaud, J. (2010). Le handicap, positionnement politique et identité subjective : le cas des pays anglo-saxons. *Les cahiers du Centre Georges Canguilhem*, 4, 69–86.

11

The Potential for Digital Health to Reframe the Role of Compassion in Patient Experience Innovation

11.1. Introduction

There is widespread concern about the "compassion crisis" in healthcare – that is, the "absence of (or inconsistency in) compassionate patient care" (Trzeciak Rivers 2017). The literature is peppered with reports of limited demonstrations of, if not a decline in compassion in healthcare (Lown 2014; Lown et al. 2015; Cocker Joss 2016). Consider the Francis (2013) report, which exposed deficiencies in patient care at the Mid Staffordshire NHS Foundation Trust and called for greater compassionate care. Similarly, Australia's Royal Commission into Aged Care Quality and Safety (2021) revealed myriad instances of substandard care, including abuse, the overuse of physical and chemical restraint, as well as neglect – consequently, it was recommended that aged care "be delivered with compassion".

Although compassion is fundamental to humanity (Williams 2018), it is particularly important in healthcare. As the Institute of Medicine (2001) observed, "health care is not just another service industry. Its fundamental nature is characterized by people taking care of other people in times of need and stress". As such, compassion matters and is an essential aspect of healthcare, rather than merely an optional extra (Fotaki 2015). This follows (at least) three key reasons. First, compassion has personal benefits. It can promote courage, understanding, healing, clinical outcomes and well-being (Davidson 2011; Feldman and Kuyken 2011; MacBeth and Gumley 2012; Clayton 2013; Gilbert 2014). Furthermore, a capacity to demonstrate compassion can increase receptivity to social support, which can

---

Chapter written by Lester LEVY, Ann DADICH and Kevin LOWE.

improve an ability to manage stress (Cosley et al. 2010). Second, compassion has social benefits. By bolstering trust between patients and healthcare professionals, it can enhance the quality of information that patients provide (Epstein et al. 2005; Sanghavi 2006). Third, compassion offers organizational benefits – it can address the oft-cited issue of workplace bullying (Huppert 2017; Zhang et al. 2018), as well as increase patients' perceived quality of, and satisfaction with healthcare (Redelmeier et al. 1995; Frampton et al. 2013; Pfaff and Markaki 2017).

The decline in compassion is attributed to myriad factors. These include: the conscious transition from a vocational model of healthcare to a professional model (Straughair 2012); the parallel marketization and bureaucratization of healthcare (Bradshaw 2009); neoliberalism, which serves to commodify healthcare (de Zulueta 2013); the pressure to be productive (Hallowell 1999; Shapiro 2012); hierarchies that create large power distances and alienate patients from healthcare professionals (van Kleef et al. 2008; Zigmond 2011) and (relatedly) reduced autonomy and freedom (Dutton et al. 2006). Collectively, these factors can contribute to "existential neglect", whereby healthcare professionals detach themselves from patients (Agledahl et al. 2011).

With the rise of digital health, it is unclear whether such innovation helps or hinders compassion in healthcare. For instance, digital technologies have opened new opportunities to: promote connectivity across geographical divides and time (Day et al. 2021; Kweon et al. 2011; Rosen et al. 2013), which was (and remains) particularly helpful during the Covid-19 pandemic (Ali et al. 2022); meet patients' and carers' changing needs and preferences, thereby offering more personalized care (Barak and Grohol 2011); foster understanding via digital storytelling (Hardy and Sumner 2018) as well as "teach or train health care professionals to provide compassionate health care which would not be previously possible" (Kemp et al. 2020). Despite these benefits, digital technologies also have a dark side. In addition to requiring patients, carers and healthcare professionals to become comfortable with using different modes of communication, if not develop new skills, they can represent an obstacle between healthcare professionals and patients and carers, creating or reinforcing distance (Swinglehurst et al. 2011; Granados-Pembertty and Arias-Valencia 2013) – or, worse still, digital technologies can encourage self-centeredness and avarice. As Day and colleagues (2021) observed:

> Technological proliferation has increased connectivity, lowered global barriers, and provided new avenues for trade and livelihood; while also fomenting greed, competitiveness and comparative individuals and societies... there are few signs that thoughtful care and consideration has been given to the sociotechnical implications of this growth, at least not to a degree that is commensurate with the rapid pace of technological development... The dispersion of information

> undoubtedly carries some putative benefits for producing more compassionate societies... Yet concerningly, in Western society at least we have witnessed an alarming reduction in humanity's capacity to understand and empathize with ourselves and one another... a trend that worryingly corresponds to the growth of virtual social networks and smartphones.

Given the opportunities afforded by digital health, this chapter clarifies the relationship between compassionate care and digital health and, in doing so, makes a case for compassionate digital health – that is, "technologies... that harness contemporary advances to actively restore, humanize and strengthen our relationships with one another as well as ourselves" (Day et al. 2021). This is achieved with reference to bona fide exemplars to demonstrate how – despite the increasing ubiquity of digital health and the decline of compassion – digital health has the potential to foster compassionate care. Following this, the chapter explicates the associated implications for scholars, healthcare professionals, policymakers as well as patients and carers. Before presenting these exemplars, the following section briefly defines the terms compassion and digital health.

11.2. Definitions

11.2.1. *Compassion*

Although compassion, empathy and sympathy are related concepts, they are different. Compassion is "a feeling of concern for another person's suffering which is accompanied by the motivation to help... [It is] feeling *for* and not feeling *with* the other" (Singer and Klimecki 2014; original italics). Rooted in an understanding of lived experiences (Hanford 2015; Denneson et al. 2018; Stevens 2018), compassion involves emotion, cognitive appraisal and prosocial motivation – that is, an intention to act to alleviate or prevent others' suffering (Gilbert 2014; Simpson and Farr-Wharton 2020). Specifically, compassion involves: "1. Awareness of an antecedent (i.e. suffering or need in another individual); 2. Feeling 'moved'; that is, having a subjective physical experience that often involves involuntary arousal of branches in the autonomic nervous system; 3. Appraisals of one's own bodily feeling, social role and abilities within the context of the suffering; 4. Judgments about the person who is suffering and the situational context; and 5. Engagement of the neural systems that drive social affiliation and caregiving, and motivate helping" (Goetz and Simon-Thomas 2017). Thus, compassion entails a tolerance for uncomfortable feelings, so as to be able to act to offer assistance (Strauss et al. 2016). However, compassion might not culminate with the action required to alleviate or prevent others' pain or discomfort (Gladkova 2010).

While compassion is action-oriented (Schantz 2007; Catlett and Lovan 2011), empathy is "the capacity to share the feelings of others… mak[ing]… it possible to resonate with others' positive and negative feelings" (Singer Klimecki 2014). Sympathy, however, is the feeling triggered by a recognition that someone has experienced misfortune (Gladkova 2010) – it involves "feelings of pity or sorrow for another" (Strudwick et al. 2019), especially someone who is perceived to be suffering unfairly (Sinclair et al. 2017).

Despite some degree of conceptual clarity about compassion, there is currently no valid and reliable scale to comprehensively measure it (Strauss et al. 2016). Although there are some strong measures (Neff 2003; Hacker 2008), they do not encompass all facets of compassion. This is likely to hinder scholarship that serves to advance understandings and demonstrations of compassion.

11.2.2. *Digital health*

Digital health is an encompassing term that generally refers to technologies that serve to promote healthcare. This includes technologies to: collect and share relevant data and information; communicate; prevent (mental) health issues; intervene early; diagnose; treat; rehabilitate; counsel; educate as well as manage and administrate (AIHW 2020; Ali et al. 2022). Digital health comprises: telehealth – that is, "the use of information and communication technologies (ICTs) to deliver health services where there is physical separation between care providers and/or the recipients over both long and short distances" (Gogia 2019); telemedicine, which is "remote clinical services in the form of patient and clinician contact"; electronic health records; wearable devices; robotics and artificial intelligence; eHealth, or electronic health (Oh et al. 2005); mHealth, or mobile health (Marcolino et al. 2018) as well as "emerging areas, such as the use of advanced computing sciences in big data, genomics and artificial intelligence" (WHO 2019). Examples include (but are not limited to): "My Health Record, fitness trackers, smartwatches, sleep trackers, wellness applications, SMS [short message service] reminders via mobile messaging, electronic discharge summaries, electronic prescribing, secure messaging, voice interfaces, medical drones, paperless hospitals, implanted microchips, [and] robotic nurse assistants" (AIHW 2020). Collectively, these examples of digital health can improve the reach of, and access to healthcare, as well as optimize effectiveness and efficiency (Wiljer et al. 2019).

11.3. Compassion in digital health

Digital health is arguably the most significant opportunity to improve health outcomes, make healthcare more accessible, reduce its cost and improve patient experience innovation, creating enthusiasm and unease in equal measure (Shaw et al. 2018; Lemire 2019). Multifaceted issues can arise from the role of digital health in patient experience innovation. These include patient safety, privacy, equity, digital literacy, as well as the principal theme for this chapter, which is to safeguard the critical "human touch" in the relationship between clinicians and patients (Kinsella 2020). If compassion is the unalloyed foundation of the conventional healthcare system, then digital health should be viewed through this same prism. Digital health can empower patients as participants in the conception of patient experience innovation as it represents a cultural as much, or even more than a technical change. Making (and understanding) this distinction is crucial to avert technological solutionism, which can dilute the "human touch" between clinicians, patients and their carers. As digital health is increasingly adopted, it is important for health systems and those who work in them to never lose sight of healthcare as a "deep human enterprise" focused on "helping people by relieving their suffering" (Lemire 2019).

In this context, it is worth pointing to Kinsella (2020) highlighting the gentler, kinder and more subtle, yet pivotal aspects of the clinician–patient interface such as compassion, empathy and trust. He observed this "relational moral competency" should not be diminished to the point that clinical capacity is reduced to technical expertise only. Kinsella promoted the notion that digital health solutions have the potential "to release more time for those patients who most need it". Day and colleagues (2021) reflected that the effects of digital health advances, which despite having the potential to significantly improve population and personal health, could detrimentally impact compassion in an unreceptive healthcare setting. Terry and Cain (2016) noted that digital health interactions lack the emotional markers and prompts that characterize in-person interactions. The unintended consequences of these exchanges are that they are more likely to be perceived as insensitive and uncaring.

Before the momentum for digital health adoption really gathers pace, more thought should be given to ensuring the healthcare ecosystem is ripe for securing and enhancing compassionate healthcare. Day et al. (2021) called out this issue through their observation that there are "few signs that thoughtful care and consideration has been given to the socio-technical implications" of the likely trajectory of digital health uptake. Striking an optimistic note, they considered there is a rich vein of evidence that "compassionate states and prosocial behavior" can be augmented by modern digital technologies. This will not happen without sustained, high levels of encouragement and support and a siren call to "courageously revisit our social contract". Wiljer et al. (2019) supported this approach. They suggested that an integrated perspective of the digital literature discourse on compassion will advance a wider understanding of compassionate care in the digitally evolving healthcare environment. This would be achieved by "providing evidence-based guidance on how digital health is to be incorporated into the practice and teaching of compassionate care". Hodges et al. (2020) extended this line of thought about the potential of digital health to undermine and weaken compassion in healthcare settings. They made a strong case for compassion as the "guiding purpose" of healthcare. While they expressed concerns about the potential adverse impact of emerging digital health technologies, they agreed with Wiljer and colleagues that these technologies can create new pathways for compassionate care. The unfavorable impacts of digital health technologies on compassion can be avoided by creating an enabling culture and environment, but this will not happen without the purposeful leadership of both health systems and health professions.

11.4. Deconstructing patient experience

11.4.1. *Patient one*

Writing in the *New England Journal of Medicine*, Gregg (2022), a medical doctor recounted, an experience she had as a patient with digital health. Previously well, Gregg experienced sudden onset multiple joint pain, weakness and an inability to undertake routine tasks. She was concerned, but confident that she would get the care she needed and scheduled an urgent telehealth consultation through her health insurer's app. She struggled to work and felt worse but was relieved that she would soon be able to share her concerns with an experienced, relatable and reassuring colleague. She assumed this colleague would thoughtfully work though a list of questions relevant to her symptoms. She sensed her doctor would be unhurried, compassionate and fully focused on her. Her reality was a "fresh-faced boy-man" who abruptly appeared on her computer screen and, without eye contact, asked how he could help. She described the nature, onset and rapid deterioration of her symptoms. The doctor nodded, tapped his keyboard, said they should check a few laboratory tests, smiled and was gone.

Not unfriendly, simply an efficient, indifferent and uncompassionate digital health experience.

Surprised by the abruptness, as well as the lack of depth and warmth of the digital encounter, she received her laboratory results via the app over the next few days. All the abnormal results were evidenced by red exclamation marks. She found the lack of follow-up about her results disheartening. She was anxious, apprehensive and distressed but still received no further contact, despite the significantly abnormal laboratory results.

Not safe medical practice, simply a deeply unresponsive and uncompassionate digital health patient experience.

She messaged the online clinic multiple times through the patient portal, with each message urgently appealing for a response, but radio silence persisted.

Shamefully detached, simply an unacceptably unsafe and uncompassionate digital health patient experience.

She eventually received a message to visit her primary care doctor to discuss her abnormal laboratory results. By now very unwell and totally exasperated, she made her way through the maze of telephone calls, was placed on-hold and was transferred. Eventually, after demanding to speak to someone, she received a telephone call from a doctor who apologized, explained her case had been overlooked, and that he would arrange for her to see a specialist the same day. The specialist prescribed medications to relieve the symptoms while the underlying cause was investigated. Unfortunately, this poorly executed digital health experience, layered on her illness, distracted her from her own medical practice routines.

The deconstruction of this digital health experience of a doctor as a patient opens a different view of the world of healthcare's heightening dependence on digital technology and its potential to undermine compassionate care. Undoubtedly, Gregg could also have had an uncompassionate, face-to-face patient experience in a physical clinic environment – this is particularly because patients increasingly find themselves as the "third party" during their in-person clinician interactions along with the computer and its ubiquitous electronic medical record (Strudwick et al. 2019). However, it is much easier to summarily conclude a digital interaction compared to an in-person interaction. It is also helplessly challenging to find your way through a digital health environment, compared to presenting to reception at a bricks-and-mortar clinic. What is compelling and disquieting in equal measure is how little needed to change for Gregg to have a medically safe and compassionate patient experience. In her digital consultation, the clinician could have amiably introduced himself, shown interest, discussed whether she was well enough to work and clarified the next steps. He should have ensured she had 24/7 contact details and asked whether she had appropriate support. None of this is difficult and all of it could be accomplished very time efficiently. It simply needed a clinician and health system that cared. Gregg unfortunately, had a patient experience reflective of a complacent and indifferent clinician and health system – an all too familiar narrative.

11.4.2. *Patient two*

The experience of another doctor, Gupta (2019), as a patient, centered on her large, rare spinal cord tumor with potentially dire consequences. As a patient, she directly experienced the "tension between technological efficiency and personal relationship building". Advanced exponential health technologies, including robotic surgical techniques, were required to add "a high degree of precision to the procedure" she underwent. Gupta revealed that those clinicians with a warm heart who were active, inclusive and compassionate listeners helped her most in navigating the most challenging phase of her life, as she dealt with this very serious tumor. Her post-illness perspective was that health systems in the digital era and those who work in them need to find a way to "bridge compassionate care with technology".

She believed that, as a health professional's time becomes "increasingly scarce and increasingly valuable", appropriately deployed digital health can credibly enhance the patient experience. Gupta's (2019) reflection on her patient experience in the digital age should echo through the entire world of healthcare – "I recognized the value of provider–patient relationships as a physician, but I truly learned the power and significance of these relationships as a patient-survivor".

A good clinical outcome and a compassionate digital health patient experience.

11.4.3. *Patient three*

Topol (2019a), a global digital health thought leader, recounted his experience following a knee replacement, the terminal result of an uncommon condition, osteochondritis dissecans, which he developed as a teenager. In this condition, the bone beneath the cartilage dies due to poor blood flow and, in his case, led to extensive knee surgery, limited physical activity and pain. His orthopedic surgeon characterized him as a perfect candidate for a knee replacement surgery as he was relatively young, thin and in good health. The postoperative rehabilitation phase was surprisingly problematic with pain, knee swelling and limited movement. During his post-surgical visit with his orthopedic surgeon, Topol described his problems and how badly they affected him. His orthopedic surgeon's blunt response was, "You should have your internist prescribe antidepressant medications". Topol described his care as devoid of empathy and compassion.

A month later, Topol's (2019a) wife discovered the term arthrofibrosis in her search for clues, which was new to him; yet this turned out to be the underlying diagnosis for his postoperative problems. Arthrofibrosis is an infrequent complication that occurs following knee replacement and one that his surgeon had not raised as a possible postoperative issue. This was surprising; although it was an infrequent complication, it was more common than the risk of infection, which he was informed of prior to surgery. He shifted his care to a new physical therapist who did help and treated him with empathy and compassion, but the experience continued to cause him anguish.

Topol (2019a) made the powerful point that artificial intelligence, a digital health technology, could have played an important predictive role in highlighting his likely challenging postsurgical period, given his particular history. This would have indicated the need for a personally tailored rehabilitation program. Pushing the boundaries, Topol suggested that a digital medical assistant in his smartphone, could have (through artificial intelligence reviewing the published literature) alerted him to his higher risk of arthrofibrosis that a customary rehabilitation program posed. This terrible problem could have been circumvented if his history of osteochondritis dissecans was included in the discussion about the risk of surgery.

Topol's (2019a) reflection was that, while the technical component of his surgery was well done, his clinical care was neither holistic or compassionate. His experience left him with a deep concern for the care of patients with chronic medical conditions. Topol described them as being "roughed up" by the health system and clinicians, as he felt he was. He believed he was treated with a "profound lack of human connection and empathy".

A poor clinical outcome and an uncompassionate patient experience.

11.5. Blending digital health with the human touch for positive patient experiences

All three doctors turned patients were insiders with deep knowledge of the inner workings of the health system; they were also digitally literate with health insurance and access to their own smartphones and computers. Despite this, Gregg (2022) described how she "had to crawl, claw and fight my way to someone's attention". Similarly, Topol (2019a) observed the "lack of compassion" in his care was "palpable". While there is an expectation of equity in care, it is instructive that two of three patients with such sophisticated and intimate knowledge of how to navigate the health system received such inadequate and insensitive care. The deconstruction of these three cases suggests that it is unlikely that "empathy is the backbone of the relationship with patients" in all patient interactions, as Topol has advocated it should be. Digital health can radically advance many aspects of the patient experience, but cannot deliver on its own, the essential human attributes of compassion and empathy (Topol 2019b).

There is an emerging discussion about the concept of "compassionate technologies", which spotlights the point of convergence between digital health and the clinician–patient interface (Day et al. 2021; Shin 2021). The suggestion is that "compassionate technologies" can facilitate a clinician's emotional awareness of, and attentiveness to patient concerns, fears and suffering. Reference has been made to a possible "digital compassion paradox", where the "human touch" and digital health are irreconcilable (Kinsella 2020). Wiljer et al. (2019) questioned whether compassionate care demands an "intimate, human-to-human interaction", suggesting that digital health patient experiences might not measure up to patient expectations of compassionate care. In this context, it is worth considering Gupta's (2019) perspective as doctor-turned-patient. Gupta proposed that the clinician–patient relationship in the digital age should preferentially commence with an in-person exchange. Once a relationship has been formed, coherently configured digital health can augment the relationship, creating "the balance between compassionate care and technological efficiency".

11.6. Conclusion

For years, there has been talk of the dividing line between traditional healthcare and digital health would being erased by the exponential adoption of digital health; but at best, progress has been sluggish and inconsistent. The advent of Covid-19, however, almost instantly legitimized many facets of digital health and the adoption of digital health picked up momentum. In this context, there has also been increasing dialogue about digital health disruption, which is essentially the transformation of existing healthcare systems by innovative digital health and operating models. The underlying basis for digital disruption is the explicit recognition of patient needs and the value provided to them. Here, value is characterized by simplicity, convenience, accessibility, equity, safety, affordability and critically an excellent patient experience. Enhancing and not diminishing the patient's experience is explicitly the intent of digital health and digital health disruption.

According to Topol (2019b), the adoption of digital health can improve the patient–clinician relationship through the "gift of time" delivered to clinicians. This "gift of time" can result when smarter technology assumes many of a clinician's routine tasks thereby releasing valuable time for authentic communication and compassionate care (Topol 2019a). However, there is a relevant concern expressed by Sparrow and Hatherley (2020) – namely, when digital health does indeed free clinicians time, "the economics of health care" will determine that time is "used to move more patients through the system". The net result of this is that, unlike the view of the digital health optimists, these new technologies might not inevitably increase the likelihood of more care and compassion. They argued that the current underlying reasons for the erosion of human contact in the patient–clinician relationship are primarily economic, "which is to say, ultimately political and technological change alone is unlikely to reverse this".

The relationship between digital health and compassion is paradoxical. On the one hand, the widespread adoption of digital health may enhance compassionate care, while on the other hand, there is the potential for a detrimental impact on compassionate care. The leadership, culture, policies and processes of the health system in concert with the mindset, values, behaviors and engagement of the clinicians will have a significant influence on whether digital health enhances or diminishes compassionate care. Perhaps health systems should pay more attention to Hodges et al. (2020) who emphasized that the ultimate responsibility for the compassionate use of digital health rests with the humans who facilitated its use in the first place. Health systems and clinicians would do well to reflect on Robinson's (2003) sentiments that health technologies do not replace "the caring of a human soul" and "the warmth of a human heart in healing the sick and injured". Hyacinth (2017) endorsed these sentiments, opining that computers will not "replace humans, for they are… devoid of compassion, feelings, empathy and life".

11.7. References

Agledahl, K.M., Gulbrandsen, P., Førde, R. Wifstad, Å. (2011). Courteous but not curious: How doctors' politeness masks their existential neglect. A qualitative study of video-recorded patient consultations. *Journal of Medical Ethics*, 37(11), 1–5.

AIHW (2020). Digital health [Online]. Available at: https://www.aihw.gov.au/reports/australias-health/digital-health [Accessed 26 January 2022].

Ali, S., Kleib, M., Paul, P., Petrovskaya, O., Kennedy, M. (2022). Compassionate nursing care and the use of digital health technologies: A scoping review. *International Journal of Nursing Studies*, 127(104161). doi: 10.1016/j.ijnurstu.2021.104161.

Barak, A. and Grohol, J.M. (2011). Current and future trends in internet-supported mental health interventions. *Journal of Technology in Human Services*, 29(3), 155–196.

Bradshaw, A. (2009). Measuring nursing care and compassion: The McDonaldised nurse? *Journal of Medical Ethics*, 35(8), 465–468.

Catlett, S. and Lovan, S.R. (2011). Being a good nurse and doing the right thing: A replication study. *Nursing Ethics*, 18(1), 54–63.

Clayton, A.R. (2013). How "person-centered" care helped guide me toward recovery from mental illness. *Health Affairs*, 32(3), 622–626.

Cocker, F. and Joss, N. (2016). Compassion fatigue among healthcare, emergency and community service workers: A systematic review. *International Journal of Environmental Research and Public Health*, 13(6), 1–18.

Cosley, B.J., Mccoy, S.K., Saslow, L.R., Epel, E.S. (2010). Is compassion for others stress buffering? Consequences of compassion and social support for physiological reactivity to stress. *Journal of Experimental Social Psychology*, 46(5), 816–823.

Davidson, L. (2011). Recovery from psychosis: What's love got to do with it? *Psychosis*, 3(2), 105–114.

Day, J., Finkelstein, J.C., Field, B.A., Matthews, B., Kirby, J.N., Doty, J.R. (2021). Compassion-focused technologies: Reflections and future directions. *Frontiers in Psychology*, 12(603618).

Denneson, L.M., Pisciotta, M., Hooker, E.R., Trevino, A., Dobscha, S.K. (2018). Impacts of a web-based educational program for veterans who read their mental health notes online. *Journal of the American Medical Informatics Association*, 26(1), 3–8.

De Zulueta, P. (2013). Compassion in 21st century medicine: Is it sustainable? *Clinical Ethics*, 8(4), 119–128.

Dutton, J.E., Worline, M.C., Frost, P.J., Lilius, J. (2006). Explaining compassion organizing. *Administrative Science Quarterly*, 51(1), 59–96.

Epstein, R.M., Franks, P., Shields, C.G., Meldrum, S.C., Miller, K.N., Campbell, T.L., Fiscella, K. (2005). Patient-centered communication and diagnostic testing. *Annals of Family Medicine*, 3(5), 415–421.

Feldman, C. and Kuyken, W. (2011). Compassion in the landscape of suffering. *Contemporary Buddhism*, 12(1), 143–155.

Fotaki, M. (2015). Why and how is compassion necessary to provide good quality healthcare? *International Journal of Health Policy and Management*, 4(4), 199–201.

Frampton, S.B., Guastello, S., Lepore, M. (2013). Compassion as the foundation of patient-centered care: The importance of compassion in action. *Journal of Comparative Effective Research*, 2(5), 443–455.

Francis, R. (2013). Report of the Mid Staffordshire NHS foundation trust public inquiry. Office of Public Sector Information, London.

Gilbert, P. (2014). The origins and nature of compassion focused therapy. *British Journal of Clinical Psychology*, 53(1), 6–41.

Gladkova, A. (2010). Sympathy, compassion, and empathy in English and Russian: A linguistic and cultural analysis. *Culture & Psychology*, 16(2), 267–285.

Goetz, J.L. and Simon-Thomas, E. (2017). The landscape of compassion: Definitions and scientific approaches. In *The Oxford Handbook of Compassion Science*, Seppälä, E.M., Simon-Thomas, E., Brown, S.L., Worline, M.C., Cameron, C.D., Doty, J.R. (eds). Oxford University Press, New York.

Gogia, S. (ed.) (2019). Rationale, history, and basics of telehealth. In *Fundamentals of Telemedicine and Telehealth*. Elsevier, London.

Granados-Pembertty, Y.Y. and Arias-Valencia, M.M. (2013). Being in front of the patient: Nurse-patient interaction and use of technology in emergency services. *Investigacion Educacion en Enfermeria*, 31(3), 421–432.

Gregg, J. (2022). The care I needed. *New England Journal of Medicine*, 386(5), 411–413.

Gupta, A. (2019). Compassionate, patient-centered care in the digital age. *NAM Perspectives*, 1–3.

Hacker, T. (2008). The relational compassion scale: Development and validation of a new self-rated scale for the assessment of self-other compassion. Doctoral Thesis, University of Glasgow, Glasgow.

Hallowell, E.M. (1999). The human moment at work. *Harvard Business Review*, 1–8.

Hanford, T. (2015). Finding words: The use of email in psychotherapy with a disorganised and dissociating client. In *Love in the Age of the Internet: Attachment in the Digital Era*, Cundy, L. (ed.). Routledge, London.

Hardy, P. and Sumner, T. (eds) (2018). *Cultivating Compassion: How Digital Storytelling is Transforming Healthcare*. Palgrave Macmillan, Cham.

Hodges, B.D., Paech, G., Bennett, J. (eds) (2020). *Without Compassion, There is No Healthcare: Leading with Care in a Technological Age*. McGill-Queen's University Press, Montréal.

Huppert, F.A. (2017). Mindfulness and compassion as foundations for well-being. In *Future Directions in Well-being: Education, Organizations and Policy*, White, M.A., Slemp, G.R., Murray, A.S. (ed.). Springer, Cham.

Hyacinth, B.T. (2017). *The Future of Leadership: Rise of Automation, Robotics and Artificial Intelligence*. MBA Caribbean Organisation, Port of Spain, Trinidad and Tobago.

Institute of Medicine (2001). *Crossing the Quality Chasm: A New Health System for the 21st Century*. National Academy Press, Washington.

Kemp, J., Zhang, T., Inglis, F., Wiljer, D., Sockalingam, S., Crawford, A., Lo, B., Charow, R., Munnery, M., Singh Takhar, S. et al. (2020). Delivery of compassionate mental health care in a digital technology-driven age: Scoping review. *Journal of Medical Internet Research*, 22(3), e16263.

Kinsella, E. (2020). Compassion in digital healthcare. *Future Healthcare Journal*, 7(3), 193.

Kweon, S.-H., Hwang, K.-H., Do-Hyun, J. (eds) (2011). Time and space perception on media platforms. *Proceedings of the Media Ecology Association*, 25–48.

Lemire, F. (2019). Caring and compassion in a digital world. *Canadian Family Physician*, 65(7), 520–520.

Lown, B.A. (2014). Seven guiding commitments: Making the U.S. healthcare system more compassionate. *Journal of Patient Experience*, 1(2), 6–15.

Lown, B.A., Dunne, H., Muncer, S.J., Chadwick, R. (2015). How important is compassionate healthcare to you? A comparison of the perceptions of people in the United States and Ireland. *Journal of Research in Nursing*, 4(1/2), 60–69.

Macbeth, A. and Gumley, A. (2012). Exploring compassion: A meta-analysis of the association between self-compassion and psychopathology. *Clinical Psychology Review*, 32(6), 545–552.

Marcolino, M.S., Oliveira, J.A.Q., D'Agostino, M., Ribeiro, A.L., Alkmim, M.B.M., Novillo-Ortiz, D. (2018). The impact of mHealth interventions: Systematic review of systematic reviews. *JMIR mHealth and uHealth*, 6(1), e23.

Neff, K.D. (2003). The development and validation of a scale to measure self-compassion. *Self and Identity*, 2(3), 223–250.

Oh, H., Rizo, C., Enkin, M., Jadad, A. (2005). What is eHealth (3): A systematic review of published definitions. *Journal of Medical Internet Research*, 7(1), e1.

Pfaff, K. and Markaki, A. (2017). Compassionate collaborative care: An integrative review of quality indicators in end-of-life care. *BMC Palliative Care*, 16(1), 1–24.

Redelmeier, D.A., Molin, J.P., Tibshirani, R.J. (1995). A randomised trial of compassionate care for the homeless in an emergency department. *Lancet*, 345(8958), 1131–1134.

Robinson, K. (2003). Technology can't replace compassion in health care. *Nursing Management*, 34(1), 1.

Rosen, L., Carrier, M., Cheever, N.A. (2013). Facebook and texting made me do it: Media-induced task-switching while studying. *Computers in Human Behavior*, 29(948/958).

Royal Commission into Aged Care Quality and Safety (2021). Final report: Care, dignity and respect: Summary and recommendations. Commonwealth of Australia, Canberra.

Sanghavi, D.M. (2006). What makes for a compassionate patient-caregiver relationship? *The Joint Commission Journal on Quality and Patient Safety*, 32(5), 283–292.

Schantz, M.L. (2007). Compassion: A concept analysis. *Nursing Forum*, 42(2), 48–55.

Shapiro, J. (2012). The paradox of teaching empathy in medical students. In *Empathy: From Bench to Bedside*, Decety, J. (ed.). MIT Press, New York.

Shaw, J., Agarwal, P., Desveaux, L., Palma, D.C., Stamenova, V., Jamieson, T., Yang, R., Bhatia, R.S., Bhattacharyya, O. (2018). Beyond "implementation": Digital health innovation and service design. *NPJ Digital Medicine*, 1(48), 1–5.

Shin, A. (2021). Compassion tech: Merging technology, consumerism and the human connection for health innovation. American Hospital Association [Online]. Available at: https://www.aha.org/news/healthcareinnovation-thursday-blog/2021-02-11-compassion-tech-merging-technology-consumerism [Accessed 12 April 2022].

Simpson, A. and Farr-Wharton, B. (2020). Cultivating organizational compassion in healthcare. *Journal of Management & Organization*, 26(340/354).

Sinclair, S., Beamer, K., Hack, T.F., Mcclement, S., Raffin Bouchal, S., Chochinov, H.M., Hagen, N.A. (2017). Sympathy, empathy, and compassion: A grounded theory study of palliative care patients' understandings, experiences, and preferences. *Palliative Medicine*, 31(5), 437–447.

Singer, T. and Klimecki, O.M. (2014). Empathy and compassion. *Current Biology*, 24(18), R875–R878.

Sparrow, R. and Hatherley, J. (2020). High hopes for "deep medicine"? AI, economics, and the future of care. *Hastings Center Report*, 50(1), 14–17.

Stevens, S. (2018). Hearing voices: The experience of associate degree nursing students to an auditory hallucinations simulation. *International Journal of Nursing & Clinical Practices*, 5(289), 1–7.

Straughair, C. (2012). Exploring compassion: Implications for contemporary nursing. Part 1. *British Journal of Nursing*, 21(3), 160–164.

Strauss, C., Lever Taylor, B., Gu, J., Kuyken, W., Baer, R., Jones, F., Cavanagh, K. (2016). What is compassion and how can we measure it? A review of definitions and measures. *Clinical Psychology Review*, 47, 15–27.

Strudwick, G., Zhang, T., Inglis, F., Sockalingam, S., Munnery, M., Lo, B., Singh Takhar, S., Charow, R., Wiljer, D. (2019). Delivery of compassionate mental health care in a digital technology-driven age: Protocol for a scoping review. *BMJ Open*, 9(7), e027989.

Swinglehurst, D., Roberts, C., Greenhalgh, T. (2011). Opening up the "black box" of the electronic patient record: A linguistic ethnographic study in general practice. *Communication & Medicine*, 8(1), 3–15.

Terry, C. and Cain, J. (2016). The emerging issue of digital empathy. *American Journal of Pharmaceutical Education*, 80(4), 1–4.

Topol, E. (2019a). *Deep Medicine: How Artificial Intelligence can Make Healthcare Human Again*. Basic Books, New York.

Topol, E. (2019b). The Topol review: Preparing the healthcare workforce to deliver the digital future. Health Education England, Leeds.

Trzeciak, S. and Rivers, E.P. (2017). Compassionomics: Hypothesis and experimental approach. *Medical Hypotheses*, 107, 92–97.

Van Kleef, G.A., Oveis, C., Van Der Löwe, I., Luokogan, A., Goetz, J., Keltner, D. (2008). Power, distress, and compassion: Turning a blind eye to the suffering of others. *Psychological Science*, 19(12), 1315–1322.

WHO (2019). Recommendations on digital interventions for health system strengthening. Report, Geneva.

Wiljer, D., Charow, R., Costin, H., Sequeira, L., Anderson, M., Strudwick, G., Tripp, T., Crawford, A. (2019). Defining compassion in the digital health age: Protocol for a scoping review. *BMJ Open*, 9(2), e026338.

Williams, G.C. (2018). *Adaptation and Natural Selection: A Critique of Some Current Evolutionary Thought*. Princeton University Press, Princeton.

Zhang, S.-E., Liu, W., Wang, J., Shi, Y., Xie, F., Cang, S., Sun, T., Fan, L. (2018). Impact of workplace violence and compassionate behaviour in hospitals on stress, sleep quality and subjective health status among Chinese nurses: A cross-sectional survey. *BMJ Open*, 8(10), e019373.

Zigmond, D. (2011). Five executive follies. How commodification imperils compassion in person healthcare. *Journal of Holistic Healthcare*, 9, 7–10.

12

Help with Prescribing Mobile Health Applications: A Partnership Design

12.1. Introduction

Among the profound changes in society and more particularly in the field of health, the digital technological revolution is one of the most entropic, yet also still one of the most chaotic. It is in fact very difficult to organize and regulate, similarly to information on the Internet, which we identified a decade ago in the context of a thesis (Flora 2012). Since the advent of the Internet and the development of interconnected digital technology, the problem is no longer accessing information, but rather the ability for everyone to find conclusive and relevant information which best corresponds to initial research, and then finding a way to treat it. As such, certain authors announced the emergence of Information-based Medicine as an extension of Evidence Based Medicine, or even of Values Based medicine (Hunink et al. 2001) linked to which we already argued that a balanced triangulation of approaches would allow an adjustment of the care relationship and consequently of quality care, by taking the changes in the behavior of care populations into account (Flora 2012, p. 45). Historically, after the exponential amount of information produced on the Internet since its emergence and over the course of these developments, recent years have seen the appearance of a considerable number of mobile health applications (or apps) and of connected objects.

In France, more than 100,000 mobile health (mHealth) and well-being applications were identified in 2017, a doubling since 2013 (Normand 2017).

Chapter written by Luigi FLORA, David DARMON, Stephen DARMONI, Julien GROSJEAN, Christian SIMON, Parina HASSANALY and Jean-Charles DUFOUR.

According to the 2021 report from App Annie, a global reference on data from the mobile application market, health and fitness "apps" recorded an 85% increase in downloads and a 70% increase in health insurance spending in one year (2021)[1].

However, in this new and expanding environment, mobile health could contribute to maintaining or improving the health status of individuals while being economically beneficial to the healthcare system (Betts et al. 2019)[2]. In 2013, PWC published that the use of mobile applications would allow European health systems to save 99 billion euros, and 11.5 billion in France alone (PWC 2013). However, risks exist at this stage that must not be overlooked, an example of which is what a public health team in Quebec highlighted by analyzing the technological choice processes in this area which they claimed could be harmful (Daudelin et al. 2015). This team sheds light on the current organization which confronts divergent interests and therefore contradictory injunctions, which can slow down the general interest, or even produce opposite effects. The report explains that, in the absence of real consideration of macrosocial dynamics due to blatant ignoring during the development of these health innovations, current technological innovations can only accidentally serve the general interest and therefore, health systems. In addition, the diversity and plethora of offerings in this area are obstacles, both for a patient and for a doctor, when it comes to choosing a reliable "app", adapted to the health objectives that they have set alone or, ideally in consultation with the care team, and when they are able do it, it is following very time-consuming research.

In addition, for many patients, there are additional obstacles linked to illiteracy and social determinants of health that can limit the choice and use of these mobile health "apps" (Regnier et al. 2018). The user interface and other usability criteria of catalogs/stores (and of apps themselves), in a context of self-measurements and self-care, for varied profiles, are important components in facilitating choice. Various mobile applications are associated with connected objects that are more or less accessible depending on the economic capacities of patients and announced benefits (well-being, primary or secondary prevention, care, monitoring or surveillance of recognized pathologies (Betts et al. 2019)).

---

1 State of Mobile 2021; App Annie, 2021. See: https://www.appannie.com/fr/go/state-of-mobile-2021/.

2 Betts, D., Batra, N., Davis, S. (2019). Forces of change – The future of health, Deloitte Insights [Online]. Available at: https//www2.deloitte.com/us/en/insights/industry/health-care/forces-of-change-health-care.html.

However, these aspects are today neglected in the usual catalogs[3]. It is all the more difficult to make a choice seeing as no catalog of health apps made up of methodologically evaluated apps currently exists in France, as it does in other countries (Trudelle 2021)[4].

In this general context, the French government, as part of the "Ma Santé 2022"[5], plan, has opened a digital health space called *Mon espace santé* (MES)[6] which notably includes a shared medical file powered, on the one hand, by health professionals (via the business software they use and which will have to evolve to become interoperable with *Mon espace santé*) and, on the other hand, by the patient themselves (by connecting directly to MES). The patient can manage access rights to their health data by health professionals and various other MES digital services.

In addition to the shared medical mile, MES also includes a catalog of "digital health services" referenced by the state. The *Mon Espace Santé* catalog of "digital health services" is a general catalog that does not offer an "intelligent/contextual" system of selection and personalized assistance in the choice of health apps adapted to the profile of the patient who consults it.

To conclude on the current context, it should be noted that nowadays, patients are getting involved with professionals in this quest for relevance in the digital environment as in all areas of health and particularly, as we will see, in the use of mobile applications, and even in their design. Thus, we evaluated in 2021, alongside Vincent Dumez – patient co-director of the *Centre d'excellence du partenariat avec les patients et le public du Centre de recherche universitaire de l'Université de Montréal* (Center of excellence for partnerships with patients and the public of the University Research Center of the University of Montreal), which he is currently vice dean of and within which he is responsible for community partnerships – the state of play of this partnership in Quebec (Dumez and Flora 2021), the number of these technical innovations being of more than 171,000 in Canada.

---

3 Often called "stores" today.

4 Trudelle, P. (2021). Évaluation des applications dans le champ de la santé mobile (mHealth). Haute Autorité de santé, Saint-Denis La Plaine [Online]. Available at: https://www.hassante.fr/upload/docs/application/pdf/202106/criteres_de_qualite_du_contenu_medical_referencement_mhealth_ens_2021-06-30_10-58-28_773.pdf.

5 "My Health 2022", in English.

6 My health space, in English.

12.2. ApiAppS research, a response adapted to the times?

To address some of these challenges, an interdisciplinary research consortium composed of university teams was formed in France[7].

This consortium proposes a research project to support decision-making in prescribing mobile health apps called “ApiAppS”.

The objective of the ApiAppS project, funded and supported by the National Research Agency (*Agence nationale de la recherche*: ANR)[8], lies in the scientific categorization design of mobile health apps that allows the establishment of a digital system to help with medical decisions in prescribing mobile apps, as a part of consultations.

These mobile apps can be available to both doctors and patients by promoting self-management for patients and supporting the doctor–patient relationship when it is deemed appropriate by the patient to discuss this with their doctor during consultations (Figure 12.1).

This proposal was also devised in order to identify, explore and eliminate existing scientific obstacles so that general practitioners can use a *system to help prescribe mobile health apps/devices*[9]*, depending on the patient.*

This proposed system was developed to be interoperable with the information sources used, which are computerized medical records and medical knowledge bases.

Even before its implementation phase, the psychosocial context of ApiAppS's prescription method was taken into account by evaluating the impact on the doctor–patient relationship, based on perceptions and expectations of citizens who

---

7 The consortium is made up of SESSTIM (*Laboratoire de recherche en sciences économiques et sociales de la santé et traitement de l'information médicale de l'Université Aix Marseille*); of DI2M (*département d'informatique et d'information médicale du Centre hospitalo-universitaire de Rouen*, creator of the CISSMEF, a catalog which has indexed principal francophone sites and documents); the DERMG (*département d'enseignement et de recherche en médecine générale de l'Université Côte d'Azur*, which during the research joined the Centre d'innovation du partenariat avec les patients et le public (CI3P)); GRePS (social psychology research group at the University of Lyon 2), and of SILK informatics (creator of management and multimedia software, of websites, training, and a specialist in the medical and social sector).

8 Project reference ANR-17-CE19-0027. See: https://anr.fr/Projet-ANR-17-CE19-0027.

9 Some apps function with connected objects.

are both patients and doctors. This is an approach that also addresses the appropriation of mobile health technologies for both doctors and patients.

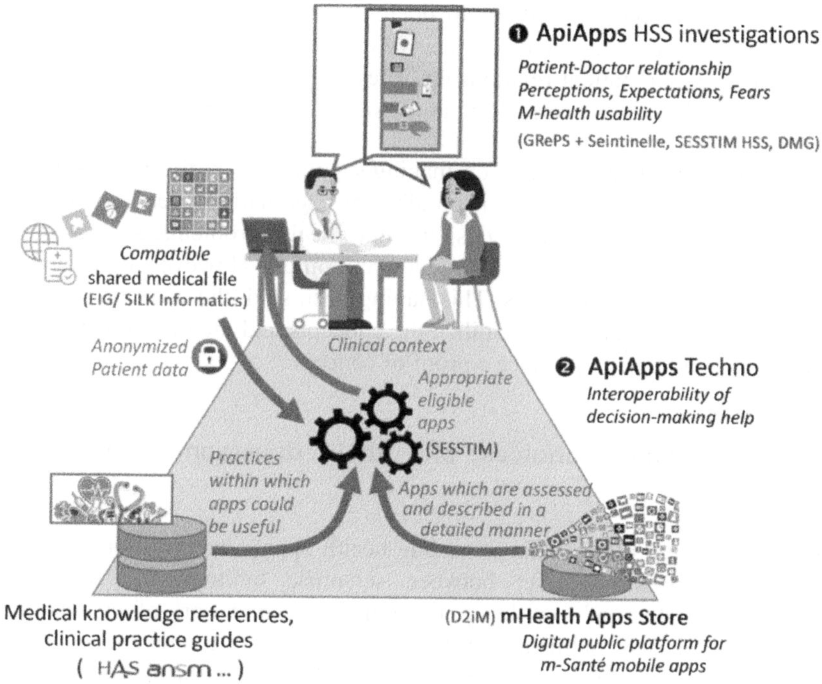

Figure 12.1. *ApiAppS working process. For a color version of this figure, see www.iste.co.uk/flora/experience.zip*

12.3. Design carried out with the participation of citizens

This first phase of studying representations and behaviors was developed as part of a research project in human and social sciences carried out by the GRePS (*groupe de recherche en psychologie sociale*: social psychology research group) which called on the "Les Seintinelles" network. Seintinelles is a network of citizens who are initially likely to be mobilized by medical cancer research, but which can currently be mobilized more widely. This network is made up, at the time of writing this chapter, of 36,618 citizens[10].

The Seintinelle network and GRePS have integrated research findings relating to the psychosocial and anthropological aspects of mobile health devices and to tools

10 A number of citizens noted on April 6, 2022 on their website: seintinelles.com.

helping with their prescription. This project aimed to better document the representations, beliefs and practices of patients linked to applications and mobile health objects and the place of health devices in the doctor–patient relationship. In addition, the needs and expectations of doctors with regard to these mobile health devices, depending on the type of device, were studied as well as the place of these devices in the doctor–patient relationship. These studies, in the field of human and social sciences (HSS), were carried out at the start of the project.

The process designed as a decision-making support system for the prescription of mobile health technologies makes it possible to eventually cover various areas of health and the majority of pathologies and other health problems, such as diabetes, cardiovascular or sleep disorders, depression and others. However, it currently only covers a part of these possibilities. This having been said, the work done so far has made it possible to develop and stabilize the concepts and theories of categorization of mobile apps and thus to produce a proof of concept.

12.4. Categorization choices and their development during this research

While the design of methods of mobile health apps categorization was initially conceived around a crossover between scientific bibliographic research and evaluation by doctors of mobile applications, a second part of evaluation was initiated on the back of publication filters. The creation of a new entity mobilizing patients based on the skills acquired throughout their life with the disease made it possible to enrich categorization quality.

The fact that one of the partners[11], the DERMG, the department for general medicine teaching and research from the Faculty of Medicine of the University of Côte d'Azur, has during the research been enriched with an innovation center for patient and public partnership (CI3P) made it possible to organize an evaluation by triangulation between hermeneutic research of the literature and heuristic research composed of singular conference parties, between doctors and patients. The tandems of physcians and patients assessors do not know each other, in the context of the medical practice, so as not to risk generating cognitive biases at this stage.

The CI3P is co-directed by a doctor and a patient[12]. It mobilizes patients within teaching, healthcare settings and research, on the basis of a skills framework

11 From the start of the project, the DERMG was responsible for bibliographic research and doctors' evaluation of apps.

12 Two of the authors of this chapter, David Darmon and Luigi Flora.

(DCPP 2015; Flora 2015). These skills mobilize the experiential knowledge resulting from living with the disease, of patients and relatives. It is from this patient involvement methodology, already used for around 10 years by the patient collaboration and partnership department (*direction collaboration et partenariat patient*: DCPP) of the University of Montreal (Flora 2015), that patient evaluators were mobilized:

– Firstly, they were involved in evaluating the apps based on their life experience with the issues addressed by the apps.

– Secondly, they were randomly assigned to apps, in order to put them in a situation wherein they would be discovering life with the illness that the app they were to evaluate dealt with.

– Finally, patient partners were mobilized by the CI3P to evaluate the contribution of these apps as an integrated decision-making support system within a consultation framework, and in a real-life situation.

As part of the research, all of these phases were studied which gave rise to medical practice theses, supervised by the DERMG within the Faculty of Medicine of the University of Côte d'Azur.

Finally, to be exhaustive, the patient co-director integrated scientific and research steering advice immediately after the decision to consider patient involvement. This project allowed for significant participation and for the emergence of diagnosis democratization (Bose et al. 2019). This project is fully a part of the digital revolution initiated within health policy in France "Ma santé 2022". In this context, a new partnership is emerging between professionals and patients in line with the WHO's 8 principles for the digital transformation of public health (PAHO/WHO 2021).

12.5. A dynamic mobilizing cross-perspectives between patients and doctors

While the described research project is today in its operationalization phase, within the finalization of this research on this first decision support device in the prescription of health apps, the initiated experience of the complementarity of knowledge of all parties gave way to a feeling of efficiency and curiosity within the consortium, such that the desire to co-design and act together led the consortium to propose developing a second research project which was submitted to and accepted by the National research agency (*Agence nationale de la recherche*: ANR).

A new project aims to develop the patient's power to act through the skills of self-measurement and self-care, a self-management of their health which they can develop, if they wish, as proposed in the care partnership with the patient approach (Karazivan et al. 2015). This design will follow the 8 principles for the digital transformation of public health from the WHO) and the recommendations of the High Authority for Health (*Haute Autorité de santé*: HAS)[13] aimed at supporting and encouraging user engagement in the social, medico-social and health sectors.

The objective of this project is, on the one hand, to design a platform to guide patients to choose their mobile applications, based on an EBM framework, and, on the other hand, to help them use these applications by making them autonomous.

This co-designed digital system aims to be integrated into the French digital health ecosystem and will take the standards and recommendations of *Mon espace santé* into account, in order to offer or prefigure a digital service for personalized recommendations/advice for the use of health apps in this space.

ApiAppS InSA, the name chosen for this new project, will include a personalized decision support module for patients in order to guide them to the choice of apps adapted to their health profile. This profile will be determined by the preexisting personal data that they agree to share. The help module will also be able to establish a dialogue with the patient to complete their profile by collecting new useful information to refine app choices (Figure 12.2).

The technical and semantic dimensions of this dialogue will be investigated in the project (e.g. what terminologies should be used for this dialogue and to integrate the personal patient health data, and possibly the data generated by the apps they decide to use, within the digital ecosystem and in the tools of health professionals). The support module will be based on formalized, explicit knowledge taken from best health practice guides and other Evidence Based Medicine sources. The catalog of health apps will be gradually enriched with new apps, co-evaluated by professionals and patients, as was the case during the first project.

The ethical and legal aspects (responsibility chains in particular) raised by such a service, one that recommends apps and encourages self-care with their use, will be studied in the project with the Legal Research Center of Paris 8 University (Centre de recherche juridique de l'université Paris 8), recognized within the fields of both medical law and health law.

13 Supporting and encouraging user engagement in the social, medico-social and health sectors, HAS recommendations are available at: https://www.has-sante.fr/jcms/p_3201812/fr/soutenir-et-encourager-l-engagement-des-usagers-dans-les-secteurs-social-medico-social-et-sanitaire.

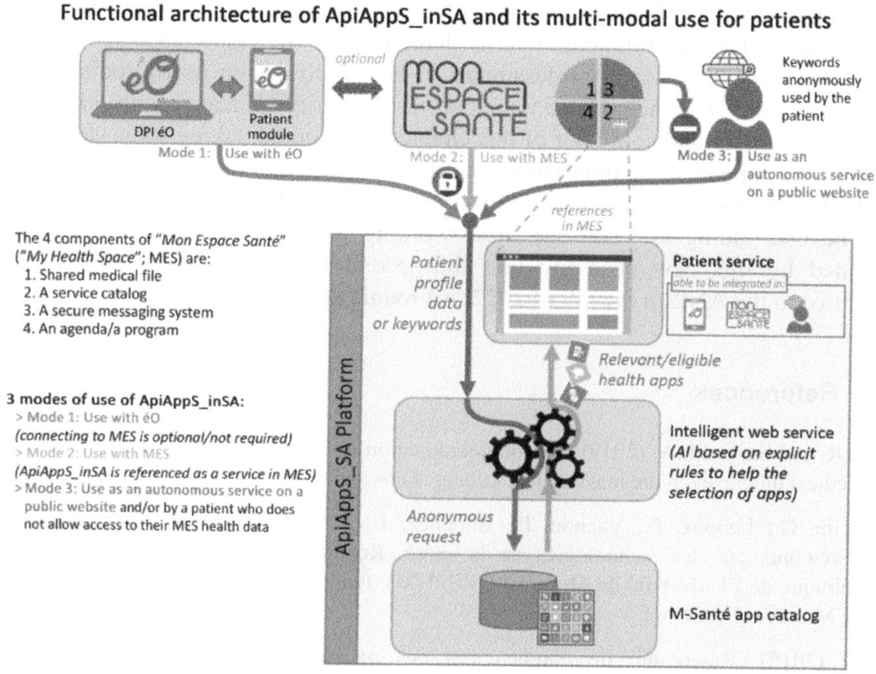

Figure 12.2. *Functional architecture of the ApiAppS_InSa project. For a color version of this figure, see www.iste.co.uk/flora/experience.zip*

This research center with which, in 2020, the Centre d'innovation avec les patients et le public (CI3P) launched a research axis on the place of the patient in the 20th century, within which the e-patient, both in terms of their care and in order to be mobilized in the health system, has a place that remains to be defined and legally supported.

12.6. Conclusion

The developments presented in this chapter propose a hierarchy, a scientifically developed categorization which makes it possible to organize the exponential universe of apps and connected objects in the field of health. Thanks to this organization, it becomes easier to find relevant information in accordance with people's needs. This service offers an interoperable decision support prescribing apps, which are integrated into consultations and freely accessible for patients and Internet users. The initiated process demonstrates the transversality and the relevance of the mobilization of the experiential knowledge of patients and citizens, in complementarity with the knowledge of professionals regarding a concrete project within the digital environment. It also demonstrates the importance of bringing together patients and health professionals in action, to design useful tools for the field of health. To conclude, as with the vast majority of teams with which the patient co-director and co-author of this chapter has worked, taking some steps back at this stage appears to be impossible as it gives credence to the actions put in place for the health of citizens, a sense of working for the health of others as the approach goes beyond "doing for" and becomes "working with". It is with this motivation animated by this new necessity that the second project presented, which was submitted to the ANR in the fall of 2022, is brought on.

12.7. References

Bose, R. and Saxon, L.A. (2019). The democratization of diagnostics: Bringing the power of medical diagnosis to the masses. *The Lancet: Eclinical Medicine*, 8, 6–7.

Daudelin, G., Lehoux, P., Vachon, P., Bouchez, J. (2015). Valeurs et expertise dans le développement des technologies de la santé. Report, Institut de recherche en santé publique de l'Université de Montréal (IRSPUM), École de santé publique de l'Université de Montréal (ESPUM).

DCPP (2015). Référentiel de compétences des patients. DCPP/Faculté de médecine/ Université de Montréal.

Dumez, V. and Flora, L. (2021). Pour une nouvelle vision du soin en adéquation avec son temps et son appropriation par la population et ses organisations. *Le partenariat de soin avec le patient : analyses*, 93–118.

Flora, L. (2012). Le patient formateur : élaboration théorique et pratique d'un nouveau métier de la santé. PhD Thesis, Université Vincennes Saint Denis – Paris 8.

Flora, L. (2015). *Un référentiel de compétences de patient : pour quoi faire ? Du savoir expérientiel des malades à un référentiel de compétences intégré : l'exemple du modèle de Montréal.* Presses Académiques Francophones, Sarrebruck.

Hunink M., Milton C. Weinstein E., Wittenberg M., Drummond J., Pliskin J., Wong P., Glasziou P. (2001). *Decision Making in Health and Medicine: Integrating Evidence and Values*, volume 1. Cambridge University Press, Cambridge.

Karazivan, P., Dumez, V., Flora, L., Pomey, M.-P., Del Grande, C., Guadiri, S., Fernandez, N., Jouet, E., Las Vergnas, O., Lebel, P. (2015). The patient-as-partner approach in care: A conceptual framework for a necessary transition. *Academic Medicine*, 90(4), 437–441.

Normand, A. (2017). *Prévenir plutôt que guérir : la révolution de la e-santé.* Eyrolles, Paris.

PAHO/WHO (2021). 8 Principles for Digital Transformation of Public Health [Online]. Available at: https://www.paho.org/en/ish/8-principles.

Powell, A. and Torous, J. (2020). A patient-centered framework for measuring the economic value of the clinical benefits of digital health apps: Theoretical modeling. *JMIR Mental Health*, 7(10), e18812.

PWC (2013). Socio-economic impact of mHealth. An assessment report for the European Union [Online]. Available at: https://www.gsma.com/iot/wpcontent/uploads/2013/06/Socio-economic_impact-of_mHealth_EU_14062013V2.pdf.

Régnier, F. and Chauvel, L. (2018). Digital inequalities in the use of self-tracking diet and fitness apps: Interview study on the influence of social, economic, and cultural factors. *JMIR Mhealth Uhealth*, 6(4), e101.

13

Beyond the Testimony: Patient Partners and Ongoing Education Program

13.1. Introduction

This chapter presents innovation-research (IR), having implanted the train-the-trainer program within primary care clinics, in which patient partners move beyond their usual status as witnesses to play a full role as trainers in practice settings. From the analysis of their contribution to the program, we have identified key elements of the enrichment brought on by the patient partner role and have drawn up some proposals to enrich the theory on patient partnership.

13.2. Train-the-trainer program an effective strategy for professional development in primary care

From a learning healthcare system perspective, numerous resources and strategies are required in order to accomplish organizational learning processes. Among them are knowledge transfer, the analysis and use of data and various training strategies in practice settings (Menear et al. 2019). Among these latter strategies, train-the-trainer approaches are increasingly recognized for their effectiveness (Poitras et al. 2021). This effectiveness arises from the fact that the most powerful modalities of knowledge transfer in the field of healthcare are those which take place between peers, due to the trust that professionals place in their colleagues (Peirce et al. 2012).

Chapter written by Yves COUTURIER, Marie-Eve POITRAS, Marie-Dominique POIRIER and Anaëlle MORIN.

These train-the-trainer strategies promote, with little costs, the relatively effective dissemination of knowledge necessary for the implementation of important innovations from an organizational point of view to professionals, the main users. Such a strategy has a certain cost advantage since the final training work is done in a real-life context, by actors already in the organization. For this reason, such an educational intervention makes it possible to effectively disseminate and implement innovations adapted to the particularities of each context (Pearce et al. 2012).

Pearce et al. (2012) emphasize that the train-the-trainer approach is positively supported by the combined use of several methods, by a so-called active andragogy by which experiential knowledge is valued, and by the implementation of material promoting learning for those trained with regard to their specific practice context. In addition, the train-the-trainer approach, which is particularly effective from an andragogical point of view, will mobilize the five modalities of professional development in an integrated manner (Wittorski 2007), namely learning: 1) on the job; 2) through the authoritative transfer of knowledge; 3) by problem solving; 4) through the observation of a third party or by the transfer of a culture; and 5) by analyzing our own actions. Thus, the train-the-trainer approach will benefit from various active andragogy strategies integrating these five modalities to varying degrees. For each of them, patients can make a positive contribution by mobilizing their experience of care.

In order to develop the train-the-trainer approach, intended for employment practitioners, a team of experts is typically formed. Some of these experts are specialized in the specific contents of training and others in andragogy. This team of experts develops training content and andragogical strategies adapted to the relevant practice context, based on professional didactics highlighting so-called active forms of andragogy and promoting the meeting of various forms of knowledge, including the experiential knowledge of trainees. Andragogy is also distinguished from pedagogy by the fact that adult learners, who are a fortiori employed, have abundant practice and, due to this, have significant knowledge from their own professional experience (Al Mosawi 2021). Ongoing or on-the-job educational programs, is typically given in a real-life context by champion practitioners to other practitioners, who will subsequently have the function of training their peers, who eventually will become trainers and so on. First-generation trainers will have been trained more broadly rather than just on the content subjected to transfer. This is the case in active andragogy approaches, for example, so as to be able to adapt their content and their training strategies to the specificities of each environment.

The combination of multiple andragogical strategies improves clinical behaviors, knowledge, abilities and the confidence of health professionals (Poitras et al. 2021). In their systematic review of scientific writings, Poitras et al. (2021) also demonstrated that increasing knowledge among trained practitioners improves patient health outcomes and the performance of healthcare organizations.

Although promising, the train-the-trainer approach encounters various limits and barriers. First, that of disciplinary self-reference resulting from training among peers in the same discipline. Keeping this between peers can reduce the transformational potential of innovation, especially in a context wherein taking into account the global nature of clinical situations is increasingly recognized. This strategy then usually gives little room for patient participation in the educational program, other than through the reminder of important but general principles, such as that of the value of patient engagement or of centering care patient priorities.

13.3. Innovation in the train-the-trainer approach through increased patient participation

Patient expertise is now widely recognized, as evidenced by the dissemination of conceptual patient partnership models. An example of this is the Montreal model (Pomey et al. 2015), which is considered to be an excellent summary of patient partnership approaches and recognizes the contribution of patients to healthcare training. In fact, such recognition of the patient's expertise has naturally led to their contribution to professional development, first of the patients themselves, and then of future professionals in the initial training context. Their role consists most often, but not exclusively, of sharing their experience of care in order to guide the ethos of future professional generations. This most recurrent testimonial approach is undoubtedly useful, but it can have the effect of restricting the role of patients, whose expertise has broader potential. In its most ambitious versions, patient partnership includes established feedback practices (Pomey et al. 2020), but it is most often circumscribed in a posture which is extraneous to action, whether upstream or downstream of it. Such feedback can also be carried out at strategic moments in the implementation of innovations, including during action, for example, within the framework of short cycles of continuous quality improvement. These short cycles present all of the stages of the continuous quality improvement process (plan, do, control, adjust), but deployed over short periods, for example, three months, in order to accomplish a small-scale change in almost real time.

The contribution of patients to professional development, in the context of the dissemination of innovations, for example, has for its part been the subject of much less work than in the initial training context. This explains a lack of knowledge about the conditions for successful patient contribution to professional development in practice environments (Fraser et al. 2017). The work of Fraser et al. (2017) has also shown a number of obstacles in this specific context, such as the resistance of professional trainers to full patient participation.

On the horizon of patient partnership, we therefore see two close borders that we can cross to expand patient partnership territory. The first concerns itself with going beyond the attribution of the expert witness status in training, by recognizing the conceptual, didactic, andragogical and operational contributions of patients. The second is that of training on the job for professionals. The F2PL intervention research project approached these new borders.

13.4. Study context

The F2PL intervention research, for *the train-the-trainer approach in primary care*, aims to support the implementation of two practice guides in the context of primary care. These guides focus on the field of practice of nurses and social workers working in groups of family doctors (*groupes de médecins de famille*: GMF), the main primary care medical organization in Quebec. The consolidation of GMFs has been an important public priority since the turn of the 2000s. This explains why these organizations are the subject of numerous innovations and, therefore, numerous on-the-job trainings. Among these innovations is a significant increase in the number of nurses working there, but above all an expansion of the scope of their professional mandate. These nurses were joined by several professionals from other disciplines, including social workers (Ministère de la Santé et des Services sociaux, 2016). These innovations have the effect of profoundly transforming primary health care by opening it to a perspective of interprofessional collaboration promoted by numerous conceptual models, such as the chronic care model (Wagner et al. 1999) or the medical home (Association of American Medical Colleges 2008). These models, among others, explicitly recognize an important role for patients as partners in care.

This intervention research consists of developing, implementing and evaluating a train-the-trainer approach aimed at supporting the use of said practice guides by these nurses and social workers. The proposed train-the-trainer approach was enriched with various change management strategies (which will not be developed here), but above all with a training design in which interprofessional collaboration and the contribution of patients as trainers was crucial. Here, the recognition of the patient through complete trainer status as a logical key to a collaborative andragogical strategy constitutes an important advancement in the partnership with patients by going beyond the sole status of patient-witness, and through the extension of the role of trainer with that of supporting changes in practices through post-training support for trainees. This last aspect was the subject of conceptualization and training, but was not implemented due to the pandemic crisis. For this reason, we will treat it in a secondary sense.

13.5. Theoretical framework

Even if few studies have focused on the impacts of the train-the-trainer approach on the skills of trainers (Kirkpatrick and Kirkpatrick 2016), this andragogical approach seems promising in terms of developing training skills (Poitras et al. 2021). Consistent with Moore and his colleagues' model (2009), the learning that is important to measure is of reactions, knowledge, attitudes, skills, confidence in putting learning into practice, the intention to apply learning and behavioral change (Kirkpatrick 2009). In addition to being adequately trained in the knowledge areas transferred to colleagues, the professional-practitioner must also be supported in the appropriation of their new role in terms of andragogical skills. Furthermore, since the train-the-trainer approach is a process of cascading professional development, it is important to offer long-term clinical support which will act on the organizational barriers of change routinization, instructed by training (Poitras et al. 2020). Trainers are therefore more than an agent of knowledge transfer, they are also an agent of post-training change.

Due to the empirical object, namely the two practical guides used in GMF/GMF (Ministère de la Santé et des Services sociaux 2019a, 2019b), we retained the concept of circumdisciplinarity, which has the same attributes as the classics of interprofessional collaboration (Couturier and Belzile 2018), but are extended to other categories of actors than just professionals (Lenoir 2000), such as caregivers and nonprofessional caregivers, including nursing assistants. The concept of circumdisciplinarity therefore makes it possible to conceive of the interdependence of actors of a disparate nature. Circumdisciplinarity therefore forms a reflexive process by which a series of pragmatically interdependent and co-active actors recognize each other's legitimacy to collaborate, regardless of their professional status, and including patients themselves. F2PL intervention research therefore recognizes the patient as being co-active in the circumdisciplinary reflective processes unfolding in the space of ongoing training in practice settings.

Finally, we retained the Montreal model (Pomey et al. 2015) (Figure 13.1) to conceptualize the role of patients, in particular the graduated continuum of the degree of patient engagement that it offers, a continuum ranging from simple information to full partnership. We also note the multiplicity and structuring of the levels of action that patient engagement can concern. The model already recognizes teaching as a legitimate level of partnership with patients, but does not distinguish initial training from continuous training. At the highest level of educational participation, the model also recognizes conceptual contribution from patients. In addition, at the bottom of the matrix-type diagram, we find a list of partnership determinants which includes the training of patients and the support that they can offer to practitioners in a work context. This matrix will allow us to logically insert the specific contributions of the work that we present here into this synthesis.

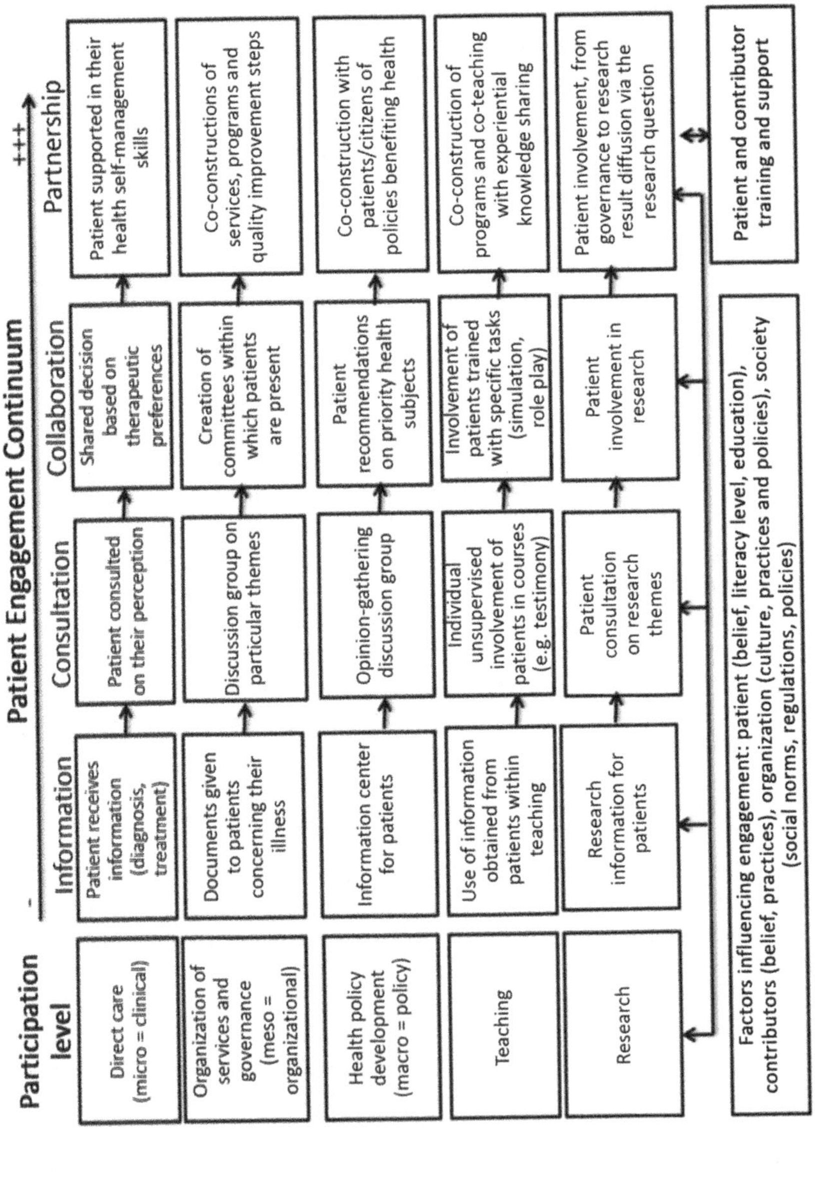

Figure 13.1. *The Montreal model (Pomey et al. 2015)*

13.6. Intervention

The F2PL intervention research therefore, among other things, carried out training with regard to the two practice guides and evaluated its implementation (process and effects) using the Kirkpatrick model (2009). Since its conception, the research team has included two patient researchers. It was subsidized by a primary care research program that very explicitly valued patient partnerships, making it a qualification and evaluation criterion for obtaining funding.

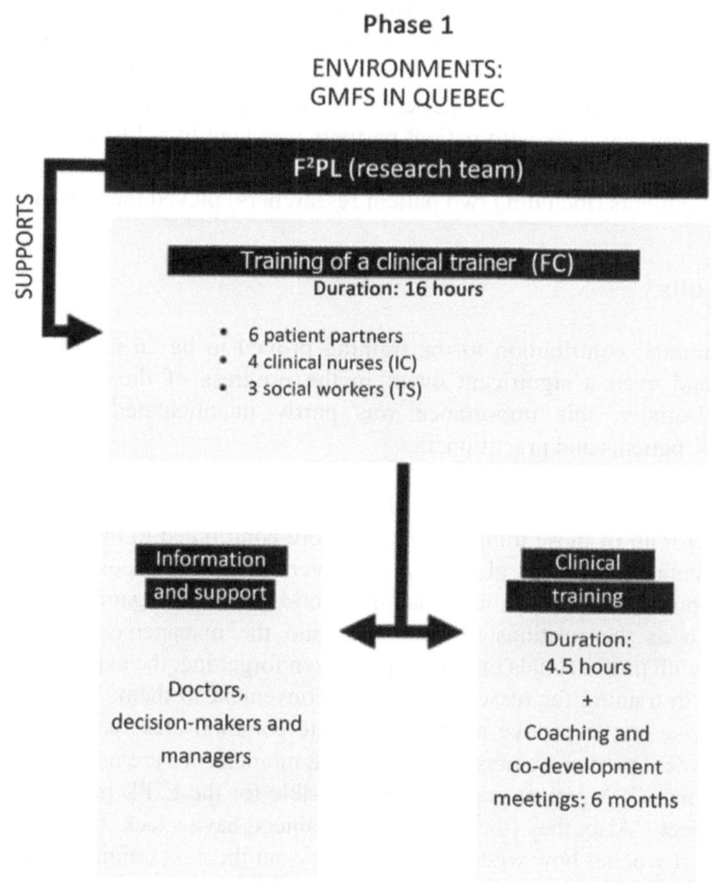

Figure 13.2. *The Front-Line Train-the-Trainer Approach (F2PL) Intervention*

The train-the-trainer approach was developed in partnership with patients, and was then offered in GMFs through a triptych design of the trainer team which included a social work trainer, another in nursing sciences and two patients (Figure 13.2).

This training was offered in six GMFs selected for their socio-demographic characteristics (metropolitan, urban, semi-urban) to social workers and nurses from these organizations. It is expected that these second-generation trainers will train all of the professionals concerned by the practice guides targeting the entirety of their territory, and then the whole of Quebec, which has more than 350 GMFs.

13.7. Methodology

We carried out a questionnaire survey among trainers and trainees, as well as individual and collective interviews with them (n = 46) and users of GMF services (n = 49). These last interviews were carried out by the patient-researchers themselves, from patient to patient. A logbook of intervention research co-development activities with patient partners was kept by all trainers. Support for patient trainers was also offered (additional specific training, support meetings, etc.). In total, six patients (including two patient researchers) played the role of trainers.

13.8. Results

The patients' contribution to the training proved to be an important source of learning, and even a significant event in the progress of the F2PL intervention research. Initially, this importance was partly unanticipated by the team of researchers, patients and practitioners.

Indeed, the inclusion of patients in the train-the-trainer approach was an enriching experience for all of those trained. This therefore contributed to the performance that we documented (Poitras et al. 2022). However, despite this positive outlook, this specific contribution from patients has in practice come up against simple practical issues, such as the relationship with time and the management of trainer trios' schedules, with professionals minimizing, or even forgetting, the expected contribution of patients in training for reasons which are convenient to them: "We will probably have to revise our respective agendas to create common areas and be able to offer dates [to patient partner trainers] because at the moment, we are never all available at the same time...". A patient partner co-responsible for the F2PL project also testifies on this subject: "Also, they [the professional trainers] have a lack, if not an absence of availability. I wonder how we are going to carry out the next training courses". It was not the relevance in principle of their contribution that was in question, but rather its conceptual and operational value to the training which de facto seemed secondary to the work plan of professional trainers. "I think we will have to further reframe the terms of everyone's involvement, because it looks like we have a team and a sub-team [between professional trainers and patient trainers]". It is important here to emphasize that this resistance was largely unconscious, incorporated into a positive but restricted representation of the role of patients in such training.

The transition from the classic testimonial logic, whose value is immediately recognized by all trainers, to a more ambitious logic of co-designers of training, then to the title of trainer in all its fullness, required a sustained effort so that it is internalized in representations and then accomplished in practice. To do this, additional ad hoc training for professional trainers on the value of the andragogical contribution of the patients' contribution was developed during the intervention:

> Ms. Maltais' presentation will become a facilitator since [during the exchanges] the intervention of the nurse who seemed the most reluctant to the participation of the patient partner in coaching meetings demonstrates an important openness to patient partnership. She says that she herself was surprised by the effect of patient partnership in the first preparatory meeting ahead of training. A barrier has just been removed.

This adjustment allowed for significant effects in the representations of patient partnerships among all participants, including patients: "Also, [after having followed the presentation of the patient partner] I found that all patient trainers better knew their roles". In fact, granting the same trainer status to patients as to professionals has had more impact than the classically interprofessional notion of training, that is, the second conceptual target of innovation. This impact shows the potential contribution of the patient partner function in the field of ongoing health training, from a perspective that we have called circumdisciplinary.

13.9. Favorable conditions for full recognition of trainer status for patients in the context of ongoing training

Among the conditions favorable to the full recognition of the status of trainer for patients in the context of ongoing training, among others and in addition to a change of status, is the creation of patient trainer duos, which has enabled solidarity between these two trainers and the balancing of the symbolic weight of trainer teams (two professionals, two patients): "Teamwork and complicity [with the other patient trainer] is a facilitator during activities with the training team". Likewise, the development of andragogical training tools didacticizing training objects for patient-trainers made it possible to insert the classic testimonial approach into didacticized objects, such as, for example, an expanded interprofessional collaboration or change management taking into account the patient's expertise. The governance of the intervention also had to integrate activities to recall the innovative intention, supporting trainers in becoming aware of the ins and outs of strongly recognizing patients as trainers in their own right. To do this, the research team continuously supported a practice community bringing six patient trainers together in order to encourage the development of their ability to play a training role fully.

Furthermore, settings wherein the experience patient partnership was more modest experienced more substantial difficulties. On the contrary, in more experienced settings, patients found it easier to manage the difficulties encountered by themselves. In the first group of environments, an erroneous representation was observed: patient partnership is above all a matter of goodwill which does not require specific training. Our study shows that this information is false and that it is easily correctable through an additional training approach for professional trainers. Measuring the degree of literacy of professionals with regard to patient partnership is undoubtedly necessary before the creation of circumdisciplinary trainer-teams in order to avoid having to slow down the training currently being developed, compensating for such erroneous representations.

13.10. An enrichment proposal for the Montreal model

Our proposal orders the logical levels on which patient partnership acts differently, starting from what appears to us as the most general to the most specific, in this case the clinic (Figure 13.3). Above all, it inserts two additional levels into action levels, namely that of ongoing training in a practice environment, which, for example, in a university context, does not have the same ins and outs as that of initial professional training, then that of support for practice changes which acts during innovation implementation. This proposal in no way changes the fundamental logic of the Montreal model, but it opens the door to consider places for the application of patient partnership which are not explicitly developed there. This proposal enriches the model, especially with regard to the mobilization of patients as closely as possible to professional and organizational practices. We have slightly edited some of the initial model's contents in order to harmonize them with the insertion of additional levels which we have added and framed in Figure 13.3.

The potentially most significant contribution of this proposed enrichment of the Montreal model concerns the beginnings of a conceptualization of the contribution of patient partners beyond the sharing of experience, through the testimonies of their participation in decisions on the general orientation of training, for the level which interests us here. We place this above the impact side of experiential knowledge on the objects of knowledge to be transferred within the training framework and on the andragogical strategies to achieve this. Thus, if testimony has certain effectiveness in raising practitioners' awareness of patients' experiences, this experience contains much more than the effect. It is full of knowledge and also contributes to the pragmatic effectiveness of training in practice environments.

Patient Engagement Continuum +++

Participation level	Information	Consultation	Collaboration	Partnership
Research	Research information for patients	Patient consultation on research themes	Patient involvement in research	Patient involvement, from governance to research result diffusion via the research question
Health policy development (macro = policy)	Information center for patients	Opinion-gathering discussion group	Patient recommendations on priority health subjects	Co-construction with patients/citizens of policies benefiting health
Teaching	Use of information obtained from patients within teaching	Individual unsupervised involvement of patients in courses (e.g. testimony)	Involvement of patients trained with specific tasks (simulation, role play)	Co-construction of programs and co-teaching with experiential knowledge sharing
Organization of services and governance (meso = organizational)	Documents given to patients concerning their illness	Discussion group on particular themes	Creation of committees within which patients are present	Co-construction of services, programs and quality improvement steps
Professional development on the job (skill-strengthening)	The non-mobilized patient	The patient consulted on their expectations	Patient testifies on their experience	Co-construction of training (goals, andragogical strategies and contents), testifies as to their experience and contributes to training as a content expert
Support for change in practices	The non-mobilized patient	The patient consulted on their expectations	Patient testifies on their experience and appreciates change	Co-construction of the support for change strategy, testifies as to their experience and contributes to support as a content expert
Direct care (micro = clinical)	Patient receives information (diagnosis, treatment)	Patient consulted on their perception	Shared decision based on therapeutic preferences	Patient supported in their health self-management skills

Figure 13.3. *An enrichment proposal for the Montreal model (Pomey et al. 2015)*

13.11. Conclusion

Overall, the study shows that patients can have a deeper role than witnessing their own experience. This testimonial tradition has a certain value, including from the point of view of the patients themselves. Their recognition as a full-fledged trainer nevertheless extends the scope of their contribution in terms of design expertise, of andragogy and of the capacity to act directly within change management. The circumdisciplinary effect of the train-the-trainer approach recognizing an enlarged role for patients enriches classic active pedagogy into an andragogy that postulates the didactic value of the overall patient experience. In doing so, practitioners trained on the job can experience an expansion of their professional development through this direct experience of clinical experience diversity.

13.12. References

Al Mosawi, A. (2021). *Training of the Trainers (TOT) Course Textbook*. Scholars' Press, Saarbrücken.

Association of American Medical Colleges (2008). *The Medical Home: AAMC Position Statement*. Association of American Medical Colleges, Washington.

Couturier, Y. and Belzile, L. (2018). *La collaboration interprofessionnelle en santé et services sociaux*. Presses de l'Université de Montréal, Montreal.

Fraser, C., Grundy, A., Meade, O., Callaghan, P., Lovell, K. (2017). EQUIP training the trainers: An evaluation of a training programme for service users and carers involved in training mental health professionals in user-involved care planning. *Journal of Psychiatric and Mental Health Nursing*, 24(6), 367–376.

Jouet, E., Flora, L., Las Vergnas, O. (2010). Construction et reconnaissance des savoirs expérientiels des patients : note de synthèse. *Pratiques de formation/Analyses*, 58/59, 13–94 [Online]. Available at: https://hal.archives-ouvertes.fr/hal-00645113/document [Accessed 25th January 2022].

Kirkpatrick, D.L. (2009). *Implementing the Four Levels: A Practical Guide for Effective Evaluation of Training Programs*. Berrett-Koehler Publishers, San Francisco, CA.

Kirkpatrick, J.D. and Kirkpatrick, W.K. (2016). *Kirkpatrick's Four Levels of Training Evaluation*. Association for Talent Development, Alexandria, VA.

Lenoir, Y. (2000). Formation à l'enseignement et interdisciplinarité : un mythe ou une exigence ? Dépasser l'interdisciplinarité et penser circumdisciplinarité. *European Journal of Teacher Education*, 23(3), 289–298.

Menear, M., Blanchette, M., Demers-Payette, O., Roy, D. (2019). A framework for value-creating learning health systems. *Health Research Policy and Systems*, 17(1), 1–13.

Ministère de la Santé et des Services sociaux du Québec (2015). Cadre de gestion des groupes de médecine de familles (GMF) et des groupes de médecines de famille-Réseau (GMF-R) [Online]. Available at: https://www.msss.gouv.qc.ca/inc/documents/ministere/acces_info/demandes-acces/2015-2016/2015-2016-285-Document.pdf [Accessed 25 January 2022].

Ministère de la Santé et des Services sociaux du Québec (2016). Cadre de gestion des groupes de médecine de familles universitaires (GMF-U) [Online]. Available at: https://publications.msss.gouv.qc.ca/msss/document-001771/ [Accessed 25 January 2022].

Ministère de la Santé et des Services sociaux du Québec (2019a). Guide pratique à l'intention des infirmières cliniciennes qui travaillent dans un groupe de médecine de famille ou un groupe de médecine de famille universitaire [Online]. Available at: https://publications.msss.gouv.qc.ca/msss/fichiers/2019/19-924-11W.pdf [Accessed 25 January 2022].

Ministère de la Santé et des Services sociaux du Québec (2019b). Guide pratique à l'intention des travailleurs sociaux issus d'un établissement du réseau de la santé et des services sociaux et qui travaillent dans un groupe de médecine de famille ou un groupe de médecine de famille universitaire [Online]. Available at: https://publications.msss.gouv.qc.ca/msss/document-002375/ [Accessed 25 January 2022].

Moore, D.E., Green, J.S., Gallis, H.A. (2009). Achieving desired results and improved outcomes: Integrating planning and assessment throughout learning activities. *Journal of Continuing Education in the Health Professions*, 29(1), 1–15.

Pearce, J., Mann, M.K., Jones, C., van Buschbach, S., Olff, M., Bisson, J.I. (2012). The most effective way of delivering a train-the-trainers program: A systematic review. *The Journal of Continuing Education in the Health Professions*, 32(3), 215–226.

Poitras, M.-E., Godbout, I., Vaillancourt, V.T., Poirier, A., Prevost, K., Débarges, B., Spence, C. (2020). Step-by-step strategies for an integrated patient-oriented research: Lessons learned from a multicentered study. *Science of Nursing and Health Practices*, 3(2), 1–9.

Poitras, M.-E., Bélanger, E., Vaillancourt, V.T., Kienlin, S., Körner, M., Godbout, I., Bernard-Hamel, J., O'Connor, S., Blanchette, P., Khadhraoui, L. et al. (2021). Interventions to improve trainers' learning and behaviors for educating health care professionals using train-the-trainer method: A systematic review and meta-analysis. *The Journal of Continuing Education in the Health Professions*, 41(3), 202–209.

Poitras, M.-E., Couturier, Y., Massé, S., Vaillancourt, V.T., Poirier, M.-D., Gauthier, G., Hudon, C., Delli-Colli, N., Gagnon, D., Careau, E. et al. (2022). Co-design, implementation, and evaluation of an expanded train-the-trainer strategy to support the sustainability of evidence-based practice guides for registered nurses and social workers in primary care clinics: A developmental evaluation protocol. *BMC Primary Care*, 23(84).

Pomey, M., Flora, L., Karazivan, P., Dumez, V., Lebel, P., Vanier, M., Jouet, E. (2015). Le "Montreal model" : enjeux du partenariat relationnel entre patients et professionnels de la santé. *Santé publique*, 1, 41–50.

Pomey, M.P., Bush, P.L., Demers-Payette, O., L'Espérance, A., Lochhead, L., Ganache, I., Roy, D. (2020). Developing recommendations for the diagnosis and treatment of Lyme disease: The role of the patient's perspective in a controversial environment. *International Journal of Technology Assessment in Health Care*, 37(1), 1–6.

Wagner, E.H. (1999). Care of older people with chronic illness. In *New Ways to Care for Older People: Building Systems Based on Evidence*, Calkins, E., Boult, C., Wagner, E.H. (eds). Springer, New York, 39–64.

Wittorski, R. (2007). *Professionnalisation et développement professionnel*. L'Harmattan, Paris.

14

The Care Partnership: Challenges and Perspectives for Healthcare Systems

14.1. Introduction

This chapter is a summary of the thesis that we defended in September 2021 to obtain the Doctorate in Business Administration (DBA) from the IAE Lyon School of Management (Université de Lyon 3 Jean Moulin) and the Business Science Institute. The thesis is entitled "The care partnership: ecosystem evidence" (Anhorn 2021).

While the care partnership has already been present for several years now, within certain institutions and medical consultations, it still does not constitute – by quite a margin – the standard within health systems, that is, throughout the care chain. The "patient at the center" notion, branded as a slogan by many professionals, has established itself as a standard in the name of which patients most often remain the object of – even benevolent – attention from professional health workers, while still not participating in the co-construction of their own project. In short: we continue to do "for" instead of doing "with". The importance of taking patients' experiential knowledge into account not only in care but also in organization and governance, in the definition of health policies, in training and research, has been widely demonstrated. Why and how to deploy this partnership within a regional healthcare system remains to be studied, and not in isolation by a few of its actors. Based on the theoretical model of business ecosystems, in which all stakeholders must share values, language and practices that aim to achieve a common objective, we operated a mixed methods research system. We deduced a theoretical contribution from it – general recommendations for the deployment of the partnership in healthcare

Chapter written by Philippe ANHORN.

systems in general – and a series of managerial, strategic and operational recommendations, for its implementation in our organization in particular.

14.2. Context and definitions

Our research took place within our organization, Réseau Santé Région Lausanne (the Lausanne Region Health Network). They focused on the care partnership with patients, and were mainly based on intervention research linked to the deployment of the anticipated care project. These three concepts are briefly described in sections 14.2.1 to 14.2.3.

14.2.1. *The Réseau Santé Région Lausanne (RSRL)*[1]

The RSRL is one of the four networks of active healthcare providers recognized as of public interest in the territory of the Canton of Vaud in Switzerland. The cantonal law on healthcare networks of 2007[2] requires all subsidized care providers[3] to join and contribute to the network in their region. The RSRL thus brings together a university hospital (CHUV, Centre hospitalo-universitaire vaudois, Lausanne)[4], four other acute care and rehabilitation hospitals, 19 medico-social centers (*centres médico-sociaux* or CMS, home help and care), 68 medico-social establishments (*établissements médico-sociaux* or EMS, medicalized retirement homes) and medicalized psychosocial establishments (*établissements psychosociaux médicalisés* or EPSM), 56 private associate members (clinics, private home care organizations), more than 800 doctors and other professionals in free practice, and finally 61 territorial municipalities whose elected officials are considered to be legitimate spokespersons for the needs of the population, for those who are sick or in good health. The RSRL directly employs nearly 100 employees (mainly liaison nurses) and has an annual budget of around 12 million Swiss francs. It is constituted in the form of a private law association. Its supreme body is the Assemblée générale (French General Assembly). This elects a steering committee made up of two representatives for each of the five groups of affiliated members (acute care and rehabilitation hospitals, EMS/EPSM, CMS, doctors, municipalities). This committee

---

1 See: https://www.rsrl.ch.

2 See: https://www.reseau-sante-region-lausanne.ch/system/files/2014/02/loi_sur_les_reseaux_2007.pdf.

3 The public health law conditions the authorization to operate or practice of providers who are not subsidized or recognized as being in the public interest (RIP) on their membership as associate members. They, in exchange for a modest contribution, receive information from the network and can participate in its activities.

4 Vaud University Hospital Center, Lausanne – in English.

can be likened to a tactical consultation table (Couturier et al. 2011), a place conducive to the definition of regional projects financed by the allocation of pooled resources (subsidies, general and member contributions). The networks in the canton of Vaud are designed to improve the coordination and continuity of care, to guide users within the healthcare system, to promote interinstitutional collaboration at the regional level and the implementation of public health programs. Their services, provided through BRIOs (*bureaux régionaux d'information et d'orientation*: regional information and guidance offices), are mainly aimed at vulnerable elderly people presenting weakening risks, functional decline and/or a loss of autonomy.

14.2.2. *The care partnership*

The partnership between patients and healthcare professionals, also called *patient partnership*, aims to rebalance power between professional and nonprofessional "knowers". It is about moving away from an asymmetrical relationship, or one of agency (Boudier et al. 2012), and considering doctors and other health professionals who, on the one hand have disease expertise, to be of equal importance, to patients or relatives, on the other hand, have expertise in living with the disease. A possible definition of the care partnership, in our context, is that appearing in Quebec in the "reference framework for the partnership approach between users, their loved ones and health and social services actors" (Laverdière et al. 2018):

> Partnership is an approach which is based on the relationship between patients, their loved ones and actors in the healthcare system (professionals and institutions). This relationship relies on complementarity and the sharing of respective knowledge, as well as on the way in which various partners work together. More precisely, the relationship promotes the development of a bond of trust, and recognizes the value and importance of each person's knowledge, including the experiential knowledge of users and their loved ones, as well the importance of co-construction. The partnership can be exercised at the level of care, at the level of the organization of care and services and also at the level of governance.

The notion of care partnership is based on a societal and ethical evolution noticeable since the 1970s in industrialized countries. For a few decades, health systems in Europe and North America have moved away from the paternalistic model, which indisputably prevailed at the end of World War II, to models in which the patient as a person, and especially as an expert on their own situation, is finally taken into account. At the origin of this advancement, we in particular find the concept of medical shared decision-making (Veatch 1972), as well as the appearance since the 1980s, in particular in the field of psychiatry, of a biopsychosocial approach to health rather than the purely biomedical one that prevailed until then (Engel 1981). The growth of the care partnership should also be compared with that of therapeutic patient education (TPE), which has appeared since 1998 as a basic concept in the WHO glossary on health promotion (WHO 1998), as well as empowerment (Fumagalli et al. 2015). Simultaneously, the concept of patient partner has established itself in certain national health policies since the beginning of the 2000s, for example in the United Kingdom in the NHS (Stuart 1999), regardless of the way in which patients actually perceive their role (Thompson 2007), and even though this approach had until then only demonstrated its influence on patient satisfaction and not yet strictly speaking, on the quality of care (Crawford et al. 2002). These notions were subsequently clarified with the definition, measurement and monitoring of patient experience (Wolf et al. 2014).

A synthesis of the thoughts and experiences carried out so far in Quebec and internationally in the field of health partnerships, the *Montreal Model* was conceived in an article published in early 2015 by a group of researchers, both patients and health professionals, based on their work carried out in 2010 at the University of Montreal (Pomey et al. 2015). The authors do a remarkable job of synthesis and simplification, in particular by representing the evolution of the possible roles of the patient (resource, coach, trainer, researcher, etc.), who is no longer as they were the day before last, the "object" of a paternalistic care system nor, as they were the next day, "at the center" of this system, benefiting from the caring attention of health personnel who give their very best to them. The patient is now part of the healthcare team (or management, training, research, etc.), which collaborates with them, placing their experiential knowledge (life with the illness) at the same level as scientific knowledge (the disease) present within the team (Figure 14.1.) As stated by Vincent Dumez, co-author of the *Montreal Model*, during the second international conference on care partnership with patients, organized by the University of Toulouse Jean Jaurès on February 25 and 26, 2021[5]: "The care partnership is not a caregiver–patient relationship, but a caregiver-caregiver one!".

The Montreal Model is today considered a founding text, particularly in Europe and North America, thanks to a very active policy of promotion, dissemination and advice, led by the Center of Excellence on Partnership with Patients and the Public (*Centre d'excellence sur le partenariat avec les patients et le public*: CEPPP)[6] created and co-directed by the article's authors.

5 See: https://partenariat2020.sciencesconf.org/.

6 See: https://ceppp.ca/fr/.

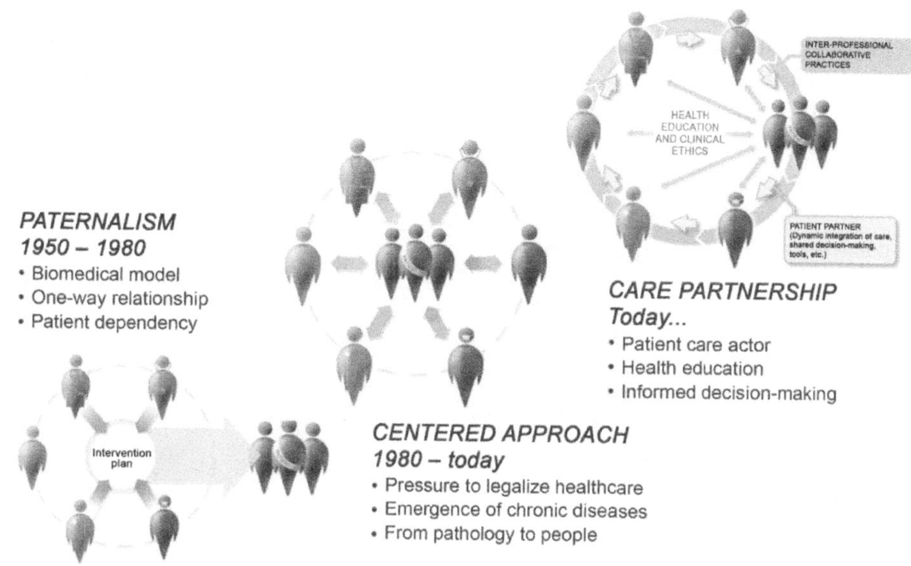

Figure 14.1. *Gradual evolution of the care partnership (according to: CPASS). For a color version of this figure, see www.iste.co.uk/flora/experience.zip*

14.2.3. *The anticipated care plan (ProSA)*

The reflections and work on the anticipated care project within the RSRL date back to 2017. That year, the network members decided to launch a project aimed at deploying "levels of care" in a coordinated manner, as they are used in Quebec to help patients determine their therapeutic objectives and ensure that these objectives are understood and applied in an identical manner by the institutions and professionals of regional health systems (Jean et al. 2016). The project team, which first carried out a literature review and an examination of existing systems in Switzerland, broadened the reflection framework to the entire field of Advance Care Planning (ACP) (Emanuel et al. 2000). This approach, born at the end of the 1960s in the United States in circles defending human rights, and in particular the right to die with dignity, developed at the same time as palliative care, especially in Anglo-Saxon countries (Sabatino 2010). ACP makes it possible to consider the question of care levels from the angle of therapeutic objectives, that is, one possible result among others (with advance directives, the designation of a therapeutic representative, etc.) of a discussion that the patient may have about their care values and preferences, with a health professional specially trained for this purpose. This approach, carried out within the RSRL jointly with the chair of geriatric palliative care at the CHUV[7], is called the anticipated care project (ProSA)[8]. It could be, in the field of somatic health, a strong vector of partnership between patients, relatives, professionals and institutions, just as the mental health joint crisis plan (plan de crise conjoint: PCC) (Ferrari et al. 2018) is already within the RSRL.

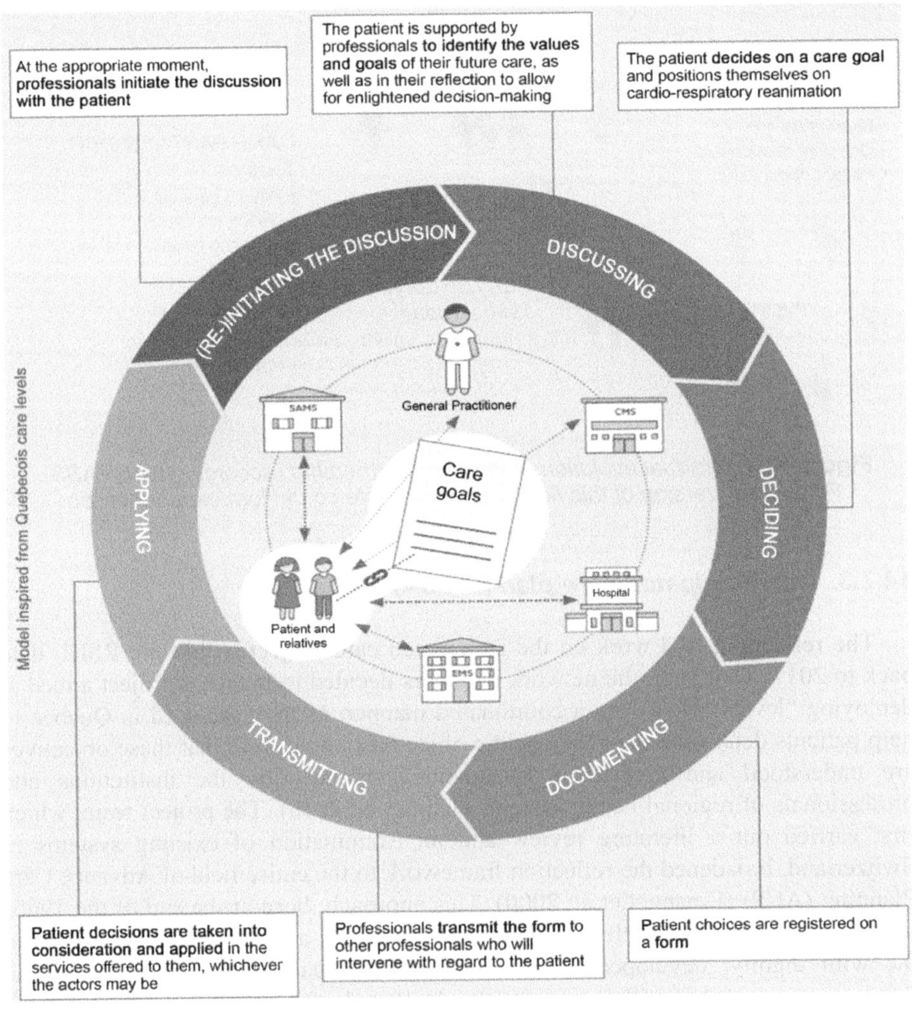

Figure 14.2. *Extract from the RSRL poster on the anticipated care plan (ProSA or PAS). For a color version of this figure, see www.iste.co.uk/flora/experience.zip*

7 See: https://www.chuv.ch/fr/fiches/chaire-de-soins-palliatifs-geriatriques/.

8 See: https://www.reseau-sante-region-lausanne.ch/projet-anticipe-des-soins-pas.

ProSA is in fact intrinsically based on the care partnership approach. It particularly consists, for health institutions and professionals jointly with the patient and their loved ones, of establishing and then continually updating the objectives of care, according to a process described in Figure 14.2, regardless of the environment in which the patient will be located (hospital, home, retirement home, etc.), and even in the event of an emergency or if the patient no longer has their capacity for judgment at the time the services are provided. After an assessment shedding light on knowledge and respective practices on issues related to anticipation, self-determination and partnership between patients and health personnel (Devaux et al. 2018), patients and members of the RSRL are today involved in the co-construction of the project's processes and tools with a view to its deployment after a test phase which took place in 2020–2021 in several healthcare settings. As part of our thesis, we followed this project in an intervention research mode. We are indeed convinced that ProSA can contribute to creating a convergence of the patient-partner care approach among the actors concerned and, in doing so, contribute to increased integration of the regional health system (Anhorn et al. 2018).

14.3. Theoretical foundations of the research

We first attempted to examine the deployment of the care partnership from the perspective of theories of organizational change (Van de Ven and Poole 1995; Kerber and Buono 2005). However, we found them difficult to operationalize in a field where change is more incremental than radical. After a detour via the sociology of translation (Callon 1986; Strum et al. 2013), we wanted to maintain an "organic" approach while returning to a framework better suited to management, and opted for that of the business ecosystem model (Moore 1993, 1996, 2006). It applies itself opportunely to the evolution of a regional health system, since it carries with it the notion of the permanent adjustment of actors for the purposes of (societal, as far as we are concerned) coordination and innovation. It was relatively simple for us to represent a regional health system (in our example: the Lausanne Regional Health Network) by drawing inspiration from Moore's business ecosystem model. "Direct clients" and "clients of my clients" are transposed into "patients and loved ones". The role of state services, included in the health ecosystem in the broad sense, is all the more interesting as it includes not only health or social action services but also those which manage other public policies (environment, land use planning, etc.), which we know, among health determinants, have an even greater impact.

14.4. Methodology

Having adopted a pragmatic constructivist epistemological position, we used mixed methods (Creswell and Plano Clark 2018). The main focus was qualitative: intervention research (Savall and Zardet 1987, 2015; Coghlan and Brydon-Miller 2014) on the introduction of the anticipated care project within a regional health network allowed us to follow around 10 clinical situations and to speak with patients, their loved ones, professionals and those responsible for the institutions involved. We were able to contextualize our observations thanks to two questionnaire surveys conducted one year apart among network stakeholders, punctuated by exploratory and explanatory interviews. In total, we collected 619 individual contributions, including 504 from professionals and 115 from patients. The quantitative data was administered and statistically analyzed with the Sphinx Déclic software, while the qualitative data (recordings and transcriptions of interviews on RedCap) were the subject of lexical analyses by grouping verbatims according to key ideas or metadata (tags) identified by focus groups.

14.5. Main research results

Our research, conducted with different methodologies, generated a large amount of data, at different times. Some of this data arrived "in packs", like the results of our questionnaire surveys, while others arrived continuously, like those from our intervention research. It quickly became apparent that presenting our results in a linear or sequential form would not do justice to the richness of the empirical work we implemented. Hence, we kept the question of how to organize and present our results open for as long as possible. In the end, several meetings and discussions, both with teams of professionals and with patients, allowed us to arrange the data in multiple forms, until they ultimately "revealed" something to us, in the way of film photographs in developing baths. In particular, since we had chosen to work with mixed methods, there was a question of illuminating certain results obtained with one of the methods, with results both similar and different, and generated by another method. In sections 14.5.1 to 14.5.4, we will highlight the main elements thus "revealed".

14.5.1. *The importance of the care partnership*

The patient care partnership is very well known within the RSRL. 85% of those questioned say that the Quebec definition is completely or at least partially known to them. This result is a happy surprise, which contrasts the results from a similar survey conducted at the same time with a sample of comparable size at the national level in France (Voyen et al. 2020), but exclusively among professionals involved in therapeutic patient education (TPE). The results of this survey showed that the concept of care partnership (patient care partner approach, *approche patient partenaire de soins* (APPS) in French, in this context) was poorly known among professionals: "13% do not know it and 47% know it vaguely". Compared with 85% of our own surveys, there would therefore only be 40% of French TPE professionals who are perfectly or partially familiar with the care partnership.

Care partnership is widely practiced within the RSRL. Nearly 9 out of 10 people responding to our surveys say they practice it systematically or occasionally. However, this figure drops to 5 out of 10 when we ask patients or those who represent them if they consider their care to be part of a partnership. The care partnership is mainly present in the clinic as well as in the organization of care and services. There is a heartening upward trend in governance and research.

The known roles of the partnership are mainly those of patient-partners in the care relationship (80%), expert patients (40%) in support of care structures, for example in the development of their protocols or for the organization of their services, and finally more and more peer caregivers or peer practitioners (from 25% in 2020 to 35% in 2021) mainly involved in supporting people suffering from a pathology similar to that which they experienced before their recovery, whether provisional, lasting or definitive.

The benefit of the care partnership is rated as essential or of great interest by 87% of respondents. The "top 3" areas in which the partnership is of essential interest are: 1) quality, safety, care economics; 2) organization of benefits and services; and 3) training. This last mention is all the more important as the care partnership dimension is still largely insufficient, or even completely absent, in professional training courses.

Between 8 and 9 out of 10 respondents consider the care partnership to be very important and that it will develop in times to come. These results from our surveys are strongly corroborated by our comprehension interviews and by our observations as part of our intervention research. The care partnership within the RSRL is therefore a major trend, and not simply an emerging or marginal practice.

14.5.2. *The need for an action plan*

Practicing the care partnership can prove to be very different depending on the moments the question is asked and depending on the generation or socio-professional sphere considered. Above all, we were shocked to discover through our surveys that it is claimed by 95% of professionals, while it is effectively only perceived by 49% of patients and their representatives!

This asymmetry in perceptions alone demonstrates the need to create a common language and shared values throughout the regional health system. Today, the fragmentation of structures, as well as that of the professional cultures that coexist there, and the quantity and heterogeneity of the rules that apply to them, are all explanations for very different practices and representations of the care partnership. The creation of a common culture is essential.

The fruits of the care partnership are not necessarily reaped in the structures that invest resources in it. It is therefore essential that its practice and financing be established within a framework that encourages and facilitates the pooling of resources, for example that of the network.

The establishment of the care partnership must move from a pilot mode to that of "default setting" in the relationship between patients and health professionals. This is the condition so that it no longer constitutes a task for professionals to "do in addition" to their already overloaded ordinary activities, and that it consists of "doing (these activities) differently". The challenge is therefore that of a transformation of practices and of the system.

This transformation must take place in a coordinated and synchronous manner. Indeed, beyond a certain experimental stage for the benefit of project financing, no actor can have an interest in playing the "good students" in the long term and in isolation. The emergence of the care partnership and its benefits can only take place in a global and simultaneous movement within the network.

These findings strongly argue for taking into account the care partnership as a strong strategic axis for the development of the regional health ecosystem, expressed in an operational action plan, the broad outlines of which we have outlined. Our proposals address the main problems that can be encountered in the introduction of a new paradigm within an ecosystem, and the change management that must necessarily accompany it.

14.5.3. *On the need to remove or alleviate structural obstacles*

The care partnership is practiced in a growing number of structures within the RSRL, and we were delighted to learn through our surveys that the transversal practice of the partnership, that is, the experience lived by patients and professionals simultaneously in several institutions or care settings, is growing from 19.6% in 2020 to 23.5% in 2021.

It is also heartening to note that 9 out of 10 of our respondents consider the care partnership as a factor facilitating continuity of care within the network.

However, we note in our comprehension interviews and our observations during our intervention research that it is not enough to be convinced of the "benefits" of the care partnership and to act directly on the factors that promote its coordinated deployment within the network. Structural obstacles appear to be persistent. They drench the enthusiasm of the most ardent care partnership promoters.

The most important of these structural obstacles have been identified by our research. These include the absence of an electronic patient record, disparate financing arrangements that prevail in different care settings and the absence of research locally producing conclusive data to support the deployment of the healthcare partnership within the regional health system.

Actors within the network must not only commit collectively to promoting the care partnership but also unite their efforts to remove or circumvent these structural obstacles.

14.5.4. *The opportunity to act in a favorable temporal context*

Finally, we were surprised to note to what extent the pandemic context that prevailed in 2020 and 2021 did not weaken, but on the contrary generally strengthened the interest and attractiveness of the care partnership, both among patients and among professionals as well as in structures within the network. Questions of ethics and solidarity were widely discussed during this period. Interest in people's anticipation and self-determination measures has been brought to the forefront, particularly with regard to advance directives for elderly or at-risk people contracting Covid-19. Unfortunately, it has still too rarely resulted in concrete measures. This "robustness" or persistence of our topic, notwithstanding a major disruptive event in the functioning of the health system (could we imagine a bigger disruption in the health field than a pandemic?) allows us to affirm that this really is a major trend and not a fad.

The question of cost control in compulsory health insurance, recurrent since the introduction of the federal law on health insurance (*loi fédérale sur l'assurance maladie*: LAMal) in 1994, cyclically gives rise to proposals linked to the quality and coordination of care. These themes are each time imbued with the political or societal trends which prevail in the field of health when political or administrative proposals are formulated. Today, the care partnership is implicitly, and sometimes even explicitly, a part of these proposals.

The cantonal context is also favorable. The care partnership is in line with the values of the political leaders in charge of health, and aligned with the strategic objectives of the General Directorate for Health (*direction générale de la santé*). It is looking precisely, within the cantonal health system, for actors capable of transforming these values and objectives into concrete and tangible achievements for the population.

Projects launched on a pilot basis by the RSRL and several partners, intrinsically based on the care partnership, such as the anticipated care project (*projet de soins anticipé*: ProSA) or the joint mental health crisis plan (*crise conjoint en santé mentale*: PCC), are now entering into their deployment phase. This moment, which consists of both a change of scale – from regional to cantonal – and an assimilation of new practices into existing operations rather than the accomplishment of additional tasks "in project mode", is particularly favorable to the generalization and intensification of the care partnership within the network. The time has come to generalize and deploy, or as the saying goes: "Scale up and spread!" (Greenhalgh and Papoutsi 2019).

14.6. Conclusion

Based on our results, we attempted, during reflections and group work with patients and professionals, to make general recommendations, returning to the theoretical framework of business ecosystems (Figure 14.3).

Moore highlighted the cooperation and competition issues of a business ecosystem during the four classic phases of its life cycle with the contemporary of the notion of "coopetition" (Nalebuff et al. 1996). By analogy, the issues that apply more specifically to a regional health ecosystem have been formulated. This generalization turns out to be plausible, even if a selection bias could probably not have been completely avoided (most of the participants in the surveys and interviews undoubtedly favored the partnership). However, the number of contributions collected, as well as the avenues already activated for future research, suggest that these results are valid.

Stage of development of the business ecosystem	Overall leadership challenges	COOPERATIVE CHALLENGES	COMPETITIVE CHALLENGES
Pioneering	Value	Defining (in partnership) the partnership objectives, launch test-projects (ProSA, PCC, etc.) at the clinical scale	Targeting projects addressing populations or trajectories which present the best rationalization potentials
Expansion	Critical mass	Generalizing partnership in clinical projects and to introduce it at the governance level (scale-up and spread)	Reinforcing the attractiveness of a network within which partnership is an efficiency and quality guarantee for performance and services
Authority	Lead coevolution	Adapting the chart and statuses, and including partnership within strategic plans	Including partnership in contracts (members, State, insurers, suppliers, etc.)
Renewal	Continuous performance improvment	Creating new partnership projects generating innovations and continuous improvement	Making sure that the partnership benefits all actors within the ecosystem, preventing external interferences

Figure 14.3. *Challenges for the deployment of care partnerships in healthcare systems (according to Moore 1996). For a color version of this figure, see www.iste.co.uk/flora/experience.zip*

14.6.1. *Conclusion and managerial recommendations*

In conclusion, in the case of the Lausanne Regional Health Network, we observed several possible effects of the care partnership on the very functioning of the regional health ecosystem.

– The care partnership can act as an important catalyst for the increased coordination of actors within the regional health ecosystem. We do know that "through regulations, reproduction and learning, [these] develop their capacity to resist entropy, allowing for flexibility, adaptation and piloting according to objectives rather than programming" (Mira-Bonnardel et al. 2012). The deployment of the care partnership precisely constitutes one of these objectives. The pursuit of this objective in an ecosystem like ours, which is non-profit and without a "leader", involves the creation of a common culture and values, the pooling of resources and the definition of a common implementation strategy. While the fragmentation of regulatory and financial frameworks encourages each actor within the system to "defend their territory" and "strengthen their positions", it seems that giving, if not power then at least a voice, to patients is the only means of forcing these actors to further coordinate their action. More and more, elderly patients, chronically ill people and their loved ones are telling us: "I don't want to repeat the same exams several times or tirelessly tell new people about my journey!", "I would like my mother's doctor to have access to all her treatments, and to be able to coordinate them", "I have written an advance care plan, but how can I be sure that it will be respected if I lose my judgment or if I am admitted to the emergency room?". How much longer will we be able to answer them: "Sorry, but that's not going to be possible", "Each healthcare structure operates with its own rules, processes, financing and costs; impossible to coordinate further", "We have been working on the electronic patient file for 25 years, but it still doesn't work…"?

– The healthcare partnership has a strong potential for the overall improvement in the collective performance of the network, that is, the benefits and services offered by its members to the population – healthy or sick – in terms of quality, safety and economizing. This notion of performance, in our interpretation of the theoretical model of business ecosystems, is assimilated into the notion of competitiveness, and justifies the interest of actors within the ecosystem in maintaining and strengthening their cooperation.

– Finally, the care partnership allows the regional health ecosystem and its members to be part of an evolution in society which tends towards greater meaning, ethics and respect. This evolution, perhaps more perceptible in Switzerland than in less prosperous countries where other aspirations remain a priority, is very marked when it comes to the rights of minorities and people in general – marriage for all, *Black Lives Matter*, *#metoo*, women's strikes, etc. – to sustainable development, environmental protection, biodiversity and the climate. This development in the field of health is also reflected, in law, by the place given to the people's autonomy and self-determination. Actors within the regional health ecosystem, whether health institutions or professionals, or patients and loved ones, are ultrasensitive to this development and must integrate it into the way they function. Subsidies, research funds, public or private labeling, certifications based on quality or on the social and environmental responsibility of companies, are all pushing the entire health system to integrate an approach such as that of the care partnership.

We make recommendations with a view to producing "actionable knowledge" and managerial impact, which is the main objective of a DBA thesis, and an important differentiator when compared to a traditional PhD in Science Management. "This must be, in our opinion, a major characteristic of DBA theses, the managerial impact of which is likely to be much more significant than that of

PhDs" (Kalika 2017). As a whole, this is presented in the form of five operational recommendations and three strategic recommendations with a view to the deployment of the care partnership within the RSRL.

14.6.1.1. *Operational recommendations*

We will here formulate five operational recommendations primarily addressed to the RSRL committee formed, let us remember, by representatives of all acute care settings within the network and which should, this being our main recommendation, include patients' representatives before working on and validating these recommendations, and then translating them into a real action plan:

– establishing a care partnership training program within the RSRL;

– organizing meets, meetings, forums and communities practicing the care partnership;

– taking care of human resources management to promote the care partnership;

– integrating the care partnership into resources, tools and methods;

– defining and implementing a care partnership communication strategy.

14.6.1.2. *Strategic recommendations*

We make three strategic recommendations here. They are primarily addressed to the RSRL committee and its partners, mainly to the Department of Health and Social Action of the State of Vaud (*Département de la santé et de l'action sociale de l'État de Vaud*: DSAS) as well as to other health networks, to the umbrella of institutions and professional orders:

– making the electronic patient record (EPR) operational as quickly as possible;

– introducing financing methods by project or target audience favoring care partnerships;

– encouraging the production of local research providing evidence on the care partnership.

Regarding the implementation of these recommendations, we propose applying the principles of implementation and evaluation in the field of health, relying first on incentives and voluntary actors as well as evaluated pilot projects. Such modalities require strong project management, obviously representative of the topic: patient/professional pairs, for example. We recommend that it be placed under the aegis of the network, co-financed and co-directed by its members, and strongly encouraged by state funding.

14.7. References

Anhorn, P. (2021). Le partenariat de soins : une évidence écosystémique ! Le cas du Réseau Santé Région Lausanne. PhD Thesis, Business Science Institute et IAE Lyon School of Management, Lyon 3 Jean Moulin, Lyon. doi: 10.5281/zenodo.5524508.

Anhorn, P., Chinet, M., Devaux, L. (2018). Projet anticipé des soins : un modèle pour des soins intégrés. *Bund, Kantone und Gemeinden in der integrierten Versorgung Rollenszenarien 2026*, 4, 39.

Boudier, F., Bensebaa, F., Jablanczy, A. (2012). L'émergence du patient-expert : une perturbation innovante. *Innovations*, 39, 13–25.

Callon, M. (1986). Éléments pour une sociologie de la traduction : la domestication des coquilles Saint-Jacques et des marins-pêcheurs dans la baie de Saint-Brieuc. *Année Sociol.*, 169–208.

Coghlan, D. and Brydon-Miller, M. (eds) (2014). *The Sage Encyclopedia of Action Research*. SAGE Publications Inc., Thousand Oaks, CA.

Couturier, Y., Belzile, L., Gagnon, D. (2011). Principes méthodologiques de l'implantation du modèle PRISMA portant sur l'intégration des services pour les personnes âgées en perte d'autonomie. *Manag. Avenir*, 47, 133–146.

Crawford, M.J., Rutter, D., Manley, C., Weaver, T., Bhui, K., Fulop, N., Tyrer, P. (2002). Systematic review of involving patients in the planning and development of health care. *BMJ*, 325(1263). doi: 10.1136/bmj.325.7375.1263.

Creswell, J.W. and Plano Clark, V.L. (2018). *Designing and Conducting Mixed Methods Research*, 3rd edition. SAGE, Los Angeles, CA.

Devaux, L., Chinet, M., Nicolas, F., Anhorn, P. (2018). Un PAS du Réseau vers l'autodétermination des patients (état des lieux). Réseau Santé Région Lausanne, Lausanne.

Emanuel, L.L., von Gunten, C.F., Ferris, F.D. (2000). Advance care planning. *Arch. Fam. Med.*, 9(1181). doi: 10.1001/archfami.9.10.1181.

Engel, G.L. (1981). The clinical application of the biopsychosocial model. *J. Med. Philos. Forum Bioeth. Philos. Med.*, 6, 101–124. doi: 10.1093/jmp/6.2.101.

Ferrari, P., Lequin, P., Milovan, M., Suter, C., Golay, P., Besse, C., Chinet, M., Bonsack, C., Favrod, J. (2018). Autodétermination et décision partagée dans les phases critiques du rétablissement. Pratiques et contenus du plan de crise conjoint en santé mentale. Réseau Santé Région Lausanne, Lausanne.

Fumagalli, L.P., Radaelli, G., Lettieri, E., Bertele, P., Masella, C. (2015). Patient empowerment and its neighbours: Clarifying the boundaries and their mutual relationships. *Health Policy Amst. Neth.*, 119, 384–394. doi: 10.1016/j.healthpol.2014.10.017.

Greenhalgh, T. and Papoutsi, C. (2019). Spreading and scaling up innovation and improvement. *BMJ*, 365. doi: 10.1136/bmj.l2068.

Jean, A., Rossignol, M., Boothroyd, L. (2016). Les niveaux de soins. Report, Institut national d'excellence en santé et services sociaux, Quebec.

Kalika, M. (2017). *Comment réussir son DBA ?* EMS Editions, Paris.

Kerber, K. and Buono, A.F. (2005). Rethinking organizational change: Reframing the challenge of change management. *Organ. Dev. J.*, 23, 23–38.

Laverdière, F., Québec (Province), Ministère de la Santé et des Services sociaux, Direction des communications (2018). Cadre de référence de l'approche de partenariat entre les usagers, leurs proches et les acteurs en santé et en services sociaux.

Mira-Bonnardel, S., Géniaux, I., Serrafero, P. (2012). Naissance d'un écosystème d'affaires. *Rev. Francaise Gest.*, 222, 123–134.

Moore, J.F. (1993). Predators and prey: A new ecology of competition. *Harv. Bus. Rev.*, 71, 75–86.

Moore, J.F. (1996). *The Death of Competition: Leadership and Strategy in the Age of Business Ecosystems*, 1st edition. HarperBusiness, New York.

Moore, J.F. (2006). Business ecosystems and the view from the firm. *Antitrust Bull.*, 51, 31–75. doi: 10.1177/0003603X0605100103.

Nalebuff, B.J., Brandenburger, A.M., Cohen, L. (1996). *La co-opétition : une révolution dans la manière de jouer concurrence et coopération*. Village Mondial, Paris.

Pomey, M.-P., Flora, L., Karazivan, P., Dumez, V., Lebel, P., Vanier, M.-C., Débarges, B., Clavel, N., Jouet, E. (2015). Le "Montreal model" : enjeux du partenariat relationnel entre patients et professionnels de la santé. *Santé publique*, S1, 41–50.

Sabatino, C.P. (2010). The evolution of health care advance planning law and policy. *Milbank Q.*, 88, 211–239. doi: 10.1111/j.1468-0009.2010.00596.x.

Savall, H. and Zardet, V. (1987). Maîtriser les coûts cachés : le contrat d'activité périodiquement négociable. *Politiques et management public*, 8(2), 162–164.

Savall, H. and Zardet, V. (2015). *Maîtriser les coûts et performances cachés*, 6th edition. Economica, Paris.

Strum, S., Callon, M., Latour, B., Akrich, M. (2013). *Sociologie de la traduction. Textes fondateurs*. Presses des Mines, Paris.

Stuart, G. (1999). Government wants patient partnership to be integral part of NHS. *BMJ*, 319(788). doi: 10.1136/bmj.319.7212.788b.

Thompson, A.G.H. (2007). The meaning of patient involvement and participation in health care consultations: A taxonomy. *Soc. Sci. Med.*, 64, 1297–1310. doi: 10.1016/j.socscimed.2006.11.002.

Van De Ven, A.H. and Poole, M.S. (1995). Explaining development and change in organizations. *Acad. Manage. Rev.*, 20, 510–540. doi: 10.5465/amr.1995.9508080329.

Veatch, R.M. (1972). Models for ethical medicine in a revolutionary age. *Hastings Cent. Rep.*, 2, 5–7. doi: 10.2307/3560825.

Voyen, M., Nguyen-Thi, P.-L., Germain, L., Pétré, B., Younsi, M., Mathieu, J., Ziegler, O., Bohme, P. (2020). Connaissance, perception et définition du concept "Patient Partenaire de Soins" : qu'en pensent les acteurs impliqués en éducation thérapeutique ? Résultats d'une enquête nationale. *Le partenariat de soin avec le patient : analyses.*

WHO (1998). Health Promotion Glossary (No. WHO/HPR/HEP/98.1). Geneva.

Wolf, J., Niederhauser, V., Marshburn, D., LaVela, S. (2014). Defining patient experience. *Patient Exp. J.*, 1, 7–19. doi: 10.35680/2372-0247.1004.

List of Authors

Ruth Laure ALAMARGUY
Université de Caen Normandie
France

Philippe ANHORN
Réseau Santé Région Lausanne
Switzerland
and
DBA Health Management
Business Science Institute
Wiltz
Luxembourg

Stephanie BEST
Peter MacCallum Cancer Centre
Melbourne
and
University of Melbourne
Australia

Anaïs CHENEAU
CREG
Université Grenoble Alpes
and
LEDI
UBFC
Dijon
France

Philippe CHERVIN
FIRAH
Montrouge
France

Yves COUTURIER
Université de Sherbrooke
Saguenay
Canada

Geneviève CYR
ESPUM
Montreal
Canada

Ann DADICH
Western Sydney University
Parramatta
Australia

David DARMON
RETINES
CI3P
Université Côte d'Azur
Nice
France

Stephen DARMONI
Rouen University Hospital
and
LIMICS
INSERM
Sorbonne Université
Paris
France

Jean-Charles DUFOUR
SESSTIM
Université Aix-Marseille
France

Vincent DUMEZ
CEPPP
CR-CHUM
Université de Montréal
Canada

Valérie FARGEON
CREG
Université Grenoble Alpes
France

Luigi FLORA
RETINES
CI3P
Université Côte d'Azur
Nice
France

Patrick GILBERT
IAE Paris Sorbonne Business School
Université Paris 1
Panthéon-Sorbonne
France

Inès GRAVEY
Mission HAD
AP-HP
Paris
France

Corinne GRENIER
KEDGE Business School
Marseille
France

Julien GROSJEAN
D2IM
Université de Caen Normandie
France

Parina HASSANALY
SESSTIM
Université Aix-Marseille
France

Marie-Eve LAPORTE
RITM
Université Paris-Saclay
France

Pauline LENESLEY
NIMEC
Université de Caen Normandie
France

Lester LEVY
AUT
Auckland
New Zealand

Kevin LOWE
University of Sydney Business
School
Australia

Anaëlle MORIN
CRMUS
Université de Sherbrooke
Saguenay
Canada

Marie-Dominique POIRIER
Université de Sherbrooke
Saguenay
Canada

Marie-Eve POITRAS
Université de Sherbrooke
Saguenay
Canada

Marie-Pascale POMEY
CR-CHUM
ESPUM
Montreal
Canada

Frédéric PONSIGNON
KEDGE Business School
Bordeaux
France

Marielle RAVOT
CI3P
Université Côte d'Azur
Nice
France

Éléonore SÉGARD
FIRAH
Paris
and
PHARes
Bordeaux Population Health
France

Christian SIMON
SILK Informatique
Angers
France

Sabrina SINIGAGLIA
ANCREAI
Clichy
France

Sharon WILLIAMS
University of Swansea
UK

Karim ZINAÏ
Almedys Life
Paris
France

Index

P, R

S, T, V

Other titles from

iSTE

in

Innovation, Entrepreneurship and Management

2024

BRASSEUR Martine, BARTOLI Annie, CHABAUD Didier, GROUIEZ Pascal, ROUET Gilles
Inclusive Territories 2: Role of Institutions and Local Actors
(Territorial Entrepreneurship and Innovation Set – Volume 2)

COURIE-LEMEUR Aline
Innovation, Collective Intelligence and Resiliency in Healthcare Organizations
(Health and Innovation Set – Volume 4)

DIMOTIKALIS Yannis, SKIADIS Christos H.
Data Analysis and Related Applications 3: Theory and Practice – New Approaches
(Big Data, Artificial Intelligence and Data Analysis Set – Volume 11)

PARMENTIER Guy
Organizational Creative Capabilities: Management Factors, Processes and Devices
(Organizational Creativity Set – Volume 1)

RUIZ Émilie
The Creative Capabilities of Open Organizations
(Organizational Creativity Set – Volume 2)

VERNIER Marie-France
Eco-Design and Ecological Transition: Questioning the Economic Model
(Smart Innovation Set – Volume 42)

2023

BOLLINGER Sophie
Management Control and Creativity: Challenges of Managing Innovation Processes
(Smart Innovation Set – Volume 41)

BOUVIER-PATRON Paul
Frugal Innovation and Innovative Creation
(Smart Innovation Set – Volume 40)

BRASSEUR Martine, BARTOLI Annie, CHABAUD Didier, GROUIEZ Pascal, ROUET Gilles
Inclusive Territories 1: Role of Enterprises and Organizations
(Territorial Entrepreneurship and Innovation Set – Volume 1)

CASADELLA Vanessa, UZUNIDIS Dimitri
Agri-Innovations and Development Challenges: Engineering, Value Chains and Socio-economic Models
(Innovation in Engineering and Technology Set – Volume 8)

DARTIGUEPEYROU Carine, SALOFF-COSTE Michel
Futures: The Great Turn
(Innovation and Technology Set – Volume 18)

PEYROUX Élisabeth, RAIMOND Christine, VIEL Vincent, LAVIE Émilie
Development and Territorial Restructuring in an Era of Global Change: Theories, Approaches and Future Research Perspectives

SAULAIS Pierre
Knowledge and Ideation: Inventive Knowledge Analysis for Ideation Stimulation
(Innovation and Technology Set – Volume 17)

2022

AOUINAÏT Camille
Open Innovation Strategies
(Smart Innovation Set – Volume 39)

BOUCHÉ Geneviève
Productive Economy, Contributory Economy: Governance Tools for the Third Millennium
(Innovation and Technology Set – Volume 15)

BRUYÈRE Christelle
Caring Management in Health Organizations: A Lever for Crisis Management
(Health and Innovation Set – Volume 3)

ENJOLRAS Manon
Innovation and Export: The Joint Challenge of the Small Company
(Smart Innovation Set – Volume 37)

FLEURY Sylvain, RICHIR Simon
Immersive Technologies to Accelerate Innovation: How Virtual and Augmented Reality Enables the Co-Creation of Concepts
(Smart Innovation Set – Volume 38)

HELLER David
Valuation of the Liability Structure by Real Options
(Modern Finance, Management Innovation and Economic Growth Set – Volume 5)

MATHIEU Valérie
A Customer-oriented Manager for B2B Services: Principles and Implementation

MORALES Lucía, DZEVER Sam, TAYLOR Robert
Asia-Europe Industrial Connectivity in Times of Crisis
(Innovation and Technology Set – Volume 16)

NOËL Florent, SCHMIDT Géraldine
Employability and Industrial Mutations: Between Individual Trajectories and Organizational Strategic Planning
(Technological Changes and Human Resources Set – Volume 4)

DE SAINT JULIEN Odile
The Innovation Ecosystem as a Source of Value Creation: A Value Creation Lever for Open Innovation
(Diverse and Global Perspectives on Value Creation Set – Volume 4)

SALOFF-COSTE Michel
Innovation Ecosystems: The Future of Civilizations and the Civilization of the Future
(Innovation and Technology Set – Volume 14)

SOULÉ Bastien, HALLÉ Julie, VIGNAL Bénédicte, BOUTROY Éric, NIER Olivier
Innovation in Sport: Innovation Trajectories and Process Optimization
(Smart Innovation Set – Volume 35)

VALLIER Estelle
Innovation in Clusters: Science–Industry Relationships in the Face of Forced Advancement
(Smart Innovation Set – Volume 36)

VAYRE Emilie
Digitalization of Work: New Spaces and New Working Times
(Technological Changes and Human Resources Set – Volume 5)

ZAFEIRIS Konstantinos N, SKIADIS Christos H, DIMOTIKALIS Yannis, KARAGRIGORIOU Alex, KARAGRIGORIOU-VONTA Christina
Data Analysis and Related Applications 1: Computational, Algorithmic and Applied Economic Data Analysis
(Big Data, Artificial Intelligence and Data Analysis Set – Volume 9)
Data Analysis and Related Applications 2: Multivariate, Health and Demographic Data Analysis
(Big Data, Artificial Intelligence and Data Analysis Set – Volume 10)

2021

ACH Yves-Alain, RMADI-SAÏD Sandra
Financial Information and Brand Value: Reflections, Challenges and Limitations

ARCADE Jacques
Strategic Engineering
(Innovation and Technology Set – Volume 11)

BÉRANGER Jérôme, RIZOULIÈRES Roland
The Digital Revolution in Health
(Health and Innovation Set – Volume 2)

BOBILLIER CHAUMON Marc-Eric
Digital Transformations in the Challenge of Activity and Work: Understanding and Supporting Technological Changes
(Technological Changes and Human Resources Set – Volume 3)

BUCLET Nicolas
Territorial Ecology and Socio-ecological Transition
(Smart Innovation Set – Volume 34)

DIMOTIKALIS Yannis, KARAGRIGORIOU Alex, PARPOULA Christina, SKIADIS Christos H
Applied Modeling Techniques and Data Analysis 1: Computational Data Analysis Methods and Tools
(Big Data, Artificial Intelligence and Data Analysis Set - Volume 7)
Applied Modeling Techniques and Data Analysis 2: Financial, Demographic, Stochastic and Statistical Models and Methods
(Big Data, Artificial Intelligence and Data Analysis Set – Volume 8)

DISPAS Christophe, KAYANAKIS Georges, SERVEL Nicolas, STRIUKOVA Ludmila
Innovation and Financial Markets
(Innovation between Risk and Reward Set – Volume 7)

GAUDIN Thierry, MAUREL Marie-Christine, POMEROL Jean-Charles
Chance, Calculation and Life

GASMI Nacer
Corporate Innovation Strategies: Corporate Social Responsibility and Shared Value Creation
(Smart Innovation Set – Volume 33)

GIORGINI Pierre
The Contributory Revolution
(Innovation and Technology Set – Volume 13)

GOGLIN Christian
Emotions and Values in Equity Crowdfunding Investment Choices 1: Transdisciplinary Theoretical Approach
Emotions and Values in Equity Crowdfunding Investment Choices 2: Modeling and Empirical Study

GRENIER Corinne, OIRY Ewan
Altering Frontiers: Organizational Innovations in Healthcare
(Health and Innovation Set – Volume 1)

GUERRIER Claudine
Security and Its Challenges in the 21st Century
(Innovation and Technology Set – Volume 12)

HELLER David
Performance of Valuation Methods in Financial Transactions
(Modern Finance, Management Innovation and Economic Growth Set – Volume 4)

LEHMANN Paul-Jacques
Liberalism and Capitalism Today

LIMA Marcos
Entrepreneurship and Innovation Education: Frameworks and Tools
(Smart Innovation Set – Volume 32)

MACHADO Carolina, DAVIM J. Paulo
Sustainable Management for Managers and Engineers

MEUNIER François-Xavier
Dual Innovation Systems: Concepts, Tools and Methods
(Smart Innovation Set – Volume 31)

UZUNIDIS Dimitri, KASMI Fedoua, ADATTO Laurent
Innovation Economics, Engineering and Management Handbook 1: Main Themes
Innovation Economics, Engineering and Management Handbook 2: Special Themes

2020

ANDREOSSO-O'CALLAGHAN Bernadette, DZEVER Sam, JAUSSAUD Jacques, TAYLOR Robert
Sustainable Development and Energy Transition in Europe and Asia
(Innovation and Technology Set – Volume 9)

BEN SLIMANE Sonia, M'HENNI Hatem
Entrepreneurship and Development: Realities and Future Prospects
(Smart Innovation Set – Volume 30)

CHOUTEAU Marianne, FOREST Joëlle, NGUYEN Céline
Innovation for Society: The P.S.I. Approach
(Smart Innovation Set – Volume 28)

CORON Clotilde
Quantifying Human Resources: Uses and Analysis
(Technological Changes and Human Resources Set – Volume 2)

CORON Clotilde, GILBERT Patrick
Technological Change
(Technological Changes and Human Resources Set – Volume 1)

CERDIN Jean-Luc, PERETTI Jean-Marie
The Success of Apprenticeships: Views of Stakeholders on Training and Learning (Human Resources Management Set – Volume 3)

DELCHET-COCHET Karen
Circular Economy: From Waste Reduction to Value Creation
(Economic Growth Set – Volume 2)

DIDAY Edwin, GUAN Rong, SAPORTA Gilbert, WANG Huiwen
Advances in Data Science
(Big Data, Artificial Intelligence and Data Analysis Set – Volume 4)

DOS SANTOS PAULINO Victor
Innovation Trends in the Space Industry
(Smart Innovation Set – Volume 25)

GUILHON Bernard
Venture Capital and the Financing of Innovation
(Innovation Between Risk and Reward Set – Volume 6)

JURCZENKO Emmanuel
Machine Learning for Asset Management: New Developments and Financial Applications

LATOUCHE Pascal
Open Innovation: Human Set-up
(Innovation and Technology Set – Volume 10)

MAKRIDES Andreas, KARAGRIGORIOU Alex, SKIADAS Christos H.
Data Analysis and Applications 3: Computational, Classification, Financial, Statistical and Stochastic Methods
(Big Data, Artificial Intelligence and Data Analysis Set – Volume 5)
Data Analysis and Applications 4: Financial Data Analysis and Methods
(Big Data, Artificial Intelligence and Data Analysis Set – Volume 6)

MASSOTTE Pierre, CORSI Patrick
Complex Decision-Making in Economy and Finance

MICHAUD Thomas
Science Fiction and Innovation Design
(Innovation in Engineering and Technology Set – Volume 6)

MONINO Jean-Louis
Data Control: Major Challenge for the Digital Society
(Smart Innovation Set – Volume 29)

MORLAT Clément
Sustainable Productive System: Eco-development versus Sustainable Development (Smart Innovation Set – Volume 26)

SAULAIS Pierre, ERMINE Jean-Louis
Knowledge Management in Innovative Companies 2: Understanding and Deploying a KM Plan within a Learning Organization
(Smart Innovation Set – Volume 27)

UZUNIDIS Dimitri
Systemic Innovation: Entrepreneurial Strategies and Market Dynamics

2019

AMENDOLA Mario, GAFFARD Jean-Luc
Disorder and Public Concern Around Globalization

BARBAROUX Pierre
Disruptive Technology and Defence Innovation Ecosystems
(Innovation in Engineering and Technology Set – Volume 5)

DOU Henri, JUILLET Alain, CLERC Philippe
Strategic Intelligence for the Future 1: A New Strategic and Operational Approach
Strategic Intelligence for the Future 2: A New Information Function Approach

FRIKHA Azza
Measurement in Marketing: Operationalization of Latent Constructs

FRIMOUSSE Soufyane
Innovation and Agility in the Digital Age
(Human Resources Management Set – Volume 2)

GAY Claudine, SZOSTAK Bérangère L.
Innovation and Creativity in SMEs: Challenges, Evolutions and Prospects
(Smart Innovation Set – Volume 21)

GORIA Stéphane, HUMBERT Pierre, ROUSSEL Benoît
Information, Knowledge and Agile Creativity
(Smart Innovation Set – Volume 22)

HELLER David
Investment Decision-making Using Optional Models
(Economic Growth Set – Volume 2)

HELLER David, DE CHADIRAC Sylvain, HALAOUI Lana, JOUVET Camille
The Emergence of Start-ups
(Economic Growth Set – Volume 1)

HÉRAUD Jean-Alain, KERR Fiona, BURGER-HELMCHEN Thierry
Creative Management of Complex Systems
(Smart Innovation Set – Volume 19)

LATOUCHE Pascal
Open Innovation: Corporate Incubator
(Innovation and Technology Set – Volume 7)

LEHMANN Paul-Jacques
The Future of the Euro Currency

LEIGNEL Jean-Louis, MÉNAGER Emmanuel, YABLONSKY Serge
Sustainable Enterprise Performance: A Comprehensive Evaluation Method

LIÈVRE Pascal, AUBRY Monique, GAREL Gilles
Management of Extreme Situations: From Polar Expeditions to Exploration-Oriented Organizations

MILLOT Michel
Embarrassment of Product Choices 2: Towards a Society of Well-being

N'GOALA Gilles, PEZ-PÉRARD Virginie, PRIM-ALLAZ Isabelle
Augmented Customer Strategy: CRM in the Digital Age

NIKOLOVA Blagovesta
The RRI Challenge: Responsibilization in a State of Tension with Market Regulation
(Innovation and Responsibility Set – Volume 3)

PELLEGRIN-BOUCHER Estelle, ROY Pierre
Innovation in the Cultural and Creative Industries
(Innovation and Technology Set – Volume 8)

PRIOLON Joël
Financial Markets for Commodities

QUINIOU Matthieu
Blockchain: The Advent of Disintermediation

RAVIX Joël-Thomas, DESCHAMPS Marc
Innovation and Industrial Policies
(Innovation between Risk and Reward Set – Volume 5)

ROGER Alain, VINOT Didier
Skills Management: New Applications, New Questions
(Human Resources Management Set – Volume 1)

SAULAIS Pierre, ERMINE Jean-Louis
Knowledge Management in Innovative Companies 1: Understanding and Deploying a KM Plan within a Learning Organization
(Smart Innovation Set – Volume 23)

SERVAJEAN-HILST Romaric
Co-innovation Dynamics: The Management of Client-Supplier Interactions for Open Innovation
(Smart Innovation Set – Volume 20)

SKIADAS Christos H., BOZEMAN James R.
Data Analysis and Applications 1: Clustering and Regression, Modeling-estimating, Forecasting and Data Mining
(Big Data, Artificial Intelligence and Data Analysis Set – Volume 2)
Data Analysis and Applications 2: Utilization of Results in Europe and Other Topics
(Big Data, Artificial Intelligence and Data Analysis Set – Volume 3)

VIGEZZI Michel
World Industrialization: Shared Inventions, Competitive Innovations and Social Dynamics
(Smart Innovation Set – Volume 24)

2018

BURKHARDT Kirsten
Private Equity Firms: Their Role in the Formation of Strategic Alliances

CALLENS Stéphane
Creative Globalization
(Smart Innovation Set – Volume 16)

CASADELLA Vanessa
Innovation Systems in Emerging Economies: MINT – Mexico, Indonesia, Nigeria, Turkey
(Smart Innovation Set – Volume 18)

CHOUTEAU Marianne, FOREST Joëlle, NGUYEN Céline
Science, Technology and Innovation Culture
(Innovation in Engineering and Technology Set – Volume 3)

CORLOSQUET-HABART Marine, JANSSEN Jacques
Big Data for Insurance Companies
(Big Data, Artificial Intelligence and Data Analysis Set – Volume 1)

CROS Françoise
Innovation and Society
(Smart Innovation Set – Volume 15)

DEBREF Romain
Environmental Innovation and Ecodesign: Certainties and Controversies
(Smart Innovation Set – Volume 17)

DOMINGUEZ Noémie
SME Internationalization Strategies: Innovation to Conquer New Markets

ERMINE Jean-Louis
Knowledge Management: The Creative Loop
(Innovation and Technology Set – Volume 5)

GAUDIN Thierry, LACROIX Dominique, MAUREL Marie-Christine, POMEROL, Jean-Charles
Life Sciences, Information Sciences

GILBERT Patrick, BOBADILLA Natalia, GASTALDI Lise, LE BOULAIRE Martine, LELEBINA Olga
Innovation, Research and Development Management

VAN HOOREBEKE Delphine
The Management of Living Beings or Emo-management

IBRAHIMI Mohammed
Mergers & Acquisitions: Theory, Strategy, Finance

LEMAÎTRE Denis
Training Engineers for Innovation

LÉVY Aldo, BEN BOUHENI Faten, AMMI Chantal
Financial Management: USGAAP and IFRS Standards
(Innovation and Technology Set – Volume 6)

LOISY Catherine, COULET Jean-Claude
Competence and Program-based Approach in Training: Tools for Developing Responsible Activities
Innovation and Responsibility Set – Volume 1)

MILLOT Michel
Embarrassment of Product Choices 1: How to Consume Differently

PANSERA Mario, OWEN Richard
Innovation and Development: The Politics at the Bottom of the Pyramid (Innovation and Responsibility Set – Volume 2)

RICHEZ Yves
Corporate Talent Detection and Development

SACHETTI Philippe, ZUPPINGER Thibaud
New Technologies and Branding (Innovation and Technology Set – Volume 4)

SAMIER Henri
Intuition, Creativity, Innovation

TEMPLE Ludovic, COMPAORÉ SAWADOGO Eveline M.F.W.
Innovation Processes in Agro-Ecological Transitions in Developing Countries (Innovation in Engineering and Technology Set – Volume 2)

UZUNIDIS Dimitri
Collective Innovation Processes: Principles and Practices (Innovation in Engineering and Technology Set – Volume 4)

2017

AÏT-EL-HADJ Smaïl
The Ongoing Technological System (Smart Innovation Set – Volume 11)

D'ANDRIA Aude, GABARRET Inés
Building 21st Century Entrepreneurship (Innovation and Technology Set – Volume 2)

BAUDRY Marc, DUMONT Béatrice
Patents: Prompting or Restricting Innovation? (Smart Innovation Set – Volume 12)

BÉRARD Céline, TEYSSIER Christine
Risk Management: Lever for SME Development and Stakeholder Value Creation

CHALENÇON Ludivine
Location Strategies and Value Creation of International Mergers and Acquisitions

CHAUVEL Danièle, BORZILLO Stefano
The Innovative Company: An Ill-defined Object
(Innovation between Risk and Reward Set – Volume 1)

CORSI Patrick
Going Past Limits To Growth

DAIDJ Nabyla
Cooperation, Coopetition and Innovation
(Innovation and Technology Set – Volume 3)

FERNEZ-WALCH Sandrine
The Multiple Facets of Innovation Project Management
(Innovation between Risk and Reward Set – Volume 4)

FOREST Joëlle
Creative Rationality and Innovation
(Smart Innovation Set – Volume 14)

GUILHON Bernard
Innovation and Production Ecosystems
(Innovation between Risk and Reward Set – Volume 2)

HAMMOUDI Abdelhakim, DAIDJ Nabyla
Game Theory Approach to Managerial Strategies and Value Creation
(Diverse and Global Perspectives on Value Creation Set – Volume 3)

LALLEMENT Rémi
Intellectual Property and Innovation Protection: New Practices and New Policy Issues
(Innovation between Risk and Reward Set – Volume 3)

LAPERCHE Blandine
Enterprise Knowledge Capital
(Smart Innovation Set – Volume 13)

LEBERT Didier, EL YOUNSI Hafida
International Specialization Dynamics
(Smart Innovation Set – Volume 9)

MAESSCHALCK Marc
Reflexive Governance for Research and Innovative Knowledge
(Responsible Research and Innovation Set – Volume 6)

MASSOTTE Pierre
Ethics in Social Networking and Business 1: Theory, Practice and Current Recommendations
Ethics in Social Networking and Business 2: The Future and Changing Paradigms

MASSOTTE Pierre, CORSI Patrick
Smart Decisions in Complex Systems

MEDINA Mercedes, HERRERO Mónica, URGELLÉS Alicia
Current and Emerging Issues in the Audiovisual Industry
(Diverse and Global Perspectives on Value Creation Set – Volume 1)

MICHAUD Thomas
Innovation, Between Science and Science Fiction
(Smart Innovation Set – Volume 10)

PELLÉ Sophie
Business, Innovation and Responsibility
(Responsible Research and Innovation Set – Volume 7)

SAVIGNAC Emmanuelle
The Gamification of Work: The Use of Games in the Workplace

SUGAHARA Satoshi, DAIDJ Nabyla, USHIO Sumitaka
Value Creation in Management Accounting and Strategic Management: An Integrated Approach
(Diverse and Global Perspectives on Value Creation Set –Volume 2)

UZUNIDIS Dimitri, SAULAIS Pierre
Innovation Engines: Entrepreneurs and Enterprises in a Turbulent World
(Innovation in Engineering and Technology Set – Volume 1)

2016

BARBAROUX Pierre, ATTOUR Amel, SCHENK Eric
Knowledge Management and Innovation
(Smart Innovation Set – Volume 6)

BEN BOUHENI Faten, AMMI Chantal, LEVY Aldo
Banking Governance, Performance And Risk-Taking: Conventional Banks Vs Islamic Banks

BOUTILLIER Sophie, CARRÉ Denis, LEVRATTO Nadine
Entrepreneurial Ecosystems
(Smart Innovation Set – Volume 2)

BOUTILLIER Sophie, UZUNIDIS Dimitri
The Entrepreneur
(Smart Innovation Set – Volume 8)

BOUVARD Patricia, SUZANNE Hervé
Collective Intelligence Development in Business

GALLAUD Delphine, LAPERCHE Blandine
Circular Economy, Industrial Ecology and Short Supply Chains
(Smart Innovation Set – Volume 4)

GUERRIER Claudine
Security and Privacy in the Digital Era
(Innovation and Technology Set – Volume 1)

MEGHOUAR Hicham
Corporate Takeover Targets

MONINO Jean-Louis, SEDKAOUI Soraya
Big Data, Open Data and Data Development
(Smart Innovation Set – Volume 3)

MOREL Laure, LE ROUX Serge
Fab Labs: Innovative User
(Smart Innovation Set – Volume 5)

PICARD Fabienne, TANGUY Corinne
Innovations and Techno-ecological Transition
(Smart Innovation Set – Volume 7)

2015

CASADELLA Vanessa, LIU Zeting, DIMITRI Uzunidis
Innovation Capabilities and Economic Development in Open Economies
(Smart Innovation Set – Volume 1)

CORLOSQUET-HABART Marine, GEHIN William, JANSSEN Jaques, MANCA Raimondo
Asset and Liabilities Management for Banks and Insurance Companies

CORSI Patrick, MORIN Dominique
Sequencing Apple's DNA

CORSI Patrick, NEAU Erwan
Innovation Capability Maturity Model

FAIVRE-TAVIGNOT Bénédicte
Social Business and Base of the Pyramid

GODÉ Cécile
Team Coordination in Extreme Environments

MAILLARD Pierre
Competitive Quality and Innovation

MASSOTTE Pierre, CORSI Patrick
Operationalizing Sustainability

MASSOTTE Pierre, CORSI Patrick
Sustainability Calling

2014

DUBÉ Jean, LEGROS Diègo
Spatial Econometrics Using Microdata

LESCA Humbert, LESCA Nicolas
Strategic Decisions and Weak Signals

2013

HABART-CORLOSQUET Marine, JANSSEN Jacques, MANCA Raimondo
VaR Methodology for Non-Gaussian Finance

2012

POMEROL Jean-Charles
Decision-Making and Action

SZYLAR Christian
UCITS Handbook

2011

LESCA Nicolas
Environmental Scanning and Sustainable Development

LESCA Nicolas, LESCA Humbert
Weak Signals for Strategic Intelligence: Anticipation Tool for Managers

MERCIER-LAURENT Eunika
Innovation Ecosystems

2010

SZYLAR Christian
Risk Management under UCITS III/IV

2009

COHEN Corine
Business Intelligence

ZANINETTI Jean-Marc
Sustainable Development in the USA

2008

CORSI Patrick, DULIEU Mike
The Marketing of Technology Intensive Products and Services

DZEVER Sam, JAUSSAUD Jacques, ANDREOSSO Bernadette
Evolving Corporate Structures and Cultures in Asia: Impact of Globalization

2007

AMMI Chantal
Global Consumer Behavior

2006

BOUGHZALA Imed, ERMINE Jean-Louis
Trends in Enterprise Knowledge Management

CORSI Patrick, CHRISTOFOL Hervé, RICHIR Simon, SAMIER Henri
Innovation Engineering: the power of intangible networks

Printed and bound by CPI Group (UK) Ltd, Croydon, CR0 4YY
16/09/2026
14963076-0004